Making
Film
in Egypt

Making Film in Egypt

HOW LABOR, TECHNOLOGY, AND MEDIATION SHAPE THE INDUSTRY

CHIHAB EL KHACHAB

The American University in Cairo Press
Cairo   New York

First published in 2021 by
The American University in Cairo Press
113 Sharia Kasr el Aini, Cairo, Egypt
One Rockefeller Plaza, 10th Floor, New York, NY 10020
www.aucpress.com

Dar el Kutub No. 25911/19
ISBN 978 977 416 985 4

Dar el Kutub Cataloging-in-Publication Data

El Khachab, Chihab
    Making Film in Egypt: How Labor, Technology, and Mediation Shape the Industry / Chihab El
Khachab.—Cairo: The American University in Cairo Press, 2021.
    p. cm.
    ISBN 978 977 416 985 4
    1. Cinematography
    2. 2 Motion pictures_production and direction
    791.4302

1 2 3 4 5   25 24 23 22 21

Designed by Westchester Publishing Services
Printed in the United Kingdom

À Papa, Maman et Zizou

Contents

Figures

Acknowledgments

M uch like coordinating a shooting day or visualizing a film, writing a book is, at its core, an imponderable quest. The various mediations through which I have worked are not without resemblance to those employed by my interlocutors in the Egyptian film industry: they include a great number of now invisible readings, conversations, observations, and interactions. This book will therefore stand, to the reader, as a reified product of much concrete labor, anticipations, anxieties, funny moments, generous assistance, and innumerable "encounters," in Deleuze's sense. I can only begin to uncover all the work invested in this book through this acknowledgments section, and I hope to be forgiven by anyone I omit.

This book would not have been possible without the participation of all the Egyptian filmmakers I met. I went to Egypt with three contacts in hand, each becoming a generous guide into the film industry: Safaa el-Leissi, Jennifer Peterson, and Hala Lotfy. I owe special thanks to Hala and everyone who worked in her production cooperative Hassala: Abdallah el-Ghaly, Abdelrahman "Mana" Mahmoud, Heba Othman, Chahira Nasef, Nayera El Dahshoury, Mona Lotfy, Wesam Lotfy, and Mohammed Rashad. I owe infinite thanks to the general manager in New Century Film Production, Ahmad Badawy, whose trust and assistance molded the course of my fieldwork. I also wish to thank Ahmed Farghalli and Mohamed Setohy for taking me under their wing in *Décor* (2014), and patiently answering my endless queries with a genuine desire to be helpful. I never spent a dull day with them or their production crew, which included Hany Abdel Latif, Ahmad Abdallah Abdel Halim, Mustafa Abu Zeid, Rasha Gawdat, Mahmoud Abdallah, Khaled Labanita, Mohammed Fathallah, Adham el-Sayeh, and Georges Ramsis.

The director Ahmad Abdalla generously allowed me on set in *Décor*, and I thank his patience for what he deemed to be my inexplicable presence. The cinematographer Tarek Hefny, the art directors Asem Ali and Nihal Farouk, the stylist Salma Sami, and the sound engineer Ahmad Saleh were also puzzled by my presence on set, but they never hesitated to answer my questions or help with my project. Their assistants were all, without exception, very helpful: I wish to acknowledge the first assistant director Omar el-Zohairy; his script supervisors Jaylan Auf and Mariam el-Bagoury; his second assistant director Renad Tarek; the assistant decorator Mohammed Ezzat; the chief builder Hussein Wezza; the prop assistant Mustafa Seyaha; the second assistant decorator Youssef el-Tarabolsy; the focus puller Moataz Mosallam; the lighting script Hany Morsy; the gaffer Mahmoud Morsi; the best boys light Ibrahim Morsi and *al-shabab* Ahmed Desha; the best boy grip Ahmad Said; the chief camera technician Hamada; his assistant Mustafa Msallem; the edit-camera Yasser Zanita; the sound assistants Ahmad Abdel Nasser and Ahmad Rashdan; the clapper Abdelsalam Radwan; the video-assist Adil; and the editor Sara Abdalla.

I was also involved in more New Century productions, and I wish to thank the directors Daoud Abdel Sayyed, Tamer Mohsen, and Ismail Farouk for allowing me on the sets of *Qudrat ghayr 'adiya* (2015), *Qitt wa far* (2015), and *al-Nabatshi* (2014), respectively. I have met many more production crew members on these projects, whose input will be apparent throughout this book: I wish to thank Tamer Fathi, Khaled Adam, Mohammed Sabry, Mohammed Mselhi, Khaled Ahmed, Amr Azkalani, Mohammed Ibrahim, Samir "Semsem" Nabawy, Mohammed Kassab, and Ahmad Abd El Aal. I would also like to thank the assistant directors Hossam Ali and Mohammed Tahawi, as well as the accountant Mohammed Hosny and the photographer Yasser Shafiey.

My fieldwork took an unexpected turn when Ahmad Fawzi Saleh, now a dear friend and one of the greatest sponsors of this research project, asked me to work with him on *Poisonous Roses* (2018). This experience has been eye opening on an academic and a personal level, and I have established long-lasting friendships with all those who have contributed to our project and, by extension, my research project. I wish to thank Fawzi, his wife Eman Hemeda, their most adorable son Hassan, Maged Nader, Mostafa Nour, Yousef Abodan, Georges Mokhtar, Ahmad Adil, Bassam Farhat and his assistants Ahmad Rashdan and Mustafa "She'bo" Shaaban, and the actors Maryhan Magdy, Ibrahim el-Nagary, Rémie Akl, Mohamed Berakaa, as well as the great Mahmoud Hemida. I would also like to thank Osama Abol Ata, Omar Abdel Wahab, Houssam Habib, Lina Aly, and Hady Mahmoud, who provided important input into my project even if they were no longer part of the movie by the time of its postproduction.

This list would be incomplete without all those who generously consented to a formal interview with me: I will thank, in no particular order, Wael Mandour, Marwan Hamed, Wahid Hamed, Tamer el-Said, Marwan el-Kahki, Abdelsalam Moussa, the late Mohammed Khan, Wessam Soliman, Sandy Samuel, Safei Eldin Mahmoud, Hani Adel, Marwan Saber, Mahmoud Lotfy, Onsi Abou Seif, Yousry Nasrallah, Maged Moussa, Karim el-Mihi, David Maher, Daoud Abdel Sayyed, Hisham Saqr, Mona Rabie, Gaby Khoury, Sherif Mandour, Marianne Khoury, Mariam Naoum, Reda Zanita, Mahmoud el-Touny, Mohammed el-Tohami, Moataz el-Kateb, Wael Farag, and Mohammed Samir.

Outside the industry, I am greatly indebted to those who made my stay in Cairo as agreeable as it was fruitful. I wish to thank Montasser el-Kaffash, Shereen Abouelnaga, Alice Hackman, Habi Seoud, Walid Abu Seoud, Hesham Aslan, Heba el-Karrar, Swagat Pani, and my childhood nanny Madeleine. I would also like to thank my mother's and my father's family in Cairo, in particular *Khalo* Yasser, who has been very enthusiastic about my academic vocation; the late *Khalo* Khaled and his wife Nisreen, whose insistent invitations have been a great occasion to relax with their kids Karim, Selim, Fahd, Taim, and Shagy; Alaa el-Karrar, Wael el-Karrar, their wives Azza and Ola, and their kids Mohammed, Mariam, Ali, Nadine, and Omar, without whom I would have spent many lonely holidays; and above all my grandmother Touta, whom I visited with great pleasure, if only to marvel at her unrelenting desire to go on against all odds.

I have yet to mention the personal and intellectual debts that I accumulated while planning and writing this book. Fieldwork for the book was completed thanks to a generous Social Sciences and Humanities Research Council of Canada doctoral dissertation award as well as a School of Anthropology and Museum Ethnography doctoral award from the University of Oxford. I wrote the manuscript while a Junior Research Fellow at Christ Church, University of Oxford. Before I started working at Oxford, I had the privilege of studying with scholars who have had a lasting impact on me. At the University of Ottawa, I would like to thank Natacha Gagné, Julie Laplante, and Stéphanie Gaudet. At the Université de Provence (Aix-Marseille I), I would like to thank the late Bruno Martinelli and Pierre

Lemonnier for introducing me to the French school in the anthropology of technology. At the University of Washington, I would like to thank Sareeta Amrute and Carolyn Pinedo Turnovsky. Lastly, at McGill, I would like to thank Will Straw and Axel van den Berg, who have been incredible and rigorous intellectual mentors.

At Oxford, I started my journey as a doctoral student with two of the best supervisors one could hope to have: Marcus Banks and Paul Dresch. Paul has retired in the meantime, yet his advice still bears its imprint on this work. Walter Armbrust, whose practical help was precious prior to my fieldwork, became a dedicated supervisor and the greatest companion one could have in a book on Egyptian cinema. To all these scholars, I am indebted beyond measure.

Several colleagues gave comments on this book in its initial stages: I would like to mention Morgan Clarke, Katherine Swancutt, Jessica Winegar, Christopher Morton, and Yasmin Moll, who kindly invited me on a panel where I started formulating the ideas presented in Chapters 5 and 6. I have been lucky to have two great friends and colleagues, Susan MacDougall and Emanuel Schaeublin, whose thought-provoking conversations and comments bear visible imprints on these pages. Many more colleagues have provided insightful comments on some part or another of the manuscript: I will thank Meir Walters, Julien Dugnoille, Kåre Poulsgaard, Riccardo Jaede, Sıla Uluçay, Sophie Chamas, and Munazza Ebtikar for their invaluable comments. Zuzanna Olszewska and Stephen P. Hughes provided important insights into how to turn the thesis into a book during a stimulating doctoral examination.

I would also like to thank Anne Routon from the American University in Cairo Press for her interest in acquiring this manuscript. Comments from two anonymous reviewers helped me bring the book into its final shape. I am grateful for Laura Gribbon's careful work on the book's production, as well as Jasmina Brankovic's copyediting of the manuscript, David Kanbergs' proofreading, and Ælfwine Mischler's work on the index. I owe special thanks to Eman Hemeda (Al Batrik) and Mahmoud Abdallah (New Century) for allowing me to use the images reproduced in these pages, including the captivating cover image. A shorter version of chapter 5 has appeared in *Visual Anthropology Review* (2016).

A little shop on North Parade in Oxford has become a second home to me. I wish to thank the owners and staff of Viny's Café—Yacine "Bijou," Ali Ali, and my dearest friend Hisham "Boshkash" Fathy—without whose daily care I would have starved both physically and spiritually while writing this monograph. Many more friends have made the writing experience enjoyable. At Wolfson College, I wish to acknowledge the never-boring nights spent with Lewis Daly, Salam Rassi, Janamarie Truesdell, Santhy Balanchandran, Seán Ó Máinseál, Rui Soares Barbosa, Grace Egan, and James Norrie. At Christ Church, I wish to acknowledge the numerous digressive conversations with Peter Hill, which, I hope, will be productive for future projects.

These acknowledgments would not be complete without mentioning the unfailing support of my parents, Walid El Khachab and May Telmissany, who have given me the most caring encouragement any human being, let alone any anxious young researcher, could have ever hoped to get. I cannot find the words to thank them for their generous work on this manuscript, especially my mom's constant readings and comments. This book is dedicated to them, and to my little bro Ziad, in the hope that he will read this one day.

Notes on the Text

Although this book is written in English, it is in fact a multilingual product. My field notes are written in a mixture of English, French, and Arabic, partly reflecting the usage in the Egyptian film industry, and partly reflecting my own idiosyncrasies as a trilingual speaker. My fieldwork and my interviews were largely conducted in Egyptian colloquial Arabic, but my interlocutors made frequent use of English and French expressions. To reflect the multilingual nature of my interlocutors' speech, I have italicized the words and expressions they used in English or in French. The reader should therefore assume that italics reflect actual speech patterns, no matter that Arabic is the main language spoken. All translations, including from textual sources, are my own.

I wish to make two more terminological clarifications. First, I use the term "filmmaker" to designate any and all cast or crew members involved in film production in Egypt. For the sake of readability, I have preferred this term to the more cumbersome "maker of film" or "film practitioner," and I never use the term "filmmaker" in the metonymic sense in which the expression has come to mean "director."

Second, I use the somewhat unusual terms "agent" and "social agent" to avoid the inevitable confusion between the term "actor" in a general sociological sense and "actor" as a cinematic profession. Any mention of "actors" is meant to refer to the profession, not the analytical term employed in anthropological writing.

I have chosen *not* to anonymize my interlocutors, for reasons that have been better articulated by Dornfeld: "Since I was empathetic to the views and situation of the producers, I felt it was unnecessary to obscure the identities of the principal subjects. This effort would probably have been futile anyway, since the names of the members of the production team would be clear to those potential readers for whom this information mattered most, that is, other . . . practitioners" (1998: 28). None of my interlocutors ever expressed reticence at having their names mentioned. In fact, many explicitly asked to be included by name, and I have done so according to their wishes.

The price of the Egyptian pound varied while I was conducting fieldwork, but it was between 6.5 and 7.5 to the United States dollar according to the national bank rates.

Introduction

Obviously, not everything that happens to us comes as a surprise.
Much is predictable enough, but what we cannot have is certainty.
—*Graeber, 2012*

One way or another, the garden is going to turn out as it turns out;
our problem is that we don't yet know how that will be.
—*Gell, 1992*

"We're screwed!" exclaimed Ahmed Farghalli. The line producer for *Décor*
(2014) had a habit of expressing his inauspicious feelings about the film's
progress every day. This time, he was irritable after having a long meeting
about the film's preparations. The meeting was held on December 8, 2013.
It was an opportunity to go over the screenplay to make sure that everyone
on the crew would be on the same page. The first assistant director, Omar
el-Zohairy, gave an official number to each scene, which would be adjusted as
Décor's screenplay evolved. The director Ahmad Abdalla explained in detail
how he intended to shoot each scene. The cinematographer Tarek Hefny,
the art directors Nihal Farouk and Asem Ali, and the stylist Salma Sami asked
in turn about lighting, movement, and colors. The script supervisors, Jaylan
Auf and Mariam el-Bagoury, came to understand the continuity between
disjointed scenes in the protagonist's parallel worlds.[1] Lastly, Farghalli asked
questions about the logistics of each scene, while trusting his production
manager Mohammed Setohy and his location manager Ahmad Abdallah
Abdel Halim to reassure the artistic crew that their ongoing demands were
being met. After the meeting, when only his production crew and I were left
in the room, Farghalli was adamant. "We're screwed!"

When I asked Farghalli why we were screwed, he gave a vague answer.
"We don't know it now, but it'll eventually happen," because "they" were

still unsure about many things. Farghalli's worries were clear: they, the artistic crew, were still undecided about many aspects of *Décor*'s screenplay that the production team had to prepare and execute. Even after holding a six-hour-long meeting to clarify the project, Farghalli was hesitant about how the film to come was going to unfold. This lack of assurance can be interpreted in two ways. On the one hand, Farghalli was concerned by the work left to the production team, which explains why he believed that the artists' indecision would screw him; on the other, he was concerned by what he did not know *now* but would know *eventually*.

Farghalli chose not to capitulate to this uncertainty, but to ask Setohy to write a to-do list with the production tasks he wanted to complete. The list included acquiring a gramophone and a ballerina box, calling Reda Zanita's camera company to rent a thirty-five millimeter analog camera as a prop, and scouting the train crossing inside the Egyptian Media Production City (EMPC). Each task was allocated to a crew member in the production team, who was expected to execute it the very next day. The gramophone, ballerina box, and camera were eventually acquired and used in different scenes in *Décor*. The scene at the EMPC's train crossing was shot on March 24, 2014.

Farghalli did not get screwed after all. Yet some things did not occur as he had expected during the preparation and execution of *Décor*'s shooting. Farghalli's initial to-do list included scouting the entrance for one of the main apartments in the screenplay—a task that exhausted the production manager Setohy and his assistants for weeks as they searched for the elusive location in Cairo. This entrance was eventually shot in Alexandria after a late decision made by the artistic crew.

Earlier in the December 8 meeting, Farghalli had asked the artistic crew how they would like to shoot the movie's *avant-titre*, the sequence prior to the beginning credits, which was to feature set-building craftsmen in action. Most of the artistic workers, including Ahmad Abdalla, Tarek Hefny, and Nihal Farouk, wanted to shoot the sequence in a documentary style, while the set was being built. Yet the art director Asem Ali, who oversaw the set building operation, warned that this strategy might hinder the progress of the scheduled building. Weeks later, and a few days prior to the shooting, the de facto compromise was to shoot inserts on actual set builders engaged in a staged building operation centered on some intentionally unfinished items. Thus, set building went largely unhindered while the *avant-titre* included some degree of "real-life" building work.

The discrepancy between the preparation and execution of this shooting day illustrates how little participants in the December 8 meeting knew about the way the *avant-titre* would be shot, let alone the rest of the shooting schedule. The fact that the gramophone, the ballerina box, and the thirty-five millimeter camera were eventually acquired and included in the film should not lead us to believe that it would have happened anyway. Yet Farghalli's lack of assurance about the future cannot be interpreted as a complete uncertainty: "much is predictable enough," to quote Graeber (2012: 26). Farghalli was confident that he would be able to execute the film through a strict division of labor between his production team and the artistic crew, by following a certain sequence of operations, using writings and images such as script copies, to-do lists, and scouting pictures.

Mediating the unpredictable yet expected future of the film-in-the-making is a central task in commercial film production. This mediation is not just about interceding in an existing social organization through technological means, but also about anticipating the future of a complex sociotechnical process. This constitutes the core conceptual problem that will animate this book, whose main contributions are situated between media anthropology, media studies, and Middle East ethnography. I will come back to the problem's theoretical significance below, but first I wish to describe the context within which I explored the problem and the way in which I gained access to the filmmaking world in Egypt.

Locating Egyptian Film Production

The Egyptian film industry has often been described as "the first," "the only," or "the most successful" one in the Arab world by scholars, critics, and journalists alike. This common perception is rooted in the industry's long-standing history of influence over the Arabic-speaking Middle East and North Africa—a history that has earned it the sobriquet of "Hollywood on the Nile" (Darwish, 1998: 12–13) or "Hollywood in the Arab world" (Dajani, 1980). Since the 1930s, thousands of movies made in Egypt have been distributed across the region, becoming a signal cultural product with a lasting influence on mass media domestically and internationally (Shafik, 1998). I grew up in a household where I was served a regular diet of Egyptian film classics and I have always wondered about the "real world" behind these dazzling on-screen performances. This interest grew into a professional one when I moved to Cairo to study the Egyptian film industry. I discovered, as Caldwell did in Hollywood (2008), that there is no self-evident, coherent whole that one can call an "Egyptian film industry." Rather, this industry is better understood as a complex world of everyday practices and representations shared by filmmakers involved in a lengthy and uneven labor process. This discovery has been shaped by extensive fieldwork among Egyptian filmmakers, which constitutes the empirical grounding of this book.

This ethnography is situated in Cairo, the beating heart of the Egyptian film industry, yet it bears little resemblance to a mainstream ethnography of the city.[2] What is distinctive about the film industry is not its gender, class, or religious components, which are often highlighted in ethnographies of Cairo, but a specific type of *working activity*. By paying attention to labor, process, and technology, my ethnography portrays a version of Egypt that has more in common with studies of Egyptian craftsmen (Elyachar, 2005), artists (Winegar, 2006), and factory workers (Shehata, 2009; Chakravarti, 2016) than it does with studies of Egyptian media and popular culture invested in questions of modernity, nationalism, and consumption (see Armbrust, 1996; Abu-Lughod, 2005; Peterson, 2011). I will situate the working activity of Egyptian film production next to a similar set of activities—industrial labor in Egypt, commercial film production outside Egypt—without trying to explain how this activity is specifically Egyptian. Thus, it is not fruitful to think about this study as another butterfly in a collection aggregating into a unified representation of "Egypt," but as an attempt to use the Egyptian context to explore broader conceptual issues concerning media labor, sociotechnical processes, and the mediation of unpredictable yet expected futures.

Recent scholarship about "the future" in Egypt has been dominated by the existential uncertainty occasioned by the January 2011 Revolution.[3] This trend has had such a gravitational pull that it might seem surprising to find so little about the Revolution in this book. It is difficult to judge the extent to which the Revolution changed the Egyptian film industry. One alleged shift is that film companies have been unwilling to invest in production after 2011, but I would dispute the claim that this reticence was primarily caused by the Revolution. I argue in Chapter 1 that investors' perception of economic uncertainty increased as satellite television channels, which were a major source of funding until the late 2000s, became unable or unwilling to pay distribution loans—a development that began before 2011.[4] More broadly, no significant changes in labor hierarchy, production activity, or technological use were caused by the Revolution. Inside and outside the industry, the Revolution appears as a contested narrative, setting a sharp "before" and "after" timeline in recent Egyptian history, and discussed among filmmakers within its own bounds. I observed many debates during my fieldwork among those who witnessed the "real" Revolution in Tahrir Square; those who did not go but supported it; those who did go but supported the 2013 military coup; those who saw the 2013 coup as the "real" Revolution; and those who did not care to engage at all. These positions coexisted within the industry's everyday conversations, but the self-referential narrative of the Revolution reproduced at the whim of lay political analyses barely touched the nitty-gritty of filmmaking.

This is not to say that filmmakers have not been affected by the events of January 2011, especially by vernacular video-making practices through which protesters braved police control to create a distinct street-level visual repertoire (see Dickinson, 2012; Snowdon, 2014; Westmoreland and Allan, 2016; Westmoreland, 2016). Ahmad Abdalla, the director of *Décor*, was involved in a video-pooling cooperative gathering and archiving digital videos about the events in Tahrir Square before being inspired to shoot *Farsh wa ghata* (*Rags and Tatters*, 2013). This earlier film used rough, on-the-ground camera movement to narrate the escape of a prisoner during the eighteen days of the 2011 Revolution. Abdalla's case is not unique. In Lebow's *Filming Revolution* project, dozens of Egyptian filmmakers, video artists, and activists engage in a fragmented conversation about the aesthetics and politics of representing the Revolution in film form (2016; 2018). It should be noted that the participants in *Filming Revolution* correspond more to "independent" cinema networks that are part of yet do not represent the whole Egyptian film industry. When it comes to the majority of movies made in Cairo, I concur with Dickinson's assessment that "unlike nonhierarchal [sic], non-profit-making media collectives which work more resolutely as a part of the revolution . . . these films . . . still uphold most of the conventions of cinematic representation, infrastructure, elitism, and modes of manufacture of old" (2012: 135).

By 2013, the daily activities of commercial film production appeared to have gone unaffected by the events of the Revolution, despite the interruptions occasioned by regular protests and the occasional curfew.[5] Such events are unpredictable, yet they become assimilated into the range of contingencies that need to be reckoned with in any film project. A striking case in point occurred during *Décor*'s shooting, a few days prior to the third anniversary of the Revolution. The set was slowly coming together after sunrise when an explosion resounded on location. "It's just thunder and lightning," quipped the assistant director Zohairy. Shortly afterward, a large cloud of smoke rose above the horizon. News started trickling onto the crew's smartphones: a car bomb had exploded near the Museum of Islamic Art, across the Cairo prefecture, about three kilometers away from our set. The shooting day went unhindered, however, and the star actress Horeya Farghaly asked me to write the following note in my diary: "In these dire circumstances, *Décor* goes on." In this spirit, privileging a narrative about the Revolution's effects on Egyptian film production would obscure its specific everyday dynamics.[6]

Several scholars have worked on the history and political economy of Egyptian film production (see Wassef, 1995; Shafik, 1998; 2007; Flibbert, 2001; Armbrust, 2004). Yet to the best of my knowledge, there is no literature on the everyday working practices of this industry. This dearth of scholarship may be due not only to a lack of interest, but also to the difficulty of accessing the industry given its interpersonal organization. I will insist on the word "interpersonal" here, as the relations binding Egyptian filmmakers are never between anonymous individuals in an open labor market, but between individuals who either know each other or know each other via someone else (a *wasta* in local terms). Gatekeepers in Cairo's film industry are all individuals in this sense, unlike industries in which large institutions such as media conglomerates, professional associations, or unions hold sway over access to film projects (see Ortner's experience in Hollywood, 2010). It is difficult to gain access to the industry unless someone who "knows you" allows you inside, which has significant consequences for the industry's political economy, as I detail in Chapter 1. My own story of access to the Egyptian film industry is therefore instructive about the way in which commercial film production is organized.

When I arrived in Cairo on August 8, 2013, I had only a handful of contacts in the industry. I knew Tarek el-Telmissany, my mother's cousin and Egypt's best-known senior cinematographer. I also knew Jennifer Peterson, a young assistant director trained at the Cairo Jesuit Cinema School, and Hala Lotfy, a well-known independent director. Without formal training in filmmaking or practical experience on set, I had not considered entering the industry through employment. I also did not want to ask for Telmissany's help as it may have positioned me as a relative and overshadowed my credibility as a researcher. Nor could I have asked Peterson or Lotfy for assistance as both women operated at the margins of the industry, where production timelines are extensive and uneven given chronic financial difficulties.

On August 14, just six days after I arrived in Cairo, protesters in Rabaa and Nahda Square were killed en masse in what became the largest single-day, state-sponsored massacre in modern Egyptian history. The city was not easy to navigate thereafter. Every Friday in the following months, violent clashes between pro-Rabaa protesters and the military would occur, and a daily curfew was established at seven o'clock in the evening. My goal was still to try and get involved in a film project to follow it from beginning to end. Therefore, I committed to contacting production companies that were working on several projects at once, even after the Rabaa Square massacre. I had heard that New Century and Sobky were still producing films, and although I did not have any contact with either company, what I did have was a name: Rasha el-Hamouly.

On an earlier visit to Cairo, in March 2013, I briefly met with one of my parents' old friends, Safaa el-Leissi, an editor turned film critic. Leissi was kind enough to connect me with Sahar el-Sherbiny, who worked in international sales in Al-Arabia, one of Egypt's major production and distribution companies. I had a brief encounter with Sherbiny that March, as I hoped to work with Al-Arabia at the time, but she informed me that the company had stopped producing films to concentrate on distribution and exhibition. Nevertheless, she gave me the names of colleagues who worked in active production companies without giving me their phone or email contact. Among those names was that of Rasha el-Hamouly, who managed the production side in New Century. Upon returning to Cairo months later, I tried calling Sherbiny to ask for Hamouly's contact, but her phone was out of service. When I called Al-Arabia's office, I was told that Sherbiny had left the company and apparently the country as well.

Anxious to be in contact with New Century, I phoned the company's office and asked if I could speak to Rasha el-Hamouly. The office assistant seemed puzzled and kept asking me whether I was a journalist, to which I would respond by reiterating that I was a researcher based at an English university. "Madame Rasha is away, you should call on another day." I phoned every day until I was transferred to Hamouly's line at last. I seized the opportunity to rehearse my pitch: "I am a researcher at Oxford University in England. . . . I work on the Egyptian film industry. . . . I wish to follow a film from A to Z in New Century." After a few exchanges, Hamouly informed me that she was no longer in charge of production in New Century and that I should contact Ahmad Badawy, the new general manager. She had the courtesy to give me his phone number, and this was the only contact I had with Rasha el-Hamouly as she left the company shortly thereafter.

I called Ahmad Badawy immediately, and after numerous phone calls and rescheduled meetings, I saw him in person. When he heard about my intended research project, Badawy agreed to support it on two conditions: first, that I did not take pictures on set,[7] and, second, that I provided him with an official letter from Oxford to confirm my research status. Once he received the letter, he agreed to invite me to the project that would occupy a significant portion of my fieldwork: *Décor*, an artistic black-and-white film directed by Ahmad Abdalla and co-written by Mohamed and Shireen Diab. I was "in" at last, through a string of interpersonal encounters.

For eighteen months between 2013 and 2015, I observed and participated in film projects at various stages of their production.[8] This book mainly covers film preparations and shooting, but it also includes a brief discussion on postproduction in Chapter 6. To mitigate the otherwise unavoidable problem of fieldwork in a media production site, which is that "too many people were doing too many things at too fast a pace for me to track them all" (Dornfeld, 1998: 27), I sought to gain some variety in projects and production phases. The workers I met were generally friendly and receptive to my research, and they would agree to be interviewed and answer my unusual queries. The project I followed most closely was *Décor*, a psychological drama about Maha, an art director working on a crass commercial movie with her husband Sharif. While rearranging an item on set one day, Maha suddenly becomes the main character in the movie on which she is working: a schoolteacher and mother to a nine-year-old daughter, married to a middle-aged cab driver named Mustafa. Maha keeps alternating between these two worlds, while remaining undecided about which life is "real." The plotline is meant to highlight the range of choices available to every woman in her life, according to the director Ahmad Abdalla. "Life is not black-and-white," as he said, "it is made of many shades of grey." *Décor* was shot in black-and-white to satisfy this moral in part, but also as an homage to the classic melodramas of the late Egyptian superstar Faten Hamama.

On set in *Décor*, I acquired the nickname Mr. X, which references a popular comedy entitled *X: Akhtar ragul fi-l-'alam* (*X: The Most Dangerous Man in the World*, 1967). The movie is a James Bond parody where the main character, Mr. X, is a world-renowned gangster with an endless capacity for fighting, disguise, deception, and seduction. When the line producer Ahmed Farghalli gave me the nickname, his crew immediately adopted it. Farghalli marshaled a pop culture reference to classify what would otherwise be unclassifiable: a doctoral candidate in anthropology on an Egyptian film set. Elsewhere, Armbrust (1996) has described how Cairenes invoke pop culture references to articulate ambiguous or problematic aspects of everyday life. By juxtaposing my presence with the character of Mr. X, Farghalli implied that I behaved in a spy-like manner as I asked expected and unexpected questions while taking endless notes on people's conversations and actions. Farghalli also implied that I was "the most dangerous man in the world" only partly as a joke, given the information I held about the film's unfolding.

In addition to *Décor*, I witnessed some preparations and some days of shooting in *Qitt wa far* (*The Cat and the Mouse*, 2015), *Qudrat ghayr 'adiya* (*Out of the Ordinary*, 2015), *el-Nabatshi* (*The Night Shift Host*, 2015), as well as preparations for a project that was eventually abandoned, *Akhir banafsigi rumansi* (*The Last Violet Romantic*). These films were all produced by New Century Film Production. I also followed and worked on another project entitled *Ward masmum* (*Poisonous Roses*, 2018), produced by Al Batrik Art Production. My access was again guaranteed by a personal relationship. In New Century, I was explicitly told that had I not been introduced by the general manager Badawy, I would not have been allowed backstage on the company's projects, and subsequent interactions with crew members were colored by being "Badawy's friend." Likewise, on *Poisonous Roses*, I attended some preparation meetings with the director Ahmad Fawzi Saleh and his ever-changing artistic crew in October 2013. I provided suggestions about the movie's artistic content in the meetings, and found in Fawzi an avid listener, even when I doubted that I was of any help in these matters. Fawzi would refer to me as *al-Duktur* because he respected "my knowledge and culture," a term soon adopted by the rest of the crew. In the summer of 2014, while I was dining with his family, Fawzi proposed that I become his assistant. I started working with him on the screenplay and, when we were ready to shoot, I worked on the film's preparations by writing partial script breakdowns, casting actors and extras, following up on production demands, and even drafting some budget plans. After an initial bout of shooting in the winter of 2014, I helped Fawzi with rewriting his screenplay in the summer of 2015 and translated it in view of a (now successful) grant application to the Doha Film Institute.

Poisonous Roses is the story of Tahiya, a young working-class woman living in Cairo's tanneries district. Tahiya is a restroom cleaner and her opportunities in life are extremely limited. She spends all her energy raising and caring for her younger brother Saqr. When Saqr announces his intention to migrate illegally to Italy in the hope of securing a better future for Tahiya and her mother, Tahiya refuses to see him leave. One day, Saqr's best friend Yehya is injured and transported to a nearby hospital, where Saqr meets a middle-class trainee doctor called Nahid. Tahiya becomes anxious about Saqr's travel and his recent love interest, and she is willing to go to any lengths to keep him by her side. The film came out in 2018, but it was unfinished at the time of writing this introduction, and the director was still unsure about its ending. This is only fitting, given that my central theoretical interest lies in the way filmmakers mediate unpredictable yet expected outcomes. This mediation occurs through a specific division of labor, production process, and technological use, as I detail next.

Labor, Process, and Technology

In addition to its focus on contemporary Egyptian film production, this ethnography is a contribution to the emerging anthropology of cinema as defined by Hoek.

> [The anthropology of cinema is] clearly distinguished from the longer history of interest in ethnographic film or the use by anthropologists of moving image technologies as a means of producing knowledge about the world. Instead, the anthropology of cinema has emerged as a part of media anthropology. It asks what the cinema is (as technology, as institution, as form, etc.), and what it makes possible (as interdiction, as pleasure, as labour, etc.), within the particular contexts of the lives of our interlocutors. (Hoek, 2016)

Setting aside Powdermaker's pioneering study (1950), the anthropology of cinema gathered momentum in the 2000s with ethnographic accounts of film production and reception in Bombay (Grimaud, 2003; Ganti, 2004; 2012; Wilkinson-Weber, 2014), Kano (Larkin, 2008), Paris (Rot and de Verdalle, 2013; Rot, 2014), Los Angeles (Ortner, 2013), Dhaka (Hoek, 2014), Accra (Meyer, 2015), Chennai (Pandian, 2015), Hong Kong (Martin, 2016), and Bangalore (Srinivas, 2016). These accounts share with media anthropology a methodological commitment to long-term fieldwork in media production sites.[9] They also reveal the concrete goals, desires, and representations of media workers in ways not possible in earlier text-centered and institution-centered media studies.[10]

Media anthropology shares with production studies the desire to reveal the less glamorous side of filmmaking (see Mayer, Banks and Caldwell, 2009; Mayer, 2011; Hesmondhalgh and Baker, 2013; Szczepanik and Vonderau, 2013; Banks, Conor, and Mayer, 2015; Curtin and Sanson, 2016; 2017). Both fields relate the everyday work of media practitioners to the political and economic structures within which they work. Such structures may be institutionalized (see Born, 2004; Caldwell, 2008), or they may well be inscribed in a more diffuse labor hierarchy (see Ganti, 2012: 202–205; Ortner, 2013: 205–210). In a similar vein, I describe the institutions and hierarchical relations constraining the everyday activity of Egyptian filmmakers in Chapters 1 and 2. This description highlights not only how workers deal with precarious working conditions (see Curtin and Sanson, 2016), but also how workers themselves think about industry norms and practices, taking heed of Caldwell's observation that "reflexive talk by these workers can be viewed as rich, coded, cultural self-portraits" (2008: 14). Moreover, to use the lighting technician Ahmed Desha's metaphor, I want to cast a light on the "shadows" (ashbah) behind the scenes of Egyptian film production, not only because their work should be brought to light and appreciated, but also because they are subject to systematic marginalization at the behest of "artistic work" conducted by hierarchically dominant cast and crew members. If I were simply to describe how artistic workers create film narratives, I would be neglecting the efforts and thoughts of workers who are not hierarchically dominant in the industry.

While media anthropologists and production studies scholars have been attentive to labor dynamics, they have had little to say about media production as a *sociotechnical activity*. This seems like a sweeping statement given the sizeable literature on "technology" in both fields. As Ginsburg, Abu-Lughod, and Larkin have recognized, "refiguring the ethnography of media necessitates a further expansion by taking into consideration the physical and sensory properties of the technologies themselves and examining the materiality of communication across cultures" (2002: 19). This expansion has a long history in media studies, from McLuhan's interest in "electric technology" (1964) to Kittler's technological media history (1999) and more recent elaborations on media infrastructures (see Parks and Starosielski, 2015; Plantin and Punathambekar, 2019). Ethnographers who work on technology's materiality and its impact on mediated content think about "technology" as an entire material assemblage (television technology, cinema technology), without examining how media workers bridge between the present and the future of complex sociotechnical processes by using everyday techniques and devices (see Spitulnik, 1998; 2002; Larkin, 2008; Eisenlohr, 2006; 2009; 2010). There are few analyses within media anthropology and media studies of the series of operations unfolding with their own sociotechnical logic during filmmaking—what anthropologists of technology have called an "operational sequence."[11]

The operational sequence is a "set of operations organized and implemented by a human group, here and now, according to the means at its disposal, including the technical knowledge it masters, to arrive at a [physical] result" (Balfet, 1991: 12). Operational sequences are designed to follow the way in which people act on matter through physically efficacious operations, and how each operation gains meaning through these acts. Filmmaking is a good example. The operational sequence in Cairo's film industry begins with inscriptions on paper aggregating into a screenplay. These inscriptions are broken down into various materials in preparations, such as scouting pictures, props, actors, sets, and costumes. These materials are reassembled, in turn, into audiovisual materials in shooting, then reworked via successive stages of postproduction until "the film" is printed. These physically efficacious operations create an ideal-typical picture of the filmmaking process, as detailed in Chapter 2. The clearest traces of these operations are written, visual, or sonic mediators such as the screenplay, the scouting picture, or the sound recorded on set. I borrow the term "mediator" from Latour, who distinguishes between *intermediaries*—objects endowed with a social meaning without having a share in its creation—and *mediators*—objects physically shaping the sociotechnical outcomes arising from a configuration of humans and nonhumans (2000: 18–19). The meaning of mediators is tied to the extended production process in which they anticipate unpredictable yet expected outcomes: for instance, how the shooting is prepared and executed (Chapter 4), how the unfinished film is visualized (Chapter 5), or how the audience's reaction is anticipated (Chapter 6).

Operational sequences present an important addition to well-established approaches to material culture in Anglo-American anthropology (see Appadurai, 1986; Miller, 1987). By allowing the analyst to map the way in which technical actions are both executed immediately *and* embedded in previous and subsequent operations, the operational sequence shows that material objects acquire meaning not just by circulating across consumption spheres, but sometimes also by breaking down the expected outcome of a complex production process into contingent tasks. Furthermore, operational sequences give more weight to the everyday technological devices that have been neglected in media anthropology and production studies.[12] Phones, cameras, laptops, or even pieces of paper do not feature prominently in media production studies, except in fleeting moments of a worker typing on a laptop (Ganti, 2012: 225) or a producer's compulsive phone use (Pandian, 2015: 42). In Sigaut's words, "The more 'rational' techniques are—that is, banal, familiar, ordinarily efficacious—the more they escape anthropology" (2003: 4).

One noted exception is Grimaud's ethnography of Bollywood, which remains underdiscussed in Anglo-American scholarship. Filmmaking, argues Grimaud, is "largely shared between individuals, material components, and the phases of the cinematographic process" (2003: 10). In consequence, "treating cinema *a priori* as a 'language' (even visual), as a 'mythology' or as the product of an 'imaginary' (that of a collective or an author) is to short-cut everything that makes its concrete and temporal thickness" (2003: 11). "Everything" in Grimaud's argument includes the sociotechnical activities and devices absent in too many studies of film production in anthropology and media studies. Such activities and devices are central to explaining how unpredictable yet expected outcomes are mediated in complex sociotechnical processes, as I detail in Chapter 3. The desire to give importance back to nonhumans in technical processes has been crucial to the field of actor-network theory, especially in its early days as a "sociology of translation" (see Latour and Woolgar, 1979; Callon, 1986; Akrich, 1987; 1993). This book avoids the actor-network language, however, because it presupposes a horizontal symmetry between humans and nonhumans in networks made of neutral "relations" or "associations" (see Law, 1992; Latour, 1996; 2005). This flattening cannot square with hierarchical organization (Peacock, 2015), and, as such, an actor-network description misses an important dimension in the everyday work of Egyptian film production.

More broadly, the actor-network language cannot describe how technological devices mediate unpredictable outcomes. This mediation is better captured by the concept of "reserve," which has been proposed by Heidegger in his writings on technology.[13] The reserve is not extensively theorized by Heidegger, but one can engage with the concept in the broader context of his reflections on objects. Heidegger distinguishes between the object in its objectness *(Gegenstand)*, an autonomous entity whose physical stuff accounts for its whole existence, and the reserve *(Bestand)*, an entity dependent on a parallel world of reserves to exist as such (Heidegger, 1994: 196–98). Smartphones are a good example. The smartphone-object is solely a mass of electronic stuff programmed with a certain software. The smartphone-reserve, in contrast, is a device always readily available to summon audiovisual content. Smartphones, cameras, laptops, and microphones can become reserves like the workers they summon to future tasks. Objects and reserves are not two different things, in this sense, but two different *moments* in the apprehension of things.

When two reserves interact, according to Heidegger, it is not in the mode of mutual "association," to use actor-network language, but mutual *summoning* to be exploited to their maximal potential.[14] This summoning remains a potential until it is actualized by another reserve, whether human or nonhuman. To provide a concrete example, when I went to scout an apartment for *Décor* with the production manager Setohy, he summoned his digital camera's potential to take scouting pictures. From a gadget sitting in Setohy's pocket, the digital camera was transformed into a reserve, used as a picture-taking device, while committing Setohy's attention to the scouting operation ahead. Of course, experiencing the camera as a reserve is possible *because* no other obstacle obstructs the object's functioning, such as the battery being insufficiently charged or Setohy not knowing how to manipulate the device. Notwithstanding these obstacles, the use of technological devices in filmmaking is better described as a mutual summoning among reserves—Setohy becomes a work-reserve and the smartphone a picture-reserve.

Through this mutual summoning, human and nonhuman reserves can mediate some unpredictable yet expected outcomes. The microphones on set illustrate this point further. The sound engineer cannot hear what happens *within* a shot unless it is recorded on a microphone, as the movement and noise on set always overshadow the specific audio content on screen. In this manner, the microphone-object can materialize sounds that would otherwise be inaudible to the sound engineer's ears. An otherwise inaudible content is summoned by the microphone-reserve, which in turn summons the sound engineer to anticipate the film's unpredictable soundtrack. For instance, how will the sound be cleaned? Will the audience hear "unnatural" glitches? Will the actor's voice sound "natural"? In this context, microphones are not just objects materializing the inaudible, or a material substratum to the cultural work of sound making. Rather, they act as reserves, just like Setohy's camera. They summon otherwise unactualized potentials—the location's image, the film's sound—to mediate the unfinished film.

The distinction between objects and reserves stands against the tendency to flatten hierarchical organization in actor-network theory, while remaining attentive to interactions between humans and nonhumans. These interactions are not symmetrical or horizontal in all cases. In Egyptian film production, they involve an uneven, hierarchically inflected summoning to apprehend what comes next in the filmmaking process. The concept of reserve has another important ethnographic merit: it allows us to explore the daily use of technological devices while remaining attentive to emic conceptions about the subject/object distinction. Egyptian filmmakers are not avid readers of actor-network theory, and they would be unconvinced that technological devices are more than just objects in their objectness, to use Heidegger's term. Acknowledging how objects can become reserves at different moments in time helps us account for different kinds of relations between humans and nonhumans, including emic conceptions of these relations.

This reflection opens a link with studies of the "extended mind" (see Hutchins, 1995; Clark and Chalmers, 1998; Malafouris, 2013). Examining how objects and subjects are summoned in a sociotechnical process in its unfolding is, in a way, trying to grasp how a complex human/nonhuman system *thinks* about an unpredictable yet expected outcome. Without being able to access my interlocutors' thoughts, I would suggest that their thought processes are not restricted to their brains; they rely on external social and material resources—what I call reserves—to apprehend unpredictable yet expected outcomes. This level of attention is necessary because it demonstrates that thinking about the future is a complex material activity with which filmmakers must reckon before attaining an outcome as seemingly straightforward as coordinating film logistics or visualizing "the film." Without being able to calculate their way out of this complexity, and without being able to rely exclusively on repetitive technical behavior, filmmakers can still mediate unpredictable outcomes through smaller, contingent tasks. This book elaborates on conceptual tools such as labor hierarchy, operational sequence, and reserves to attend more accurately to the way in which such outcomes are mediated in complex sociotechnical processes.

Mediating Futures

The anthropology of cinema and, more broadly, empirical studies of media production have seldom theorized the expected futures faced by media workers. This neglect is sometimes due to the extended present in which ethnographies are written (see Ganti, 2012; Ortner, 2013), where workers simply "work" without acknowledging that their activity always involves anticipation (What will the *avant-titre* look like on screen? How will we get the ballerina box?). This processual awareness is better evoked by Grimaud (2003), Hoek (2014), and Pandian (2015), who wrote their ethnographies with a structure reflecting the making of films from inception to exhibition.[15] The futures described in these ethnographies are broadly characterized as being "uncertain." Grimaud writes, for instance, that "making a film in Bombay is playing the game of a laborious and uncertain quest" (2003: 7). Pandian expands on this thought:

> Wherever I followed filmmakers like Krishna and Vishnu—the streets and studios of Chennai, the sandstone plateaus of central Karnataka, the soaring bridges of Kuala Lumpur, the mountains of Switzerland, or the deserts beyond Dubai—I found a milieu of tremendous uncertainty. Consider the enormous complexity of filmmaking as a technical and material process. Accidents come in endless varieties: the excitement that crests and wanes with every new story; the protean play of light, wind, and other natural forces shadowing every take; the unforeseeable needs that inevitably trail shot footage into editing and composing studios; the constant failure of actors and equipment to act and react as they should. Directors, cameramen, designers, and editors struggled with this caprice, but I also found them constantly anticipating and improvising with chance events. (2015: 6)

Here Pandian uses a notion of uncertainty that is pervasive across all social sciences: an unknowable and unpredictable future that can surprise agents with its "caprice" and "chance events"; a future with existential consequences on an individual, societal, and/or planetary scale.[16] These conceptions do not adequately grasp how Egyptian filmmakers like Farghalli apprehend their activity's outcome, because while Farghalli is a human being caught in the same existential dilemmas posed by a fundamentally uncertain future, his conception of the film-in-the-making is somewhat more assured. This assurance is neither the conceit of expert prediction nor the poise of resignation, but an implicit recognition of the difference between uncertainty and what I call "imponderability." Throughout the book, I will consider the term "imponderable" equivalent to the expression "unpredictable yet expected." While an uncertain future is *unknowable* and *unpredictable*, an imponderable future is *expected* even though all the courses of action leading to it cannot be weighed in the present. Both futures cannot be predicted by Farghalli, but his attitude toward each one is different.

The difference is modest yet significant. First, it situates the filmmaker's engagement with "the future" beyond the existential concerns visible in current anthropological studies on political, economic, and ecological crises.[17] Wondering about the outcome of Brexit, the migration crisis, or environmental degradation is a lived concern, but it is not the *only* future on the minds of people working, moving, cultivating, cleaning, cooking, acting, playing, making films—in short, engaging in a wide range of everyday activities that are not always geared toward uncertain existential matters. Often, they are geared toward futures with an expected outcome, yet whose actualization comes after an unpredictable series of events leading, say, to the making of a film. In line with Bryant and Knight's project for an "anthropology of the future" (2019), I wish to highlight a different "orientation" through which filmmakers apprehend future actions and ends. Imponderable outcomes are distinct from uncertain outcomes because they have a strong weight of expectation attached to them. They are also distinct from *probable* outcomes because there is no *a priori* way of calculating weights on the outcome's actualization; of "pondering" courses of action in the etymological sense of the term. Farghalli could not determine the exact chances that he would acquire the gramophone and the ballerina box in advance, yet he was not gripped by an existential doubt about it. Whether the ballerina box is bought or not, whether the apartment's entrance is shot in Cairo or not, the agent's attitude toward "the future" varies significantly according to whether s/he expects what comes next.

Imponderable outcomes escape the agent's capacity to envision all courses of action leading to them. They can never be solved by direct action but can only be *mediated*. The idea of mediation has been used in various ways across the social sciences, and it is not my intention to expand on its extensive philosophical genealogy (see Boyer, 2007; Guillory, 2010). What is common across these uses is a definition of mediation as a way in which two entities or states of affairs enter in a relation with the intercession of a third one. What varies is the nature of the entities in question, the nature of the relation, and the nature of the intercessor. In media studies, mediation can be about media technologies interceding between media producers and remote audiences to communicate a certain content (McLuhan, 1964; Thompson, 1995; Peterson, 2005). It can be about media institutions and contents interceding in "the general circulation of symbols in social life" to contribute to how audiences make sense of their world (Silverstone, 2002: 762; see also Baudrillard, 1972; Silverstone, 1994; Couldry, 2008). It can even be about media messages and infrastructures interceding between dominant ideologies and a dominated audience to achieve hegemony (Martín-Barberio, 1993; Aouragh, 2012).

In media anthropology, the term has taken on more meanings. Eisenlohr writes about the "paradox of mediation" (2009: 273–74), by which he means that the very technologies carrying media content across distant space-times seem invisible in local media use. This tension has been signalled in Bolter and Grusin's theorization of the dialectic between immediacy and hypermediacy (2000), but also in ethnographic works on digital technology (Born, 1997; Miller and Slater, 2000; Mazzarella, 2006; Boelstorff, 2008; Villi and Stochetti, 2011) or at the intersection between religion and media (Engelke, 2010; Pype, 2012; Meyer, 2015; Moll, 2018). In such contexts, media technologies "seem to vest the mediation [with the divine] in which they take part with some sense of immediacy, as if the use of microphones or film would yield some extraordinary experience that brings people closer to the divine" (Meyer, 2011: 25). In material culture studies in the mold of Appadurai (1986) or Miller (1987), mediation broadly describes the various objects, social relations, representations, institutions, and conventions interceding among humans in their daily life, which is never lived in an "im-mediate" manner so to speak (see also Mazzarella, 2004; Boyer, 2012).

With all the meanings accrued by the term "mediation," one might argue, as Stankiewicz did with the term "imagination," "that the concept no longer holds together in any meaningful way and that its semantic excess and ambiguity tend to thwart, or stand in for, more careful ethnographic attention to the processes and practices by which people come to know and think about themselves and others" (2016: 797). The "mediation of everything," as Livingstone has called it (2009), is symptomatic of academic interest in a world where media forms, institutions, contents, infrastructures, and technologies are proliferating, yet it may not be a useful analytical tool on its own. One possible response to this assessment has been to create more specific concepts corresponding to different kinds of "mediation." Prominent examples include "remediation," a process whereby older media forms and content are reused in newer media forms (Bolter and Grusin, 2000; Rajewsky, 2005), or "mediatization," a process whereby everyday life becomes structurally incorporated into media forms and institutions over the long run (see Hjarvard, 2013; Hepp and Krotz, 2014; Livingstone, 2014).

In this book, I use a similar strategy of specification, but I am interested in a "mediation" that has yet to be addressed by the literature in anthropology and media studies. I am interested in the way in which social agents attempt to overcome imponderable outcomes in their everyday activity. This attempt transforms unpredictable yet expected futures into smaller, contingent tasks by relying on existing labor hierarchies, operational sequences, and technological devices. The film *Décor*, as it was anticipated on December 8, 2013, became a series of concrete tasks such as getting a ballerina box, scouting a train crossing, and arranging a staged building operation. These tasks were executed using assumptions about the filmmaking division of labor, its anticipated operational sequence, and various to-do lists and scouting pictures summoned by reserves. This entire process is what I would call a "foremediation," an intercession between a present and a future state of affairs in a given project, in which labor, operational sequence, and technology act as intercessors. This concept is not meant to argue that there is a deeper, better, more original mediation to consider prior to all mediation, but that there is a different type of mediation involved in thinking about the future of a complex sociotechnical process. The prefix "fore-" highlights the anticipation involved in bridging the present and future of complex processes—an anticipation that is not only a production imperative, but also a lived and conscious concern among media workers.

The concept of "foremediation" contributes to media anthropology and media studies in two ways. First, it affords more accuracy in describing how workers think about and execute a sociotechnical activity in which they are entangled. Insofar as this activity engages human and nonhuman agents in a present extending to the near- and far-future, conceptualizing how agents think and act in order to anticipate their activity's unpredictable yet expected future, in contrast with a broadly uncertain one, becomes more specifiable through the idea of "foremediation." Second, and more important, the concept gives an analytically precise term to address the ways in which humans "manage," "mitigate," "cope with," "deal with," or "imagine" unknowable futures. Such metaphors are common in the anthropological scholarship on risk and uncertainty, where facing the future may involve probabilistic calculations (Beck, 1992; Zaloom, 2004; 2009), anticipatory scenarios (Samimian-Darsh, 2013; Hannerz, 2016), visual simulations (Kinsley, 2010; 2012), or hope in means of improvement (Miyazaki, 2004; Appadurai, 2013), in promises (De l'Estoile, 2014; Hetherington, 2014; 2016), or even in divination (Zeitlyn, 2012). These various methods of confronting the future do not capture specifically how agents break down imponderable outcomes within an extended production process. What interests me is not whether agents eventually succeed in actualizing their objectives—they may well fail—but rather to understand *how* hierarchical labor relations, operational sequences, and various technological devices "foremediate" these outcomes.

Since the neologism might hinder readability, I will not use the terms "foremediation" or "foremediating" in this book, preferring the simpler "mediation" and "mediating" in the specific sense of an intercession between the present and the future in a production process. I do not mean to use these terms in order to replace or call into question the wide-ranging meanings of mediation outlined earlier, but to point out that the discussion surrounding these meanings should be enriched by considering how complex sociotechnical activities have an anticipatory dimension. When building a boat, erecting a building, writing a book, or even making a film, the expected outcome's actualization cannot be predicted in advance, because it is impossible to assign a specific weight to each possible course of action leading to it. Had Farghalli tried to envision every part of the logistical elements needed to shoot *Décor*, he could never have known exactly what they might be because the actions that needed to be taken by all workers involved in the project were not known on December 8, 2013. Still, this process engages social agents such as Farghalli in a mediation—in the narrow sense in which I use the term—whereby they expect to reach a certain outcome through certain labor hierarchies, production practices, and technological devices, even if the outcome's actualization is not as they had initially imagined. Mediating the futures emerging from this activity is central to this book's argument and, more broadly, to the ethnography of media production.

What Comes Next

Overall, this book is animated by two objectives. The first one is to describe the everyday work of film production in a seldom-studied film industry. This description extends the effort launched by Becker's study of "art worlds" by giving appropriate weight to "all the people whose activities are necessary to the production of the characteristic works which that world, and perhaps others as well, define as art" (2008: 34; in the Egyptian art world, see Winegar, 2006). Egyptian film production provides a wealth of empirical insights on an industrial, late capitalist, urban version of Egypt, while exploring how makers of film—like makers of buildings, boats, and books—mediate the futures of their everyday sociotechnical activity.

The second ambition is to show *how* these imponderable futures become mediated, knowing that they go beyond the agent's ability to weigh different courses of action leading to their anticipated outcome. To this end, I expand on writings in media anthropology and media studies to address the labor hierarchies, production operations, and technological devices through which this mediation occurs. I am not so much interested in everyday "negotiations" of uncertainty in this sense, but in the way in which different agents at different moments in a complex production process apprehend what needs to be done to get "the film" made, without knowing in advance how it will be made. To paraphrase Gell, the film "is going to turn out as it turns out; our problem is that we don't yet know how that will be" (1992: 57).

The argument proceeds in six chapters, each adding a new layer to the analysis of the mediation between the present and the future of filmmaking in Egypt. In Chapter 1, I lay out the historical, political, and economic groundwork upon which Egyptian film production is built. I describe how the industry is organized around interpersonal relations, which in turn explains why I focus on individual agents and their interpersonal interactions in discussing how imponderable outcomes are mediated. The sociotechnical activity of filmmaking in Egypt is described in more detail in Chapter 2, where I discuss the industry's hierarchical labor organization, its personalized mode of apprenticeship, and its operational sequence. Since technological devices have received little coverage in studies of media production, I devote Chapter 3 to these technologies in various guises, starting from emic conceptions of "technology" in Cairo and moving on to their commodity status and their use as "reserves" in film production. The remaining chapters focus on three imponderable outcomes in filmmaking and their mediation by film-makers: coordinating the shoot, visualizing the film, and anticipating the audience's reaction. I examine the logistical groundwork underlying film shooting in Chapter 4, with attention to the imponderability of budgeting, scheduling, transportation, and execution. I then explore the visual and sonic mediators summoning filmmakers to visualize the unfinished film in Chapter 5. In Chapter 6, I analyze the different ways in which filmmak-ers anticipate an "enchanted" reaction from their imagined audience, while instilling it into the film's fabric.

The architecture of this book is not in itself suggestive of filmmaking as a process, but it gives a sense of the way in which filmmakers antici-pate the future. Each chapter title evokes a different way of apprehending the future in/of Egyptian film production—as an industry, as a process, as a reserve summoning to eventual tasks, as logistics, as visualization, as enchanted viewing. This sense of anticipation is built into the interludes between each chapter. The seven vignettes in grey shading act as a narrative foretelling of the chapter to come and of the next interlude.

I have chosen to focus on *Décor* throughout the book for the purposes of narrative continuity: to ensure that the reader will be familiar with the project's cast of characters and its overall story in order to highlight the conceptual work around labor, process, technology, and mediation in Egyptian film production. I would stake that the experiences described in *Décor* have broader relevance to the Egyptian media industry, based on the range of projects and experiences I gained in this domain. Collectively, the vignettes tell the story of *Décor* since my initial involvement with the proj-ect in September 2013 until its projection at the Cairo International Film Festival in 2014. I have tried to evoke the way social agents encounter the events to come without assuming what has happened next. What comes next will not necessarily happen, but it is expected to happen, which has consequences for the way in which filmmakers envisage the future.

These consequences are well illustrated in the story behind Figure 1, which summarizes this book's core argument with a single snapshot. On the surface, this picture is of an asphalted road like so many, surrounded by two rows of streetlights and fading away into the arid horizon. This seems like a clichéd evocation of the future as a horizon disappearing in the distance, yet it was never meant to be interpreted in this way by its makers. The picture was taken on October 4, 2012, while Ahmad Fawzi Saleh, his

1. The streetlight road; Credit: Houssam Habib or Maged Nader. Photograph ©Al Batrik Art Production.

assistant Maged Nader, and the cinematographer Houssam Habib were scouting locations for *Poisonous Roses*. This road, located in the rich Fifth District in New Cairo, grabbed Fawzi's attention as a possible location to shoot a scene where the protagonist Saqr would walk alone, engulfed by the barren landscape, defeated by the cruelty of his fate. This scene occupied such an important place in Fawzi's mind that the "streetlight road" *(shari' 'awamid al-nur)* became a staple in our screenwriting sessions, and we discussed it as though it were integral to the fabric of the eventual film. Fawzi regularly went over its scouting pictures to nourish his imagination, and we would move the scene around within the screenplay according to the flow of our discussions.

The scene was never shot, because it was taken out of the screenplay's final version. What ended up happening has no bearing on the way in which Fawzi wrote the scene. He still anticipated a shooting day in the nondescript "streetlight road," no matter whether it would be shot or not, because he had this picture in hand. The picture, in turn, was a small part in the wider breakdown of "the film" into concrete tasks and images—it contributed to mediating the film's imponderability into contingent decisions about its screenplay, its shooting location, its visual style, and its antici-pated audience. Sometimes these decisions bore fruit, other times they did not. Yet they leave traces like this picture, allowing us to understand how the unfinished film's future is mediated, not because the streetlight road was never shot, but because it embodies the way in which filmmakers have anticipated its shooting.

Inside Immobilia

The Immobilia is an iconic building in the history of Egyptian cinema. Standing just north of Abdel Khaliq Tharwat Street in downtown Cairo, the building has hosted many production companies, housed many movie stars, attracted many cinephiles to its cine-clubs, and even featured in films like *Hayat aw mawt* (*Life or Death*, 1954) and *Qissa mamnu'a* (*Forbidden Story*, 1963). The majestic white building has its entrance in a small dark alley, behind a grand metal door leading onto marble stairs in a huge, badly lit lobby. Sand and dirt accumulate on an unlit neon sign bearing the Arabic caption of a long-gone production house: "The Heliopolis Company for Film Production." The failing lights and the deteriorating interior cement the impression that this building was iconic in a bygone era, but is now falling into disuse.

I am filled with excitement and angst when I first enter the lobby on September 2, 2013. This was the very first time I would visit a production company—what I had envisioned for a whole year as the start of my field research. Not caring much about the storied building, I go straight to the sixth floor, where I have an appointment with the general manager of New Century, Ahmad Badawy. The company's name hangs on the wall next to the eleva-tor doors, looking just like any of the innumerable signs peppering downtown office buildings. The sign reads "Dollar Film." At the time, I did not realize that Dollar is in fact the distribution arm of New Century, and that its office had been in the Immobilia build-ing since 1949.

Three middle-aged men sit in the office, two on waiting chairs and one behind a small desk in what looks like a very narrow ves-tibule. The man behind the desk stands up. "Yes, sir?" he asks with the half-upright, half-suspicious tone characteristic of gatekeepers in Cairo. "I'm here to meet Mr. Ahmad Badawy." "What?" exclaims the man as he leans in. I had spoken too softly as usual. "I have an appointment with Mr. Ahmad Badawy."

The man walks behind his desk, opens a glass door leading further into the office, and asks me to sit down on a small leather couch next to the entrance. This room is bigger than the vestibule, yet it feels narrower because of the large desks covered in boxes, papers, and computers. Behind the desks, a young man in a dress shirt and a young hijabi woman stare at me in silence, while the reception man enters another narrow corridor. One or two minutes later, he comes back saying "*Itfaddal!*" politely nudging me to come through.

I enter the first room to the left, and I see Ahmad Badawy sitting on a rolling chair behind a very large desk. This room breathes better: surrounded with salmon pink walls are two green leather couches, a small wooden chair, a small coffee table with an antique ashtray, an old dresser filled with old company books, a photo of Omar Sharif visiting the company, and a narrow window giving just enough light to a wooden bookshelf behind the desk. As soon as I step into the office, Badawy stands up to greet me: "How are you? We meet at last!" I smile. "Yes, finally. . . ."

Badawy is wearing a red polo shirt and jeans, a casual outfit that cannot conceal the signs of exhaustion on his face. He still seems somewhat enlivened and invites me to sit down. "Do you want something to drink?" asks Badawy in accordance with the mandatory courtesy. "I've got tea . . . ," says the reception man, who still stands by the door. "Okay, I'll take a tea without sugar, and make it slightly heavier." The man smiles: "*Mashi.*"

I sit on the small wooden chair next to the desk across from Badawy's chair. "So what are you doing, exactly?" he asks. I start with my standard answer about writing a PhD dissertation on contemporary Egyptian film production and wanting to follow a production operation from A to Z, but Badawy still looks unsure about what I want. "On a very practical level, I want two things," I state candidly. First, I tell him that I want to be physically present in the making of a production project. Second, I want to interview the main people involved in the production after their work, to ask them about their thoughts on cinema and the film they are doing. "Is there a way you can do all that without disturbing the work? Without taking any pictures . . . ?" I jump on the occasion, sensing Badawy's positive tone: "Sir, all I do is exactly like you see me right now [I had a notebook on my lap]. I take notes in this little notebook and, at night, I write longer notes. You can read over these notes if you'd like. That's all I use for my project." He is willing to help me, he says, but he wants to see official paperwork from Oxford first.

We have a lengthy conversation afterward—about his life, about my life. When he learns that I grew up in Canada, he asks, "So how are you finding the country?"—expecting, I suspect, a diatribe about how bad things have gotten in Egypt. "It's not too bad. . . . Problems before and after the Revolution aren't different in nature, but in magnitude: traffic *(zahma)*, order *(nizam)*, security *(amn)*, cleanliness *(nadafa)*, et cetera. It's not so different, it's just worse." Badawy in turn laments the state of the country, and I consciously play into the narrative that it was much better in the 1960s. "It was much better only five years ago!" he exclaims, adding that filmmaking does not bring enough revenue anymore. "Yesterday, for instance, all Egyptian movies in the entire country made a hundred and forty thousand [Egyptian] pounds." I feign surprise: "In all of Egypt?" "Yes," he answers with a plaintive tone. "Last Eid, movies would make three or four million pounds a day."

"Why do you want to do this project?" he suddenly asks with a hint of curiosity. "I'm interested in making the Egyptian style of film production known outside of Egypt. . . . In books, I only read about American and Indian film production, when the Egyptian model is also important and needs appropriate consideration. . . . I'm among the only people who can do it, because I speak Arabic well . . . and I'm also from a film family." "Really?" He looks intrigued. I put on another soapy smile. "Yes, on my mother's side, I'm from the Telmissany family." Badawy raises his eyebrows as if he were pleasantly surprised—a noteworthy event considering his placid demeanor. After a slow month, I feel like I have a way in: now is the time to treat this appointment as an interview.

"What projects are going on right now?" I ask. "We're finishing shooting *al-Ashshash* [*The Collector*, 2013]." "Ah! Is it done now?" "No, we still have six days left . . . but we're planning on finishing before the Great Eid season." He adds that *al-Ashshash* will not really suit my study, but he tells me about a more appropriate project directed by Ahmad Abdalla and written by Mohamed Diab, called *Décor*. I make an impressed expression, and I deliberately show that I am taking notes. Once I get proof of my Oxford affiliation, he tells me, I can get introduced to Ahmad Abdalla and Mohamed Diab. "It'll be an important film for you and for people abroad." He says little more, but I sense that what he means is that the film will raise Egypt's artistic reputation on the international film scene. I tell him that I would also be interested in seeing commercial movies destined for the Egyptian market, as I need to examine different examples of production. He smirks: "Even if you want to dabble in properly Egyptian filmmaking, you'll really like working on Ahmad Abdalla's film."

1
Industry

S etting aside early experiments in film production, the emergence of an Egyptian film *industry* is traditionally dated to the mid-1930s (Darwish, 1998; Shafik, 2001: 38–40). This coincides with the establishment of Studio Misr, which opened its doors in 1935 under the auspices of nationalist tycoon Talaat Harb. Many more political and economic factors are behind this emergence, however, including the relative freedom allowed to Arabic-speaking filmmakers under British colonial rule, the close intertwinement between cinema and nationalist expression, the influx of theater actors and directors into film production, and the growing construction of exhibition spaces in Egypt (Shafik, 1998: 12–14). This construction reached an all-time high in the late 1950s, with over four hundred cinemas built up to that point (Flibbert, 2001: 112).

Studio Misr was initially a production company, yet it quickly became central to the whole industry because it owned its own filmmaking infrastructure. This included shooting studios and a complete postproduction facility, with all the necessary equipment to edit, mix, and print movies. Soon after its founding, the Studio became a focal point for commercial film production, even as Egypt's average output reached forty-eight films per year from 1945 to 1952 (Shafik, 1998: 12). As Armbrust indicates (2004: 84), Studio Misr's contribution to the industry did not lie so much in financing film projects as it did in leasing shooting studios and, crucially, postproduction equipment to smaller production companies. The Studio's importance was (and remains) infrastructural in this sense. Moreover, as will become apparent, "the 1930s and 1940s were important because it was at this time that the basic economic patterns of Egyptian film production were set. Except for the 1960s, when the cinema was nationalized, variations on these economic patterns persist" (Armbrust, 2004: 83).

From the late 1950s to the early 1970s, President Gamal Abdel Nasser's regime gradually took over most private production, distribution, and exhibition companies, while seizing all studios and laboratories. These moves were paralleled by the creation of two key institutions devoted to developing the newly nationalized industry. In 1957, a national film organization was created to promote the industry domestically and internationally. Although it underwent several changes in structure and mandate in its early days, this organization was consolidated as the General Film Organization (GFO) in 1963 (Shafik, 2001: 28). The GFO's mission was, broadly, to "promote" national film products, but it quickly became a source of direct funding for film production (Telmissany, 1995: 70). Thus, production throughout the 1960s was concentrated in the "public sector" *(al-qita' al-'am)*, even though some private companies were operating (with notorious difficulty) during this period (Flibbert, 2001: 115).

A second key institution was established in 1959: the High Cinema Institute *(al-ma'had al-'ali li-l-sinima)*. It remains a prime training ground for screenwriters, directors, cinematographers, art directors, graphic designers, editors, and sound engineers.[1] It is a central networking institution in today's industry, where successive generations of filmmakers make contacts that will later become useful when they work and employ their *ma'had* friends.

Nationalization was not an exceptional event, as several economic sectors were nationalized under Nasser, including textiles, mining, banks, and, most famously, the Suez Canal Company. In film production, as in other sectors, the overall effects of nationalization were twofold. On the one hand, national economic interests were divorced from colonial ones, leading to the development of an autonomous national economy under centralized state control. On the other hand, central control led to an increasing reliance on a bureaucracy that became too burdened—and too burdensome—to allow economic expansion, especially in the wake of Egypt's defeat by Israel in 1967 (Khouri, 2010: 54–57). Today, the state retains only limited control over film funding and distribution—a major issue in the 1960s, when filmmakers were bound to deal with the state bureaucracy to finance and distribute their products.

After Nasser's death in 1970, President Anwar Sadat promoted a general program of economic liberalization conventionally known as the "opening" *(infitah)*. State funding for film production dropped sharply.[2] All of production, distribution, and exhibition were once more privatized, and the Cinema Industry Chamber (*ghurfat sina'at al-sinima*) was reestablished.[3] Yet, as Flibbert observes, "the film industry in the Sadat era remained mired in a morass of state regulation and oversight" (2001: 123), a statement that may be extended to today's industry. Major studio facilities such as Studio Nahhas and the EMPC remain under state control. Egyptian filmmakers must interact with state bureaucracy to clear the censorship process, to get ticket sales approved by the tax authorities, and to secure shooting permits (see El Khachab, 2017). As Flibbert mentions, "state tax policy treated the industry more like a source of revenue than anything else. According to one observer [Samir Farid, a prominent film critic], tax collectors were sent to cinemas every single day of the week to collect the state's share of receipts, including on weekends" (2001: 124). Such stories of tax burden are common in the industry to this day.

All in all, one can distinguish four critical periods in the Egyptian film industry's history. From the mid-1930s to the late 1950s, the industry was consolidated during what is known as its "Golden Age." From the late 1950s to the early 1970s, the industry was nationalized under Nasser, and various state institutions emerged to promote national production/distribution. From the mid-1970s to the early 2000s, film production was once more liberalized as part of Egypt's "opening." From the early 2000s until today, the industry is witnessing significant changes in its financing patterns as well as a wider transition to digital cinema technologies.

Into the New Millennium

The industry underwent two major changes in the early 2000s. The first was spawned by a specific event, according to many of my interlocutors: the wildly popular release of *Isma'iliya rayih gayy* (*Return Ticket to Ismailia*, 1997). The film, a youth-oriented comedy starring emerging comedian Mohammed Heneidy, reaped unprecedented gains in domestic theaters and across the Arab world. This is said to have driven the industry into an era of prosperity on the back of light comedies and a new generation of movie stars: Ahmad Helmy, Ahmad el-Saka, Mona Zaki, and Mohammed Saad, to name some of those who are still active today. This regained prosperity contrasts with the drought of the 1990s, when production outputs fell to historical lows.[4] The 2000s witnessed a short-lived boom in commercial film production in comparison, but I doubt that it was caused by a sudden shift in audience taste toward comedy and younger stars. What coincided with increasing profit making were the larger investments made in the form of distribution loans by major satellite television channels in the Gulf, including ART and Rotana.

Distribution loans were instrumental in financing film production throughout the 2000s.[5] This model of production is sometimes called "brokerage" (*samsara*), and the producer dismissively dubbed a "broker" (*simsar*). The label evokes the small-scale brokering agents on Cairo's property market, who extract gains from transactions between private buyers and sellers without generating any wealth of their own. A *simsar* producer makes movies with the distributor's money. This is a problem, according to the well-known cinematographer Marwan Saber, because the producer has no incentive to make a "*high-quality*" product, as "he already made his money before the movie is done."[6] According to several interlocutors, "brokerage" production culminated in the rise of the film company Good News, which was eventually dissolved in the late 2000s. Good News is credited with having increased all wages in the industry by a great margin, most notably among stars,[7] and it has been at the center of regular money laundering accusations.[8]

Satellite channels largely stopped giving out loans by 2010—an event whose explanation remains mysterious, according to most of my interlocutors. As independent director Hala Galal asserted, it seemed like production was halted "because the sheikh has changed his mind," alluding to the common stereotype according to which Gulf-based investors (or "sheikhs") can shift colossal sums of money on a whim. The producer Sherif Mandour, on his part, explained this event as an aftershock of the 2007–2008 financial crisis. In his view, the crisis affected global advertising businesses in such a way that advertising revenues significantly dropped in Gulf-based satellite channels, thereby limiting their investments in film production in Egypt.

Since the early 2010s, film financing in Egypt has become a matter of individual investments. While I was conducting my fieldwork, the two most active financiers were Walid el-Kurdi in New Century and Ahmad and Mohamed El Sobky in their respective companies. These producers make movies out of pocket and shoulder all the risk in distribution. Major producers of the 2000s like Al-Arabia, Oscar, Al-Nasr, or Al-Masa were unwilling to do this without distribution loans. Other companies have resorted to a strategy of local co-production,[9] where resources are pooled on discrete projects among several producers.[10] A well-known co-producer is Mohammed Hefzi, head of Film Clinic, who admits to never going beyond 50 percent equity in investing on a single project. This contrasted with New Century's or Sobky's financing strategy in those years, or with "independent" financing strategies that relied strictly on international film festival funds and meager state resources.

The second major change in the postmillennial industry is technological. The advent of digital filmmaking has made analog shooting and postproduction technologies obsolete, including analog cameras, negative rolls, Moviola editing suites, as well as coloring and negative labs. This change is often narrated as an "inevitable" and "natural" development, according to a deterministic narrative of technological change equally prevalent in Euro-American societies (see Pfaffenberger, 1992). As one might expect, however, the actual passage to digital technologies was far from automatic. The earliest digital cinema technologies were nonlinear editing suites such as Lightworks and Avid, which arrived in Egypt in the early 1990s. According to the prominent editor Mona Rabie, the first digitally edited film was Youssef Chahine's *al-Muhagir* (*The Emigré*, 1994), but digital editing suites were more rapidly adopted in the television and advertising sectors. This early connection between digital editing and television/advertising explains why major postproduction companies today work with clients in all media sectors.

While nonlinear editing suites were well established by the early 2000s, color grading and mixing still relied on analog methods, which meant that derelict studios maintained an important role in postproduction. Since the late 1950s, the postproduction infrastructure had been under state control, most notably in Studio Misr (which was reprivatized in the early 2000s) and the EMPC (which was built in the mid-1990s under President Hosni Mubarak's auspices). These two sites were the only places where one could edit, color, and mix a film in Egypt until the advent of digital postproduction.[11] Such technologies were initially imported in the late 2000s by today's biggest private postproduction studios: Aroma and TimeCode. Digital color grading technologies (DaVinci, Luster, Base Light) and digital sound technologies (Pro Tools) made local postproduction affordable and comparable in quality to non-Egyptian facilities. As the mixer Mohammed Fawzi recalls, the costs of local postproduction between the late 1990s and the mid-2000s were equivalent to the costs of better-maintained facilities outside Egypt, where some larger Egyptian companies would finish their films.

While digital postproduction tools were becoming more and more popular, the Egyptian media industry continued to use analog cameras until the late 2000s. By the early 2010s, however, digital cameras had become the norm. The workflow between shooting and postproduction all the way to printing was digitized.[12] Since digital cinema cameras produced digital material, it became possible simply to transfer the film's files from a camera to backup hard drives to computers equipped with postproduction software, until a final film file was exported, printed, and projected. This shift has not had a significant impact on the industry's ownership structure: large sums of capital and access to distribution deals are still concentrated in the same hands. The narrative according to which digital technologies "democratize" access to media production has therefore not materialized outside the industry's margins. To add another caveat, one should not assume that this digitization process led to a "dematerialization" of filmmaking, *pace* editors who worked with greasy negatives on Moviola machines. Filmmaking was just "rematerialized," with a renewed significance attached to computers and hard drives as opposed to negatives and chemical solutions (see Chapter 3).

With significant changes in capital and technology, the contemporary film industry could be described as a collection of small- to medium-sized companies working with different sources of funding (private capital, local coproduction, festival/state funding), contracting their own cast and crew, renting equipment, securing shooting locations, and seeking postproduction services to make and sell movies on a project-by-project basis.[13] The myriad companies in today's industry are mostly inactive: some exist in name only while others produce one movie without being able to survive beyond it. In the most recent Euromed Audiovisual report, a survey of 378 commercial films found that almost 75 percent of all films between 2002 and 2012 were produced by only twenty companies (2013: 52). This pattern may be attributed to a variety of factors, not least of which is the chronic unavailability of capital. Since 2013, several major productions—including Marwan Hamed's *al-Fil al-azraq* (*The Blue Elephant*, 2014) and Sherif Arafa's *al-Gazira 2* (*The Island 2*, 2014)—have been halted for months at a time because producers were unwilling to invest more in them. I would argue that one of the main reasons behind this unavailability of capital is the tight local/regional distribution and exhibition market.

The distinction between production, distribution, and exhibition is formally recognized in Egypt, but these phases are consolidated within a few companies bound by a de facto oligopoly over domestic exhibition, whose current shape can be traced to the early 2000s. Over this period, the two largest theater-owning groups have been Renaissance (the distribution arm of Al-Arabia, which is headed by Isaad Younis) and the trio composed by Al-Nasr (headed by the late Mohammed Hassan Ramzy), Oscar (headed by Wael Abdallah), and Al-Masa (headed by Hesham Abdel-Khalek). Smaller exhibitors include Dollar Film (a holding of Walid el-Kurdi, head of New Century Film Production), Misr International Films (headed by Gaby Khoury), and the United Brothers (headed by Farouk and Walid Sabry). Until the late 2000s, the major producers were the major distributors/exhibitors. This market set unattainable standards for smaller production companies—most notably, the demand to hire major movie stars. For bigger companies, however, the oligopoly guaranteed that box-office revenue could be integrally recovered without dividing shares between a distributor and an exhibitor.

In addition to domestic exhibition, television sales have been a standard source of revenue in the industry since the establishment of terrestrial television in 1960 (Amin, 1996: 102). The Egyptian film industry quickly gained popularity across the Arab world by producing the very rare Arabic-language film content on national television channels in the region. The regional predominance of Egyptian films can be attributed to the absence of any significant competition, although political conflicts with neighboring nations, as well as increasing imports of Hollywood productions, had severely constrained the market share of Egyptian movies in the Arab world by the 1970s (Flibbert, 2001: 77–78). From the 1990s to this day, however, serial drama production sponsored by large satellite channels in the Gulf has financially dwarfed the national film and television sector.[14] Although these Gulf-based channels stopped sponsoring the film industry via distribution loans by the early 2010s, they remain the main buyers of Egyptian media products outside the country.

Overall, it is difficult to secure accurate figures on the revenue generated by commercial films in Egypt. Big production companies have the most accurate numbers on domestic ticket sales, because they hire a representative *(mandub)* traveling with each film copy to report back on theater revenues. Since financial transactions are largely cash-based, there remains some degree of doubt in the records kept by the company and the numbers reported by the sales representative. Without direct access to these records or numbers, one cannot trust the numbers available in public.[15] What obeys a more conventional distribution is the *share* of revenues secured by producers. Unless otherwise agreed, exhibitors conventionally secure 50 percent of revenues in addition to the tax on each ticket; distributors secure 10 percent of the revenue; and the rest (roughly 35 percent) is given to the producer.[16] Needless to say, these shares lose relevance when the same company produces, distributes, and exhibits the film. The question in this context is just "how many copies can you print and how many days can you stay in theaters," as the assistant director Habi Seoud once told me.

There have been notable exceptions to this pattern: El Adl Group, the now defunct Good News, both Sobky companies, Hany Gerges Fawzi's company, and Film Clinic have been distributing their movies without owning theaters. Although it is difficult to know why specific production/distribution companies are more successful under these conditions, I would argue that it is primarily about their ability to adhere to their distributors' demands, as well as their ability to cultivate interpersonal relations with them. One could argue that these producers are more successful because they are better attuned to the audience's tastes, but this argument can only mean that they are better attuned to what the distributors *think* are the audience's tastes, since these producers have no direct access to their audiences. From a producer's perspective, then, local exhibition and selling television rights to satellite channels in the Gulf—and only by extension a movie's popular appeal—constitute the hallmarks of commercial success.

The distributors' demands concern movie stars above all, and marginally the director, the screenwriter, and the storyline.[17] This star system explains why 20 to 50 percent of a film's budget can be given to two or three stars: because these stars act as the central currency between producers and distributors. A rigid star system has been a crucial feature in the national and regional distribution market since the 1940s (Flibbert, 2001: 64). The luxury of hiring a star can only be afforded by medium to large productions today. According to Euromed Audiovisual data, the average movie budget in 2008 ranged from five to twenty million Egyptian pounds, while the range was between seven and thirteen million by 2013. From sparse yet grounded evidence, I would suggest that the range for an average production dropped to five to ten million Egyptian pounds between the late 2000s and the floating of the Egyptian currency in 2016, while larger productions spent around twenty-five to thirty million Egyptian pounds. Smaller productions could spend as little as three hundred thousand and as much as a million and a half Egyptian pounds before 2016. The main difference in the budget of these productions is star salary. A major male star like Karim Abdel Aziz could command a salary rumored to reach between five and ten million Egyptian pounds in 2014.[18] For a major female star, the range is less intimidating: Mona Zaki, for instance, was rumored to have commanded a salary of one million Egyptian pounds in 2013.[19]

Star salaries are not standardized; they are negotiated on an individual basis with different companies. While they vary according to the company, the degree to which they are perceived as being "deserved" depends on the star's commercial success. While preparing Daoud Abdel Sayyed's *Out of the Ordinary*, a star asked for two million Egyptian pounds to make the movie. New Century refused to pay and eventually booted the star off the project, because they did not value the star's commercial status enough to pay the full amount. In a movie like *Décor*, led by a minor female star and two minor male stars, the overall star budget was around two million Egyptian pounds, in a film whose budget was around ten million. This sets star salary at about 20 percent in an average-sized production, though this proportion can reach 30 to 50 percent in a larger production. For example, in *Suni'a fi Misr* (*Made in Egypt*, 2014), the star Ahmad Helmy was rumored to have commanded a salary of ten million Egyptian pounds, which is equivalent to what was spent on the remainder of the film. In this context, as Shafik soberly states, "little remains for props, set, costumes, transport, and wages" (1998: 27). The script supervisor Mariam el-Bagoury imaged it in another way: "Stars look like *aliens* on set." They are better dressed than everyone else, they perform better than other actors, but because they get a greater share of the budget, they are often the "shining stars in a bad production."

Overall, the pattern of production in the contemporary Egyptian film industry remains similar to the one established in the 1930s. Flibbert describes it as follows,

> Most of the producers in this period made only one or two films per year, revealing the disorganized, almost speculative nature of early production and its financing. Domestic and foreign distribution generally was undertaken by the individual producers themselves. A few of them, such as Togo Mizrahi and Studio Misr, led the way by their consistent efforts to make and distribute several films each year. But the vast majority of production was done by much smaller-scale operators, who either entered the business temporarily or failed to last more than a short while. (2001: 111–12)

While today's industry shows similarities to that in the 1930s, it carries the weight of successive historical legacies, including extensive dealings with state bureaucracy (since the 1950s), a much larger pool of trained workers (since the 1960s), and previously unavailable funding and distribution outlets in regional and international television channels (since the 1960s) and/or festivals (since the 2000s).

An Interpersonal Political Economy

Notwithstanding some marginal cases, the contemporary Egyptian film industry is concentrated in Giza, on the west bank of Cairo. This has been the case since the 1930s, when early studios in Alexandria were overshadowed by the building of Studio Misr in the Haram neighborhood in Giza (Flibbert, 2001: 64). The High Cinema Institute, the National Film Institute, Studio Nahhas, and Studio al-Ahram were built in the same area. Many production/distribution companies, as well as the biggest casting companies, equipment rental companies, and postproduction companies, have offices in Dokki and Mohandessin, two upper-end neighborhoods in Giza. Even the EMPC, which was built on the outskirts of Cairo, is located within accessible distance to Haram by car.

This geographic concentration comes with advantages comparable to what has been noted in the case of post-1980s Hollywood (see Storper and Christopherson, 1987; Scott, 2002). While Hollywood and Cairo operate on vastly different scales, both industries are vertically disintegrated, which means that the production process is not single-handedly controlled by large conglomerates. Under these conditions, geographical concentration eases access to information concerning new projects, makes face-to-face interactions in ongoing projects easier and more affordable, gives access to a large, skilled workforce, and eases access to the institutions regulating the industry. It also provides a distinctive geographic milieu in which conventional landmarks are accessible to shoot (for example, the Hollywood sign in Beverly Hills, the Qasr al-Nil bridge in Cairo). Thus, geographical proximity is a prime advantage in maintaining the long-term interpersonal links on which the Egyptian film industry is based. In fact, cinema, satellite television drama, and advertising share the same labor market and the same shooting/postproduction infrastructure. The Egyptian media sector constitutes a consolidated "market" in this sense: *al-su'*, as it is known in the industry's insider language.

"The advantage in an industry like Egypt," said New Century's general manager Ahmad Badawy, "is that everyone knows everyone else." The production manager Khaled Adam disagreed: he thought that the worst thing in Egypt is that you always deal with individuals *(afrad)* and not companies *(sharikat)*. This is a problem, he said, because some individuals have a monopoly over specific professions, such that they are not motivated by competition to improve their services. The problem is exacerbated when Adam fights *(yi'fish)* with someone, because he becomes unable to work with this person (and possibly their company). Interacting with companies would ideally be different, according to Adam: if someone else decided not to work one day, his own work would not be affected because there would always be someone to replace the absentee. To Adam's disappointment, this is not the case in the Egyptian film industry. Whether seen in a positive or a negative light, all institutions in today's industry work thanks to the interpersonal sway of individuals connected with other individuals.

Ganti's ethnography of Bollywood likewise emphasizes "the centrality of face-to-face interaction in the Hindi film production process" (2012: 191). Unlike in Hollywood, where professional intermediaries like "publicists, agents, or personal managers" abound, Ganti argues that "personal relations and Bombay-based social networks serve as the mediating and gatekeeping force within the industry" (2012: 193). This description is perfectly applicable to commercial film production in Egypt, where interpersonal relations, by which I mean direct relations between named individuals, are central in grasping the economy of film production. This networked labor market is characteristic of commercial film production outside Cairo and Bombay, including in Dhaka (Hoek, 2014: 79–84), London (Blair, 2001), Paris (Darré, 2006: 127), and post-1980s Los Angeles (Christopherson, 2008; Ortner, 2013: 160–63). What is specific to the Egyptian case is the extent to which this interpersonal logic governs training patterns and institutional transactions beyond the tightly knit circles of film production (even in interactions with state bureaucracy, see El Khachab, 2017). For instance, in a strictly institutionalist account, one might think that the production companies specializing in film, television, and advertising would contract different types of workers. The interpersonal account traced below will show, however, why film workers with good contacts can have access to the television and advertising markets as well. In fact, most film workers tend to seek employment in all media sectors, where more advantageous salaries allow them to maintain a steady income outside filmmaking seasons.[20]

Ganti notes that kinship networks "provide a source of personnel, a site for training, and a form of organization for the film industry" in Bombay (2004: 55). This description is somewhat applicable to Egypt as well. For instance, my mother's family, the Telmissanys, are famous for the director Kamel Telmissany, the pioneering documentarians Abdel Qader and Hassan Telmissany, as well as the star cinematographer Tarek el-Telmissany (who was initially trained by his father Hassan). Networks of kin, in this case, are a "source of personnel" and a "site of training." Workers who grew up in a film household gain insider knowledge that allows them to navigate the industry, but I would argue that this advantage is not structured specifically by kinship networks. More broadly, the interpersonal links cultivated within a given family, and between the family and the wider industry, are more central to the industry's organization. Being affiliated to the guild of filmmakers, in this sense, is more important than the nature of the affiliation (by kin or, say, by training in the High Cinema Institute). Therefore, kinship per se is not a "form of organization" in the Egyptian film industry, except insofar as certain families control core production/distribution/exhibition companies over generations.[21]

In the industry's insider language, all private companies are associated with specific names. Al-Arabia is known as "Isaad Younis' company"; Oscar is known as "Wael Abdallah's company"; InCast, a major casting agency, is called "Hazem el-Aswany's company"; and TimeCode, a major postproduction company, is called "Mohammed Abul-Saad's company." This pattern is indicative of the industry's interpersonal workings, where a production company seeking to cast some extras is better described as Ahmad Badawy asking Hazem el-Aswany to get a deal on extras. If Aswany's deal is not suitable, Badawy may try to get a better deal with Sayyed Rashed, or Ibrahim Safina, or Ahmad Tammam. All these "casting agents" *(regiseir)* do not necessarily have established companies, but they have enough manpower and contacts to service any production team with extras. Ultimately, the institutional description (the production company hires a casting agency) is less accurate than the interpersonal one (Badawy hires Aswany).

While there is a clear sense in which some service-lending companies are larger and more influential than others, this size advantage is based on interpersonal links with production companies as opposed to institutional ones. To give a concrete example, TimeCode was only created in the mid-2000s, yet it quickly rose to prominence in the industry. This is partly, one may argue, because it offered access to some of the latest digital postproduction equipment with highly qualified technicians. More important, however, the company was headed by Mohammed Abul-Saad, who had acquired a long-lasting reputation in the postproduction business in the 1990s, all the while cultivating personal links with several major players in the industry, such as well-known director Sharif Arafa. I cannot dwell on each major company extensively, but I wish to give a brief idea of the way in which companies entertain interpersonal links by outlining how *Décor* was produced and distributed by New Century Film Production. With enough evidence, however, this interpersonal description could be extended to the whole industry. Indeed, the most accurate diagram of the industry would be a gigantic network of filmmaker-nodes connected with other filmmaker-nodes via common working trajectories.

The current owner of New Century is Walid el-Kurdi. In 1949, his father Ismail el-Kurdi founded Dollar Film, which ranked among the country's biggest distributors until the industry was nationalized in the 1950s. Since Walid el-Kurdi never came to Cairo, his general manager Ahmad Badawy made all daily decisions in his name and with his approval. When *Décor* was initially proposed by Mohamed Diab and Ahmad Abdalla to New Century, Badawy accepted on the condition that Horeya Farghaly (the star actress who had collaborated on several New Century productions) was included in the project. Diab had previously worked with New Century on the movie *678* (2010). Abdalla did not know Kurdi or Badawy but was recommended by Diab. After stars Khaled Abol Naga (with whom Abdalla worked on several projects) and Maged el-Kedwany (who is well-known as a character actor in the industry) were added to the project, Badawy reached a deal with Abdalla and Diab on *Décor*.

On the production side, Badawy hired Ahmed Farghalli to be the line producer for *Décor*. The two worked together at Good News. They were both assistants with Nabil Sobhi, a well-known line producer who incidentally manages studio rentals in Studio Misr (where New Century regularly rents studio spaces). Like his colleagues, Farghalli's team included friends, relatives, and recommended candidates. His production manager Mohammed Setohy worked with him while they were at Good News under Nabil Sobhi. The location manager Ahmad Abdallah Abdel Halim was his high school friend. The production assistants included Hany Abdel Latif, who studied at the same university as Farghalli; Mahmoud Abdallah, Ahmad's brother; Georges Ramsis, Jr., the son of a well-known line producer in Egypt; Adham el-Sayeh, who was recommended by the director Ahmad Abdalla; and the list goes on.

The creative crew was chosen by Ahmad Abdalla to include the assistant director Omar el-Zohairy, the cinematographer Tarek Hefny, the art directors Asem Ali and Nihal Farouk, the stylist Salma Sami, the sound engineer Ahmad Saleh, and later the editor Sara Abdalla. Ahmad Abdalla had worked with Zohairy, Hefny, Farouk, Saleh, and Abdalla on previous projects. Asem Ali came highly recommended for his work in Nadine Khan's film, *Harag wa marag* (*Chaos and Disorder*, 2012), while Salma Sami came recommended for her work as assistant to Nahed Nasrallah (the most famous costume designer in Egypt). Each crew member, in turn, brought his or her own assistants. Zohairy brought Jaylan Auf (movement script supervisor), who came recommended by Ahmad Abdalla personally, and Mariam el-Bagoury (costume script supervisor), who came recommended by Kawthar Younes (who had previously worked with Zohairy's mentor, Wael Mandour).[22] Zohairy also hired the casting agent Ahmad Hashem, with whom he had worked previously.

The cinematographer Hefny hired the focus puller Hossam Mohammed and the gaffer Mahmoud Morsi, who worked with him on previous movies and commercials. The art director Ali brought his usual assistant, Mohammed Ezzat, as well as his usual builder, Hussein Wezza, while his colleague Farouk brought a prop master with whom she had been working, Mohammed Seyaha. One could go down the hiring cascade by describing how the gaffer's crew, or the builder's crew, or the prop master's crew were hired based on interpersonal links. I could also indicate how *Décor* was distributed in Renaissance cinemas in addition to New Century cinemas given Isaad Younis' good relations with Walid el-Kurdi. Yet, I will spare the reader these details and clarify some basic assumptions in this interpersonal network.

Working relations in the Egyptian film industry are based on friendship, kinship, or sustained interaction at work. When personal relations are not direct, so to speak, they are established via a *wasta*, an intermediary individual. While the term *wasta* has a somewhat nepotistic connotation in Egypt, the actual role played by various interceding parties in hiring decisions is crucial. While talking with the assistant director Zohairy and the stylist Sami one afternoon in New Century's office, the production manager Khaled Adam said, "It's important to have a *wasta* to enter the industry, but once you're in, where you end up is a matter of *shatara* [skill]." The importance of *shatara* will be addressed in Chapter 2, but what matters here is Zohairy's reaction to this statement. He asked Sami, "Did Nahed Nasrallah recommend you?" "Absolutely!" she answered matter-of-factly, going on to recount a situation in which the famed costume designer vouched for her in another job. In *Décor*, this vouching process was evident in the case of the costume script supervisor Mariam el-Bagoury and the director Ahmad Abdalla, both introduced to their potential hirer by an intermediary individual.

In the few cases where a worker is hired without prior connections or intermediaries, s/he is hired based on reputation *(sum'a)*. The Arabic term *sum'a* is straightforwardly equivalent to the English word "reputation," but I am inclined to understand it in its literal sense—as something that is heard (about someone). The art director Asem Ali, for instance, claimed that he would not work on a television serial drama because it would bring his reputation down in cinema circles. He willingly worked in the advertising sector, however, where ephemeral productions did not affect his name in "the market" to the same extent. Word of mouth is vital to the creation and sustenance of one's reputation within the industry. This occurred to me while Khaled Adam was chatting with Zohairy on the same afternoon in New Century's office. "Who are your friends in the industry?" asked Adam, who did not know Zohairy very well at the time. Zohairy replied with a long list of names, while Adam jumped in periodically to say, "I know him" or "I've never worked with him." These types of conversation are frequent in the film industry; they allow the interlocutors to make up their minds about each other based on the people they know while keeping tabs on connections that could become useful when it comes to getting work or contracting someone in the future.

The importance of reputation is perhaps best seen in the case of actors. Being a star, after all, is a matter of reputation among producers and distributors. Likewise, working regularly as a secondary actor or as an extra requires attention to one's reputation among directors, assistant directors, and casting agents. Although I have spent little time with actors, I can say that their reputation among production and direction crew members is built on two bases: first, their ability to execute well (in the director's or the producer's estimation) a role in which they have been cast, and, second, their on-set behavior (for instance, their politeness and punctuality). Actors who are judged to be skilled at a given role are likely to be cast in a similar role in later film projects, which is why typecasting is a common phenomenon in Egyptian cinema. If an actor's behavior is rowdy or disrespectful, however, s/he might disqualify him/herself from future working opportunities. I witnessed this in casting brainstorming sessions among production and direction crew members in *Poisonous Roses* and *The Cat and the Mouse*, where certain names were immediately excluded from the conversation, even if they would have been adequate to the role.

Nearly all cast and crew members are hired on a contract-by-contract basis. No one is permanently hired by production companies except the general manager, the accountants, some company representatives, and the office maintenance staff. Contracts can be made for a lump sum to be paid over pre-agreed installments or for a weekly/daily salary.[23] The accepted notion is that all salaries are based on previous salaries within a given company.[24] This means that raises can only come through individual negotiation *or* a simultaneous increase in rates within a given profession, which is difficult to accomplish in the absence of effective unions.[25] Conventionally, salaries are collected every "week," meaning every six shooting days, with a 10 percent payment *('arbun)* given upon signing the contract.[26] While paper contracts are signed, they are not binding in practice. Workers in Egyptian media production, whether in advertising or television or film, frequently complain that they work without getting paid on time, and sometimes without getting paid at all. A video-assist worker once complained about his low pay on a New Century production, but still sang the company's praises. "They're respectable," he said, because at least they pay all the money on time without withholding it, a situation he deemed exceptional in the industry. This sentiment is well summed up by the colorist David Maher: "The issue isn't the salary. The salary is okay, but good luck collecting it."

One might think that this contract system translates into an open labor market where crew members circulate as they wish, but the practice is different because hiring is nested in an implicit order of decision-making. The producer hires the director; the director hires the assistant director; and the assistant director hires the continuity script supervisors and the second assistants. Likewise, the director hires the cinematographer and the art director, who in turn hire a gaffer and a prop master, who in turn hire their first and second assistants. While hiring decisions are ultimately under the producer's purview—s/he is the one paying after all—these decisions are in practice left to each team's head or sub-head, even when it comes to replacing crew members who leave (or are made to leave) the project. According to the line producer Ahmed Farghalli, this hiring structure poses problems "art-wise and production-wise" *(fanniyan wa intagiyan)*. For instance, a director might not like a star's makeup artist who does not give him/her what s/he wants, but the star might insist on keeping him/her anyway because s/he likes him. The production team therefore needs to manage a conflict that would not have arisen had hiring decisions been concentrated, say, in the director's hands.

In short, all workers in the Egyptian film industry either have a personal contact with their hirer, or they know a person who knows their hirer, or they have a list of achievements such that their name circulates widely enough in the industry for them to become hirable. This hiring pattern— nested contracting based on interpersonal relations—has consequences for the way in which workers are brought into the industry, hierarchical superiors are considered, and career paths are traced. I will discuss these elements in greater detail in Chapter 2, but it bears noticing how this interpersonal logic permeates working relations even in the way institutions interact within the industry.

Local Models of the Industry

This chapter has striven to give a sense of the Egyptian film industry's overall shape, its historical evolution, as well as its central organization around interpersonal relations. The extent to which this form of organization permeates the industry is not always underscored by Egyptian filmmakers. In local understandings, the gang-like nature of interpersonal networks *(shilaliya)* is on par with divisions between "commercial cinema" *(al-sinima al-tugariya)* and "independent cinema" *(al-sinima al-mustaqilla)*. The idea of independent cinema was pushed by a group of filmmakers in the late 1990s as an alternative to the mainstream. Much like in the American indie industry, "independent filmmaking sees itself as different from, and better than, Hollywood in its ethos and practices of making films" (Ortner, 2013: 30). In Egypt, the whole so-called commercial enterprise is not Hollywood, but "the market": the permeable job market between advertising, television drama production, and cinema. While independence is articulated by opposition to this commercial mainstream, the nature of the opposition is unclear. Is it opposition to mainstream production patterns? To mainstream sources of funding? To mainstream stories and plotlines?

According to Hala Galal, an independent filmmaker who claims to have been among the first to identify as an "independent" in the 1990s, independence means being "independent from the market's conditions" *(mustaqill min shurut al-su')*. These conditions include commercial conventions about film length and plotlines: "all movies should have a little comedy and a little drama," in Galal's words. This transforms movies into "tin cans," that is, a mass-market product. In contrast, independent director and head of Zero

Productions Tamer el-Said argues that independence is being "independent in administrative decisions" *(mustaqill fi-l-qararat al-idariya)*. In this view, the artistic process must be independent from the commercial interests prevalent in the market, which means that independent cinema must have a different production model with a different infrastructure. With this idea in mind, the independent director Hala Lotfy, head of the production cooperative Hassala, refused to hire her cooperative's equipment to mainstream productions. "Imagine an independent movie needs to be edited, but I agreed to lend my editing stations to Aroma or some other company?" This poses an unwelcome dilemma. Rental revenues are not worth the sacrifice of what Lotfy sees as Hassala's mission: to help filmmakers *own* their movies.

For independent producer Mohammed el-Tohami, independent cinema seeks to reach the same public as commercial cinema, but by presenting an alternative viewpoint. "The only movies I like are the ones that can go to the streets," he said. Contrary to zero-budget films, which are made in a "do-it-yourself" fashion, independent cinema seeks to build the industry *(sina'a)*.[27] And contrary to art-house cinema exhibited in limited venues, independent cinema seeks a mass public. This wish is echoed by Hala Lotfy, who argued that her ultimate goal would be to distribute to the public, who could watch her movie and give back money that she could use to make new films. Implicit in Lotfy's argument is a distinction between "movie theaters," where she wants to distribute her movies and attract audiences, and "the market," which is the corrupt distribution structure standing between her and her anticipated audience.

The criteria for independence are still unclear. Is independence determined by production conditions, as Galal and Said seem to suggest, or by the target audience as Tohami argues? One possible answer, which was articulated by aspiring director Abdallah al-Ghaly, is that "there is no such thing as independent cinema." I was a little startled when he made this remark on a late January evening, because he worked as an assistant director with the adamantly independent Hala Lotfy. Ghaly doubled down: "Independent cinema has not produced an *alternative* cinema," he said, it just gave an individual platform to directors such as Ibrahim Battout and Ahmad Abdalla. He said he was totally disillusioned with independent cinema in Egypt because younger directors are still condemned to either make movies within commercial conditions or "beg for grants" *(nishhat fandat)*. Independence is not a fact from this viewpoint, but a promise that aspiring directors like Ghaly can make their own movies on their own terms—a promise that has never been fulfilled, in the young director's view.

This promise is precisely what Mohammed Rashad, another assistant director with Hala Lotfy, sees as being characteristic of "independence." One should not try to classify a film, in his view, because what counts most is what the director wants to make of the film. "I have the right, as an independent filmmaker, to make movies with my own conditions, and I have the right to present it to a wide audience" and to accrue revenue in the process, as he suggested. Rashad's argument has a distinctly normative flavor, seeking to assert what independence *should be* rather than what it *is*. His claims seemed to reach a limit when he mentioned that Atef el-Tayeb, a well-known director in the 1980s, made movies according to criteria that were, incidentally, shared by the market. "So he's kind of an independent filmmaker," he said hesitantly, perhaps because he could see the contradiction in his own argument. On the one hand, Rashad wanted to commit to a rigid distinction between "independence" and "the market"; on the other, he wanted to commit to the director's individuality, even if his/her work lies within the market's conditions.

A more cynical take on the boundary between independent and commercial production was articulated by the director Ahmad Fawzi Saleh, who does not identify as an "independent" even though his aesthetic choices lead him to being categorized as such by industry insiders. According to Fawzi, people who show off as "independent" just want to get into the commercial industry but cannot because they lack the necessary connections. The assistant director Omar el-Zohairy, who worked with both so-called "independent" and "commercial" directors, spoke in a similar vein. He argued that independents often do not like the market because they get no work there, "but no one ever asks if s/he is good enough to work in commercial cinema." In this sense, a lot of people working in independent circles make movies independently until they get their opportunity in the market, which raises questions about the boundedness of each circle and the integrity of the positions taken by these social agents.

I would argue that the emic distinction between independent and commercial filmmakers is an instance of "boundary-work," whereby a professional community traces its outer limits by exclusionary means (Ganti, 2012: 7). What Galal, Said, Ghaly, or Rashad are doing in seeking to define "independence" is to assert their adhesion to an independent side in a game where the important thing is to take a position. This game is equally well played by social agents adhering to the commercial side of the industry. When I told the cinema journalist Walid Abul Seoud that I was researching the model of commercial film production in Egypt, he immediately replied,

> There's no such thing as commercial cinema in Egypt, because all cinema is made according to the market's standards. So there's no independent cinema either. Everyone who says they're independent, like *Heliopolis* [dir. Ahmad Abdalla, 2009], *Fi shaqqat Masr al-Gadida* [*Inside the Heliopolis Apartment*, dir. Mohammed Khan, 2007] . . . all these are made within the market's conditions.

Implicit in Abul Seoud's claim is that commercial cinema is a standard that cannot be escaped, thereby delegitimizing so-called independent cinema by arguing that the whole field is occupied by commercial enterprises.

The assistant director Karim el-Mihi staked his position in a different way when he said that his projected documentary, *The Crisis of Egyptian Film Production*, would be a commercial documentary. This is a somewhat unorthodox idea in a context where documentaries survive thanks to film festivals without access to movie theaters. Mihi still wanted his documentary to be commercial because, in his own words, "I don't want it to be independent." He continued: "I don't even understand what independent means??! What is it independent from?" He added that independent filmmakers seem to "make movies for themselves" and "cherish them like their own babies," without wanting to reach wider audiences. Mihi's argument is directly contradicted by Tohami's or Lotfy's vision of an independent cinema that would reach mass audiences. The crux of their disagreement is whether the market's standards are the only ones that can reach a mass audience—as in Abul Seoud's narrative—or whether there is a different way to address such audiences. No matter how the disagreement is resolved, what matters is how social agents commit to a given position in a game of position-taking.

Standing between independent and commercial circles, Zohairy argued that each world had its advantages and disadvantages. One of the main problems of independent cinema, in his narrative, is that it does not concern itself with the "*quality*" of the product, especially among filmmakers in downtown Cairo.[28] This is confirmed by the common representation among workers in the commercial industry that the independent scene is full of "amateurs," whereas only the market houses "professionals," along with its attendant training ground: the High Cinema Institute. Later in the conversation,

Zohairy recognized that he had learned a lot from working with independents: above all, how to concentrate his film to create lower production costs while maintaining a similar filmmaking "*quality*." This explains why major film companies are increasingly hiring independent filmmakers, in his view, because they already make quality movies at a low cost.

Zohairy seemed to be contradicting himself. How can independents not care about "*quality*" yet be hired because they make "*quality*" movies? The answer is that, within the same conversation, Zohairy drew two different boundaries in his attempt to position himself between the commercial and the independent: one between the downtown film scene and the rest of the film industry, and another between would-be "independents" and "nonindependents" within this industry. What he did is not exceptional, given the multifarious meanings associated with independent and commercial cinema, but it is instructive with regard to the way in which the boundary between independent and commercial cinema shifts according to where workers position themselves. The distinction remains, at its core, one between individuals and the social relations they entertain. This is well illustrated by Zohairy's example, as he could fall in either camp depending on the set of social relations he chooses to invoke.

What is common to the commercial and independent sides of the industry is that they both work through interpersonal relations. If independents tend to work more with independents, it is because they have better connections with each other, while gaining access to "the market" and its distribution outlets is difficult for them precisely because they lack these connections. Difficulties with access to local distribution channels is, I would argue, the central difference between the commercial and independent sides of the industry. On separate occasions, the director Ahmad Abdalla and independent producers Mohammed Samir and Mohammed el-Tohami described the situation as though there are two tight circles that never come into contact: one representing the oligopolistic industry and another representing people with little access to it.

I should mention that the labels "commercial" and "independent" have no bearing on the inherent commercial aims of these filmmaking enterprises. Although their sources of funding and their target audiences may differ (local exhibition as opposed to film festivals), both so-called independent and commercial cinema seek, in part, to sell film products. As Ahmad Fawzi Saleh argues, one can try to make films with a different aesthetic, but all Egyptian filmmakers rely on the same labor market to get all the people who will work on their projects and the money that will help substantiate their daily existence. And even people making "independent" films distribute their movies in Europe or in regional film festivals, where they are still bound by a market that has its own rules, albeit different ones to the Egyptian one.

"Let's See . . ."

Preparations are well under way in *Décor* by mid-November 2013. I come into New Century's office around two o'clock in the afternoon and I sit alone with the production assistant Mustafa. It is still early. Hany, another assistant, walks in shortly afterward. He had been scouting a sketchy apartment in the Abbasiya neighborhood. "It was absolutely not in reference!" he says about the mismatch between the apartment and the artistic crew's demands. He adds that the area around the apartment "isn't clean enough" and that no one ever shot there before. "People were asking me if I'm the guy who'll set up the gas when I was taking pictures. . . . Who the hell had the idea of sending me there?" Setohy, the production manager, who is in the office by then, answers that the apartment was suggested by a real estate broker *(simsar)* but that they did not get to see pictures beforehand.

Ahmed Farghalli walks into the office around five o'clock and, two hours later, the art directors Asem and Nihal sit down with Farghalli and Setohy, while Hany and I sit next to them in complete silence. Farghalli starts showing pictures of all the apartments scouted by the production team on his MacBook. Scrolling through them at a rate of one or two pictures per second, Farghalli indicates the neighborhood in which each apartment is located, pointing at specific pictures to give a sense of the apartment's interior. "That's the entrance, that's the kitchen," he indicates while pointing at the screen in a mechanical manner.

Asem and Nihal comment on each apartment with short judgment calls. "It looks nice *(hilw)*." "That won't work *(ma yinfa'sh)*!" "It needs to be more contrasted," says Nihal about a kitchen where the floor and the wall have nearly identical colors. They discuss specific aspects of the apartment: its size, its hardwood floors, what the windows look onto. Asem makes a recurring comment about wanting "good angles" *(zawaya kwayisa)*, but I am not sure whether he means good camera angles or good corners to build the set (because *zawya* means both "angle" and "corner"). They generally seem to be looking at the apartments with the specific location into which they will have to transform the space in mind: a location is "good for" Mustafa and Maha's apartment, or Sharif and Maha's apartment, or Dr. Magid's clinic.

Farghalli shows Asem and Nihal a villa I scouted with Setohy on Boules Hanna Street, next to New Century's office. "It can work both as an apartment *and* a clinic for Dr. Magid," says Farghalli with a smile, relishing the opportunity of shooting two locations in one villa. "The villa looks great," the art directors muse, but they remain undecided because there is no garden. Farghalli shows them the villa's garden with an air of innocent objection, but the art directors are unconvinced. "It seems a little small." "Ahmad Abdalla might change his shot from a garden to the front reception." "If Ahmad Abdalla is okay with it, I'll be okay with it."

Neither Asem nor Nihal write anything down; they just comment on what they see, leaving Farghalli and Setohy to keep notes on approved apartments. When the art directors leave, Farghalli gathers Hany, Mustafa, Setohy, and Ahmad Abdallah Abdel Halim to arrange a tentative schedule for viewings in person that coming Friday. Each production worker receives an assignment in a different neighborhood: Hany will contact people in Garden City, Setohy will contact people in Heliopolis, and Ahmad will take Setohy's contacts in Dokki and arrange viewings later in the afternoon. "I'll be arranging viewings from ten in the morning," concludes Farghalli, while Setohy meticulously notes down all the locations on a sheet of paper. Each crew member notes down his assignment.

A few days later, I sit again in New Century's office with Farghalli, Setohy, Ahmad Abdallah Abdel Halim, and the accountant Hosny. They are waiting to meet with the artistic crew to settle on the scouting locations that will be viewed in person. As soon as Asem walks in, Farghalli announces that the villa where they could have shot two locations has just been rented out for a year. "I've brought you a better clinic," he immediately says while showing some pictures to Asem on his computer. "It looks nice," says Asem reservedly, adding that it would take too much work to clean and decorate the latter villa. Nihal, Tarek Hefny, Ahmad Abdalla, and Omar el-Zohairy arrive later to look through Farghalli's scouting pictures.

Ahmad Abdalla asks Farghalli to scroll quickly through the first two apartments as he agrees to check them in person. "I like the checkered floors," he mentions after a brief glance. The following apartment is not in style. "It's too modern, it doesn't look 1960s at all," says Ahmad Abdalla. Farghalli switches folders quickly. Next up is an apartment with a view on the Nile in Dokki. Ahmad Abdalla looks unconvinced: "I don't like duplexes. . . ." "There are very clear pictures of the Nile," says Tarek, arguing that it would not work, as Mustafa and Maha's apartment is meant to be in Alexandria. "But it's got nice levels," pleads Asem. "Let's see . . . ," concedes Ahmad Abdalla in an unconvinced tone.

Farghalli scrolls some more and the crew comments more. I have not eaten much all day, so I am fighting to concentrate on the dense exchanges. Farghalli is about to show some apartments in Alexandria when Ahmad Abdalla interrupts the proceedings. "We need to be clear about how we're going to transition between internal and external shooting in Mustafa and Maha's apartment." When asked how *exactly* he will shoot the transition, Ahmad Abdalla shrugs: "I don't know yet." Asem and Nihal insist that it will be impossible to find an identical window in Cairo and in Alexandria to shoot the transition.

After much discussion, they agree to shoot all the internal scenes and the transition in Cairo, then to shoot the building's external scenes in Alexandria. Farghalli is still showing apartments, but as they have reached this conclusion in the meantime, it seems clear that whatever external façade will be chosen in Alexandria depends on the Cairo apartment's internal look. There is collective agreement to settle on the Alexandria building later.

2
Process

There is a genuine sense in which filmmaking is a teleological process. "The film" is the filmmakers' ultimate goal, a *telos* toward which the production is marching. This is not to say that "the film" is an ideal artwork waiting to be carved out of formless matter. Rather, to echo Grimaud's remark, cinema forces us to decenter "the analysis of creative processes that have so far been a little too centered on a screenplay, an author, an imaginary or a language, since filmic material, in order to be constituted, implies multiple little contributions, each with its own temporality, and not all of which can be reduced to them [that is, a screenplay, an author, an imaginary, or a language]" (2003: 11). To describe the filmmaking process, one needs to recognize that "the film," although it does not exist now, is expected to exist later, and that its existence depends on a specific series of operations happening, "each with its own temporality." In this sense, the film's future is not *uncertain*, because its outcome is known and expected, but it is *imponderable* given the varying ways in which filmmakers can arrive at their destination.

This chapter describes the division of labor, modes of apprenticeship, and operational sequence underlying the journey toward the film. Before setting foot in Cairo in 2013, I had never seriously thought about the patterns of work I would encounter in the Egyptian film industry. I was wholly driven by exploring the various uses to which technological devices were put, and I wrongly assumed that labor was marginal to these uses. Quickly, I realized not only that my notes were filled with references to work tasks, contracts, salaries, career paths, and so on, but also that these references were vital to understanding the filmmaking process itself. While labor hierarchies shape core assumptions about *who* is responsible for dealing with specific imponderable outcomes, the workers' embodied apprenticeship and the operational sequence in which they are engaged shape *how* and *when* they deal with it. The incorporated predispositions of filmmakers and the step-by-step nature of the filmmaking sequence inform the everyday practices of Egyptian filmmakers as well as their conception of the film's future.

The intricacies of the Egyptian film industry's division of labor are too numerous to discuss in a single chapter. The detail of professional hierarchies and production operations has been abridged in two tables in the appendix to this book. This chapter instead synthesizes some important assumptions about the process of commercial film production in Egypt, with an eye to showing how these assumptions underlie the mediation of unknown yet expected futures. First, I describe the general concern with hierarchy in working relations, with attention to the distinction between artistic and executive labor. Second, I describe existing modes of apprenticeship and promotion in the industry. Third, I illustrate how the operational sequence of Egyptian film production is understood to move from one stage to the next via mediating writings, images, sounds, spaces, and times. After introducing these assumptions in turn, I come back to the crucial fact that they are not evenly shared by all workers in the industry, which puts in perspective the way in which different social agents engage with what I have described as a singular "process" of film production.

Labor Hierarchies

There is an enduring, conscious, and vertical sense of hierarchy in Egyptian film production. This is striking insofar as commercial filmmaking is not vertically integrated, meaning it is not centralized in conglomerates that own all production components within a single corporate structure. Since cast and crew members are hired on an interpersonal basis, one might have expected working relations to look something like an actor-network, where each crew member occupies an equivalent node in a web of interpersonal connections. Yet the emphasis on hierarchy is widely prevalent. On the ground, I was struck by the way in which workers down the ladder tended to address their superiors as "chief" *(ya rayyis)*, while superiors would address them by their names or nicknames. This usage runs down the hierarchy, such that all workers stand to be at once someone's chief and someone's subordinate.

The line producer in *Décor*, Ahmed Farghalli, answered to no one on set. His commands were religiously followed by his crew members, to the point where some lamented that their obedience shaded into undignified submissiveness *(ta'ris)*. However, when the general manager Ahmad Badawy walked on set on the morning of a difficult shooting day, Farghalli became noticeably tenser and more agitated. In his own chief's presence, Farghalli could have hardly behaved otherwise. "When Badawy comes, everyone starts running around," said the production assistant Hany Abdel Latif, who argued that crew members would run without apparent reason just to perform that they were working in front of their superior. Likewise, the usually relaxed and authoritative Badawy would become tense and extra careful when he received phone calls from his own chief, the producer Walid el-Kurdi.

What matters, in this sense, is the interpersonal recognition of chiefs and subordinates, of people who issue commands and people who obey. These hierarchies are consciously recognized, discussed, and sometimes resisted. For example, on the set of *Décor*, the assistant director Omar el-Zohairy once reprimanded his script supervisor for asking an actress to change costumes when there was no need. Zohairy wanted to ensure that his assistant never repeated this mistake, but the script supervisor saw no mistake, arguing that the director Ahmad Abdalla had asked her to tell the actress to change costumes. Zohairy immediately took a pencil and paper to draw a little diagram of the direction team's hierarchy, including the director, the assistant director, the script supervisors, and their trainees. This diagram expressed a clear and consistent representation of the division of labor within the direction unit, which was shared by all the crew members I interviewed on the matter. Zohairy went on to explain how the director discharges all executive details onto the assistant director, which means that decisions concerning costume changes—as well as decisions concerning actors' schedules, continuity issues, and changes of lighting—needed to go through the assistant director before they went to the director. "This is illogical," exclaimed the script supervisor, but Zohairy had already prepared his retort: "There's the logic of life and the logic of work."

Zohairy's reprimand reinforced the industry's conventions *('urf)*, which indeed would have required a subordinate to report to his/her immediate chief over a logistical decision. The term *'urf*, which literally means "what is known," is used in practice to talk about social customs or conventions in Egypt. Within the film industry, the term designates the shared implicit knowledge imparted to insiders through informal apprenticeship. This emic notion is useful in thinking about how industry-specific conventions can conceptually merge with broader ones. For instance, the hierarchical logic pervading the film industry and constituting an important aspect of its *'urf* extends to artisanal and mechanical crafts as well (see Elyachar, 2005: 96–136; Chakravarti, 2016: 49–97). Indeed, there seems to be a historical link between the organization of masculine labor in various mechanical crafts of European origin in Egypt, including cinema, car mechanics, and industrial manufacture.[1] This continuity is evident in the master-to-apprentice mode of enskilling; the systematic attribution of superior technical skill to the master; the master's exclusive right to "stand at the machine" *(yu'af 'al-makana)*; and a horizontal model of career advancement, where a skilled apprentice who wants to become a master needs to leave his workshop and open a new one on his own (Elyachar, 2005: 113).

With this context in mind, Zohairy's steadfast distinction between life and work masks the continuities between the two realms. The gendering of working relations is one such continuity. The Egyptian film industry is an overwhelmingly masculine environment, and women are largely underrepresented, except among actresses and extras. When Farghalli once signaled that there were eight women working behind the scenes in *Décor*, I asked, "Is that unusual?" I thought that eight women out of forty to fifty crew members represented a low percentage. "Absolutely," replied Farghalli. "If there's more than one woman in production or direction, it's already a lot." Women on the crew tend to come from well-educated, relatively wealthy backgrounds, such that they are excluded from the drudgery of "masculine" labor like production legwork or set-building craftsmanship. Although women can work in direction, cinematography, and art direction, they are overall better represented in "feminine" jobs like costume script supervisor, stylist, or editor. This distinction between masculine and feminine labor extends beyond the film industry, but it colors the way in which certain filmmaking tasks—managing clothes, makeup, and hairstyles, sitting at the editing machine, building props and sets—are perceived within the industry.

Zohairy's reprimand highlighted another important continuity between class and hierarchy in the film industry. There is a certain ambiguity to the term "class" in the Egyptian context. On the one hand, there is a strong emic discourse of "classism" *(taba'iya)*, which is indistinctly applied to class in a sociological sense or hierarchical relations more broadly. When the script supervisor Jaylan Auf described the disparity in the treatment of a child star as opposed to schoolboy extras in the comedy *La mu'akhza* (*Excuse my French*, 2014), she used the term *taba'iya* just as she might have described the treatment of a business owner as opposed to his employees.

On the other hand, the academic literature uses the term "class" to distinguish between objective social strata. This differentiation either occurs on economic grounds, as evident in ethnographies of the "working class" in Egypt (see Singerman and Hoodfar, 1996; Hoodfar, 1997; Ghannam, 2002; Shehata, 2009; Chakravarti, 2016), or on cultural grounds, as evident in ethnographies of the "middle class" or "upper middle class" (see Armbrust, 1996; de Koning, 2009; Peterson, 2011; Schielke and Shehata, 2016). While economic class is understood as a sociological position determined by one's source of income, cultural class is understood as a habitus in Bourdieu's sense (1977), an embodied predisposition to act based on a given educational background. The definitions do not correspond to one another, nor do they correspond to the emic usage, which makes it difficult to pin down which groups are united by the term "class" when it is used in everyday life in Egypt or in the academic literature on Egypt.

Without being able to resolve this difficulty, I would argue that the hierarchical relations among film workers are *homologous* to the ones entertained by people in different economic or cultural classes, but the people who occupy homologous positions are not necessarily the same. This explains why Auf would describe actors and extras in the same way as she would describe business owners and workers, but it highlights the crucial difference between the two things: that the actual children who are stars and extras are not necessarily higher- or lower-class outside the industry. While these patterns of stratification can intersect—car drivers tend to come from working-poor families; artistic crew members tend to come from wealthy, educated families—these trends are not systematic. Well-educated workers can work at the lower end of the industry's pyramid, just as workers hailing from working-poor families can make it to the top. Mobility within the industry is more common than mobility across economic or cultural classes, although it remains constrained, as I detail in the next section.

This homology is further illustrated by the distinction between manual workers (*'ummal* or *sanay'iya*) and non-manual workers, whether they are involved in office-based work or artistic work. The distinction is marked by using the term *usta* to designate the chiefs involved in manual work on set (such as the gaffer, the key grip, the chief builder), a term equally applied to master craftsmen in Cairo (Elyachar, 2005: 100). This distinction is not based on one's position in the industry's hierarchy, because an *usta* is better positioned and better paid than some office-based workers (such as assistant editors and production assistants). Instead, it is based on a general sense that manual workers are involved in "unclean" or "unseemly" work, whereas office-based workers and artistic workers "look clean" *(shakluhum nidif)*. This representation is not about hygiene or uncleanliness, of course, but a thinly veiled comment on class belonging, as manual workers tend to come from economically and culturally disadvantaged backgrounds. Again, this disadvantage does not systematically map onto the industry's hierarchies, yet it informs apprehensions of status within the industry.

In sum, labor hierarchies provide a widely accepted model for the organization of work, a model based on embodied interpersonal interactions, which are sometimes difficult to set apart from ordinary gendered and classed interactions in Cairo. For instance, the overwhelming male presence on set imposes a constant burden on female workers to remain "professional" in an environment where mixed-gender contact is always possibly fraught with unwanted flirtation. This was a regular topic of conversation among female workers in *Décor*, who were acutely aware of the inconvenience of being female on an Egyptian film set. Likewise, interactions between chiefs and subordinates with different economic or educational backgrounds are fraught with the kind of classism prevalent in Cairo. The stylist Salma Sami once explained how hairstylists and makeup artists are generally considered "craftsmen" *(sanay'iya)* in Egypt, which means that some superiors treat them in a "classist" *(taba'i)* way, in the broad sense in which Auf used the term earlier. "You tell them, 'That's not what I want, that's what I want,'" said Sami, mimicking a bossy chief with her pointed index finger. Craftsmen can become unresponsive to this snobby treatment, she said, arguably because they feel demeaned by it socially, even though the stylist remains in his/her right to boss them around according to industry conventions.

While some hierarchical distinctions go beyond the film industry, some are specific to it. One such distinction is between "artistic" *(fanni)* and "executive" *(tanfizi)* labor. While artistic workers are responsible for designing all aspects of the film's audiovisual content, executive workers execute the labor necessary to actualize artistic work. The main artistic head is the director, and his/her artistic crew includes the cinematographer, the art director, the stylist, the sound engineer, and the editor, in addition to the star actors. All remaining workers receive different executive tasks to aid the artists' creation. The assistant director Habi Seoud once joked that a director colleague wanted all cast and crew members to "imagine" things *(yitkhayyalu hagat)*, but he was adamant that "some people cannot be asked to imagine; it would be worrisome if they imagined anything!" The line between artistic and executive work translates into different salary grades, different decision-making powers, and even different meals on set. More crucially to the book's argument, both types of workers get assigned, de facto, specific responsibilities toward the film's imponderable outcome. While the artistic worker is concerned with "the film" and its audience (see Chapters 5 and 6), the executive worker is concerned with coordinating the film's logistics and execution (see Chapter 4).

This distinction is implicit in many interactions on set. We have already encountered it when Zohairy had to explain to his script supervisor that the director, who "has a purely creative role," discharges certain logistical details onto his assistant director. As Zohairy put it, the assistant director lays out "the course of execution of a film" *(al-masar al-tanfizi li-l-film)*. His position is pivotal, standing between the line producer (who concentrates all authority over logistical matters) and the director (who concentrates all authority over artistic matters). The assistant director and the line producer hold two types of executive authority in this sense, both of which are at the mercy of the artistic crew's demands. The first type is exemplified by the assistant director, yet it includes positions like the cameraman or the assistant decorator. These potent assistants are next in line to artistic crew members, and they are required to execute their bosses' demands while "enlarging [their] horizon of thought," to use the art director Asem Ali's expression. Although final decisions remain in the hands of artistic workers—and ultimately the director—the assistant director, the cameraman, or the assistant decorator can have some input into the film depending on their personal relations with their chiefs. Professionally, however, they remain bound by a hierarchical relationship between the artistic work of their superiors and their own executive work, which ensures that artistic demands are being met.

The second type of executive authority is exemplified by the line producer, who never intervenes in artistic matters except when they involve additional costs or logistical burdens. For instance, when I caught Farghalli discussing the star actress' look with the stylist Salma Sami, he explained that he cannot be interested in the look per se, because his job involves financial or logistical problems alone. What interested him was to ask why the actress needed a wig if her natural hair fit the character, as a wig involves additional costs with minor artistic impact, in his estimation. The production team can restrict similarly small artistic decisions, most often in cinematography, art direction, or styling, but they have little recourse to stop the director's major artistic decisions given the prevalent model of production described in Chapter 1. Indeed, negotiations over major budget changes are handled between the director and the producer/financier directly, such that the production crew manages the budget without holding much leverage over the director, whose artistic authority trumps their financial or logistical concerns in practice. Ultimately, the production team needs to provide everything the direction team wants. As a production assistant once imaged, working in production is like being a "luxury servant" *(khaddam shik)*.

Unlike the above-the-line/below-the-line distinction in Hollywood (Wasko, 2003: 33), the distinction between artistic and executive labor is never mentioned as an explicit principle of labor organization in Egypt. Moreover, while the distinction is systematically operative between artistic superiors and executive subordinates within the same team, it is not always neatly recognized across teams, including among unit heads who hold an executive position (such as the line producer, the assistant director, the cameraman). Thus, sound engineers are sometimes treated as executive workers because they seem to be appendages to the sound-recording equipment, with no artistic say on the material beyond "pressing the record button," as is sometimes joked. The stylist, likewise, is subject to denigration by other chiefs. Farghalli saw no use to the position, since he considered styling work to be about "clothing actors," which can be done by a lowly actor's assistant *(labbisa)*. Moreover, the stylist's authority over the actor's look is very often overlooked by stars, who may judge that they are more apt at choosing nice clothes. In *Décor* and *Poisonous Roses*, however, both the sound engineer and the stylist were given authority over the sound material and the costumes, respectively, just like the screenwriter decided on the film's plotline and dialogue, the cinematographer decided on lighting, or the art director decided on set and prop design.

The distinction between artistic and executive work is reproduced in critical appraisals of films among industry insiders. The director Daoud Abdel Sayyed, for instance, argued that there was a central distinction between directors with a "vision" *(ru'ya)* and "*technicians*," although he said there are varying degrees of skill within these two categories. "The difference between them," he explained, "is the difference between a car driver and a taxi driver: both have a car, and both will arrive at their destinations, but one can drive the car as he pleases, ... the other is bound to drive on a specific path until his destination." While a director with a vision is more likely to have disagreements with the producer, because s/he needs to confront his/her views with the producer's views, a technician will only want to know which screen-play s/he needs to make, how much money s/he will receive, and how much time s/he has to make it. Directors with creative ambitions tend to assert their distinctiveness in similar terms, shunning the taxi drivers within their profession in the same way as they would shun the executive work necessary to make their films.

In a sense, labor hierarchies in the Egyptian film industry separate the "creativity" *(ibdaʿ)* of artistic work from technical or logistical concerns. Artistry in this context does not simply lie in individual skill, but also in the hierarchical relations binding cast and crew members together. For example, Omar el-Zohairy could be deemed a "more creative" individual than Ahmad Abdalla, yet the specific hierarchy binding him (as an assistant director) to Abdalla (as a director) makes him liable to obey all commands given by his superior, and likewise within all teams. This creates a situation where, independently of one's personal proclivities, the worker holding the role of cinematographer, art director, or, better yet, director receives every-one's deference in artistic matters. This authority is not absolute, and it is indeed challenged by technical imperatives and artistic disagreements, but this ideal-typical model of creation cannot give the final say to execu-tive workers. While filmmaking involves a great deal of collaboration in practice, only a limited number of workers can legitimately influence the final film product. These workers, in turn, can claim authorship over "their work" given their direct authority over certain artistic decisions, not neces-sarily because they executed all the tasks required to make the film.

Thus, the association between a director's artistic views and the movie's content is not unmediated, as an unrefined version of auteur theory would have it, but it is precisely possible *because* the industry's division of labor isolates the artistic worker's individuality. The notion of creativity that is thereby implied is a negative one: the artistic worker is someone who can *exclude* creative possibilities from the film, independently of whichever possibilities s/he chooses to include. The artistic worker's commands are never disobeyed, except when disobedience comes in the wake of an artistic disagreement, such as a director disagreeing with the cinematographer's lighting choice or a star disagreeing with the stylist's costume choice. What remains clear is that the distinction between artistic and executive labor is a central assumption guiding the way in which Egyptian filmmakers divide their day-to-day tasks and, by extension, cope with the imponderability of their activity's future.

Apprenticeship

All novices in the film industry are not socialized in the same way. My own apprenticeship is atypical: I gained access to New Century as a researcher, and what I learned is based on the personal connections I made thanks to this status. On my very first day on an Egyptian film set, I sat right next to the director Ismail Farouk with the general manager Ahmad Badawy and the star actress by my side. I was brought a fast-food meal and a soft drink, and I freely conversed and joked with the director. Needless to say, this is not the usual way in which crew members are introduced to a set. This was the product of my position as Badawy's friend, a "guest" on set, and accessorily a doctoral researcher. Within the industry's hierarchy, I was conceptually near the top, while most novices start training at the very bottom.

What is common to the apprenticeship I underwent and the one undergone by novices is the personalized, embodied, hands-on nature of training. In the final shooting days in *Décor*, the gaffer Mahmoud Morsi intentionally hit a spotlight leg carried by one of his second assistants. The assistant seemed surprised and angry, as he was going down the stairs with such heavy equipment, yet Morsi did not budge and uttered a brief "watch out!" *(khalli balak)*. I looked at him with puzzlement, thinking that it was a very dangerous move, but Morsi shrugged it off and said he wanted to build his assistant's awareness. Morsi said he thought his assistant was a little dazed, and he wanted to "wake him up," as it were; not to be cheeky, but to teach him that he should always be aware of his surroundings. What may be taken as a social norm—"be careful"—is instilled through a physical action—hitting the equipment—which leads to the incorporation of a technical skill—how to carry a spotlight leg around the set. Unsuspectedly, Morsi went on to throw a tennis ball to another assistant, who alertly caught it on his way to getting more equipment out.

Although trainees in direction, cinematography, art direction, styling, and sound engineering have usually received formal education prior to working in the industry, most notably at the High Cinema Institute, they are typically "retrained" in a hands-on manner once they start their careers. It is very common to hear Institute graduates saying, "I learned nothing until I started working in the industry." This is certainly an exaggeration, just as it would be an exaggeration to say that I "knew nothing" about Egyptian cinema before doing fieldwork. The High Cinema Institute trains students across filmmaking fields—screenwriting, direction, camera work, production design, editing, sound engineering, and production—in a range of theoretical and practical courses, ranging from film criticism and analysis to the use of specific pieces of equipment. The pedagogical framework, however, is not up to date with trends in global film industries and does not allow students to experiment with new equipment. "Learning nothing" is therefore a revealing statement about the state of formal film training in Egypt, as well as a comment on the dominant mode of apprenticeship in the industry. This apprenticeship is not a linear socialization process aimed at acquiring knowledge; it is very much a "sociotechnicalization" process, where social expectations are incorporated by the worker along with a specific technical know-how.

Any novice acquires a habitus specific to his/her position within the industry's hierarchy (Bourdieu, 1977: 72–73), as well as a savoir-faire, or "know-how," specific to his/her craft (Martinelli, 1997; Chamoux, 2010). These French notions designate incorporated pre-dispositions to act, organized around master-to-apprentice transmission in "real-life" learning situations. While I use the notion of habitus to describe the incorporation of general dispositions to behave in a hierarchical industry, I use the notion of know-how to describe the specific kind of practical knowledge incorporated by workers in the exercise of their craft. The distinction is important insofar as some workers have one without the other. A worker can have a certain know-how without having acquired the expected habitus (being polite to co-workers, being attentive to hierarchy on set), while a worker with an acceptable habitus might not have sufficient know-how to execute his/her job well (carrying spotlight legs around the location).

This know-how is evaluated according to a certain measure of skillfulness *(shatara)*. The Egyptian word *shatara* is a generic term: it implies a sense of both "being good at something" and "doing things right." When a pupil is said to display *shatara*, to be *shatir*, it implies that s/he is good at school *and* conforming to certain norms of appropriate conduct. In the Egyptian film industry, the word is rarely used in its latter, normative sense. When the art director Nihal Farouk mentioned that her ex-boss, the art director Ali Hossam, was *shatir*, she was not comparing him to a well-behaved pupil but suggesting that his set designs were skillfully executed. On another occasion, Sharif Nabil, who had also worked under Hossam, mentioned that his boss was no doubt *shatir* because he was trained by Onsi Abu Seif, who is widely recognized as Egypt's greatest living art director.

When filmmakers talk about each other's *shatara*, in short, the evidence invoked is past work or past training.

The substance of the skill in question is variable, however, and it is sometimes difficult to describe it when the result is not a physical product (such as past set designs offering some visible evidence to evaluate the skill of an art director). A good example of this difficulty is the skill of production workers. When I told the production manager Michel Makram that I was interested in studying production, he immediately replied, "You know, production is more about practice *(mumarsa)* . . . so you should come by my office this week, and we'll see." Makram implied that he would train me in production because he could not verbalize what being a skilled production worker entails. While his answer reinforces the idea that apprenticeship is an embodied, hands-on affair, it also expresses the unease with which production skill is articulated by industry insiders.

I came to understand why skillfulness is integral to the position of production crew members within their team's hierarchy when I asked the line producer Ahmed Farghalli about the difference between a "production executor" *(munaffiz intag)* and a "production assistant" *(musa'id intag)*. Farghalli argued that the executor and the assistant have the same tasks but that there is a difference of experience *(khibra)* and skill *(shatara)* between them, which makes the executor hierarchically superior to the assistant. Skill trumps experience, however, because with the right set of skills, someone who has worked for a year can become a line producer, whereas someone who has worked for five years can still be an assistant. The difference lies in what one can do and how well one can do it, in Farghalli's opinion. What matters is not longevity within the industry, then, but the ability to get products, contracts, or even services as cheaply as possible; the ability to work flexible hours going over the conventional twelve-hour shift; the ability to withstand pressure on location; the ability to "think on your feet," especially when a mistake is made and needs to be corrected; and the ability to "have a nice tongue" *(lisan hilw)*, which means being able to talk smoothly to avoid paying extra money or avoid tricky situations (such as a passerby starting a fight on location). All these practical skills combine into a specific production know-how that can be acquired with experience, but experience—or more accurately longevity—is no guarantee of skill or promotion.

Skillfulness is therefore vital to understanding how trained workers perform their tasks, which are incorporated as predispositions to act. When a worker is asked to execute a certain task by a superior, s/he has a reservoir of embodied knowledge to engage in this task with assurance. Consider the way in which gripping technicians lay down dolly tracks before a shot:

> Toukhy (the key grip) is supervising the operation, while about four or five of his men work on the track. The track is made of two foldable metal tracks (looking almost exactly like a train track, but made from some light metal). The tracks are tied together by a little mechanism and settled by little door stubs, with one or two inserted under every track (the grips have a whole box of door stubs, which they bring along whenever they set a track). One grip uses a level device to check whether the track is straight, and once it's checked, he makes sure all door stubs are in place. Then they bring the Panther dolly and settle it on the track (it takes some time, because they need to align all wheels in the right direction). They push it back and forth a little to check its movement. (Field notes, December 24, 2013)

There is a certain automaticity with which the grips' bodies carry and lay out tracks in a well-defined division of labor between the key grip (who supervises the operation), the best boy (who measures the track's flatness), and the assistants (who arrange the tracks according to the key grip's commands). Throughout this operation, there is no sense in which grips are at the mercy of uncertainty: their work enacts an embodied habitus within a certain division of tasks and a know-how of the "right way" to do them.

This skilled know-how is obvious with specialized cinema equipment, but it is subtler in the case of everyday digital technologies, which appear as commonplace appendages to the filmmaker's personal life. I have never heard anyone talking about the acquisition of computer or smartphone skills in the same sense as "learning a craft" (*yit'allim san'a*)—as a gaffer would learn to carry spotlights or as a grip would learn to lay down tracks. Nevertheless, digital technology skills have become integral to the industry's work, and familiarity with computer software has become the single most important prerequisite for the work of preparation and postproduction. To use Boyer's words, "screenwork has quietly emerged as the norm of professional practice" (2013: 26). Not unlike other skills, technological learning is a personalized, embodied, hands-on process. An economical anecdote in Chennai captures how this learning process works in Cairo:

"He worked in advertising for a decade, learning how to use the Avid digital editing system without bothering to read the manual. 'If I press this button, what happens to the visuals?' Now many of the biggest Tamil films pass through his studios" (Pandian, 2015: 221).

Much as with this Tamil editor, learning digital skills in Egypt involves a combination of experimentation with technological devices, online reading on specialist websites and forums, as well as personal mentoring by tech-savvy colleagues. Since "a technique is never known until one has acquired its experience by a more or less lengthy apprenticeship" (Sigaut, 2009: 42), it is important to situate these learning moments within a lifelong trajectory, beyond the times when a gaffer throws a tennis ball at his assistant or an editor clicks away on her computer. These skills are inhabited over time, throughout a worker's life, and it is difficult to approximate their temporal extension within a single fieldwork stint. "It's like when you get used to your house," said the editor Sara Abdalla about her "human" relationship with Final Cut Pro software. "You know where you've put everything, you know how to move in it, you're at ease in it, and you won't be annoyed if you want to bring people to look around. You know it's your space."

Insofar as career promotion is somewhat related to skill in the film industry, one can map the filmmaker's embodied enskilling onto his/her team's hierarchy. The gaffing and gripping teams are instructive in this sense. Trainees hang out near equipment, watching what their crew does (see Martinelli's discussion on the "apprentice's gaze," 1997). Assistants pack, carry, and unpack equipment, while remaining attentive to their chief's directives. The chief directs the whole operation with the assurance of a masterful technician, an *usta*. When I asked the gaffer Mahmoud Morsi about the difference between each worker on his team, he marked a pause. "Is it a matter of task definition?" I asked. "No," he answered, because everyone in the lighting subteam is expected to know how to carry lighting equipment, how to plug lamps, how to rig lamps on stands or on walls, and so on. "Is it a matter of experience *(khibra)*?" "No," he asserted once again, because some gaffers have little experience, yet they manage to climb quickly to the top of the profession—very much like what Farghalli described among production crew members. This sentiment is regularly echoed across teams involved in manual work. The equipment manager Reda Zanita argued that promotion is a matter of "personal ambition" *(tumuh shakhsi)*, while the grip Ahmad Nader said, "It depends on each person's understanding; how much he understands how things are going."

In the end, Morsi said that the hierarchy was a matter of knowledge *('ilm)* and skill *(shatara)*. In this sense, chiefs are supposedly the most skilled at all tasks required within their teams, while the best boys are second-best, and so on down the ladder.

Some roles in the industry have no implicit career trajectory, but most teams' hierarchy constitutes a roadmap to one's possible career advancement or promotion—what is locally known as "flipping up" *(yi'lib)*. Promotion is synonymous with status and salary increase, which is why it tends to occur in between projects. It is also irreversible in some sense, because one cannot come back to a lesser role once one progresses to a higher one. This leads to an odd situation where once a crew member is promoted to the rank of director, s/he will refuse to work as a script supervisor or assistant director even when there is no other work, not because s/he lacks the professional competence but because s/he would be "regressing" down the ladder. This perception explains why the director Ahmad Fawzi Saleh once advised a cameraman not to take up a cinematographer position in an unknown production, because it would close doors to him as a cinematographer *and* as a cameraman. Once he got promoted, he would not be able to go back to an assistant role. Knowing when to "flip," therefore, is integral to career strategy in the industry.[2]

Once I asked Mariam el-Bagoury, the costume script supervisor in *Décor*, whether she wanted to become a director one day. She candidly answered: "Yes, it's my goal." When I asked whether she would like to become a first assistant director, she answered yes again, to which I said, "Would you be an assistant director your whole career?" "No, just to become a film director," she replied. Bagoury's statement reinforces the commonsense notion according to which becoming a director necessarily involves a linear progression, from trainee to script supervisor to assistant director to director. The script supervisor Jaylan Auf expressed dismay at this imagined career path, arguing that each position requires an independent skillset, something which Bagoury herself recognized. "Art isn't about [script breakdown] tables," she added, acknowledging that she did not learn much as a costume script supervisor that would become useful in her work as a director. Yet, to remain realistic about her career chances, especially as a woman within a male-dominated field, Bagoury said that she needed to commit to the conventional career path.

Although it is possible to become a director without going along this path, especially among so-called "independent" filmmakers, skipping steps is unusual within the industry. It is even more unusual because the superiors on each team have the authority to hire crew members and to promote them—which is not strictly the case with directors, who are hired by the producer. Since hiring and promotion are so personalized, novices tend to remain under their initial contact's patronage until they make more contacts in the industry. The general perception is that crew members (especially younger or less powerful ones) are under constant threat of not working if they do not abide by their superiors. The inequality inherent in this hiring system leads to what is known as *ta'ris*, a vulgar term that literally means "to prostitute oneself" but is more widely used to designate unwavering approval and support of one's superior (what one might call "sucking up" in English). I very frequently heard that *ta'ris* is part of the industry's conventions *('urf)*, and that it constitutes its very structure—or, to use the clapper Abdelsalam Radwan's metaphor, "it's the woodplank upon which the structure is built."

The overall perception is that sucking up to a superior is disingenuous and cynical, but there is still great weight put on loyalty to the chief. This is another way in which the blurred boundary between professional and personal interaction can become problematic: when hiring seems to depend on nepotism or personal likeability, not skillfulness. The distinction matters to filmmakers because, in principle, only workers judged to be skilled *(shatir)* ought to get promotions, with the higher skill leading to the better position in the industry's hierarchy. The irony, of course, is that the objective criterion of skillfulness is judged by the very same superiors who gage likeability on a subjective basis, and the superiors who make hiring decisions are accorded great autonomy in their judgment. Evaluations of skill are not neutral in this sense, because their consequences are brought to bear by the very superiors who control hiring. As Darré points out in the French film industry, "The mode of recruitment, by cooptation at each level—of creative collaborators by the director; of assistants and trainees by the team heads—allows for the reproduction of the group and its ideology. What is selected, at the level of entrant trainees, is above all the 'adequate habitus'" (2006: 127).

There is an unresolved tension, therefore, between skill and nepotism when it comes to promotion within the Egyptian film industry. The common belief remains that considerations of skill will ultimately prevail. In a casual conversation with his production crew, the line producer Farghalli mentioned once how Tamer Fathi, who was sitting next to him, started working as a lighting technician before becoming a well-respected production manager, and how Khaled Adam, who also started in a smaller job, became a line producer. Farghalli was quick to add that they fired many friends and family members from the crew because they were not good enough to do the job (including Ahmad Badawy's brother and Farghalli's own cousin). More broadly, there is a sizeable number of current line producers and production managers who started their careers as runners or with some small job on set, then slowly climbed their way to the top. This kind of mobility is still constrained by labor hierarchies, as well as the overall bias against women and lower-class crew members—or, in other words, workers who have a different habitus from the dominant educated men in the industry. What remains clear is that the habitus and know-how acquired by workers via personalized, hands-on apprenticeship is crucial to the way in which they execute their daily tasks and conceive their career trajectory under the patronage of hierarchical superiors.

Operational Sequence

Labor hierarchies and modes of apprenticeship are integral to understanding how filmmakers work and how novices are enskilled, but they are insufficient to describe the future-orientation implicit in much of the filmmaking process. This orientation is never just one of uncertainty toward a diffuse and distant future; it is one where the film is apprehended as a clear outcome whose actualization remains unpredictable. Apprehending this imponderable outcome requires a heuristic understanding of the operational sequence behind the film. This sequence does not determine film production on the ground, but it informs the social agent's understanding of the operations yet to come. In practice, it is difficult to know whether a project will ever become an actual film while it is being made. Media anthropologists solve this difficulty by arguing that "the film" has no real beginning or end, that it is an ever-changing process/product whose circulation entails various definitions as it moves across sites of production and consumption. This solution is most clearly presented in Grimaud (2003), Hoek (2014), and Pandian (2015), where the authors meticulously show how films get modified throughout their writing, shooting, postproduction, and circulation in movie theaters and beyond.

This position is sound in some sense: it is indeed the case that *Décor* gained a different meaning and shape when it was just a screenplay in

Cairo, or a rough cut watched by the mixer in Greece, or a projection at the 2014 Cairo International Film Festival. However, when it comes to describing how filmmakers apprehend their work, it is unhelpful to stress the malleability of "the film" to the extent that it assumes that the outcome is conceived as being equally malleable. On the contrary, there are conventional horizons of expectation about films in Egypt. Filmmakers do maintain a qualitative distinction between the operational sequence of filmmaking and the distribution/exhibition of the film product. This sequence should not be understood as a model for the way in which films *ought* to be made, but as a sociotechnical tool allowing filmmakers to probe the future and to understand the day-to-day work of commercial film production. Moreover, the directionality of the sequence should not make us think that it is linear in practice, but that it is *conceived* as a linear process, where each stage leads to the next through a series of audiovisual mediators, starting with the screenplay.

In Egypt, all operations in film preparations emanate in some respect from a screenplay. In its "broken down" guise, the screenplay serves as a checklist of elements to be gathered in anticipation of shooting. Scouting fills the screenplay's main locations; set design/building arranges the location in accordance to the screenplay's description; casting/fitting selects and dresses the characters in the screenplay; and image testing selects the tools by which the screenplay is transformed into concrete images. The well-known screenwriter Mariam Naoum insisted that the screenplay is supposed to leave artistic workers some room to imagine their own aspect of the film (acting, cinematography, set design), but the assumption was still that there is a screenplay to guide the whole process. There is a clear directionality between screenwriting and preparations in this sense. This directionality is not linear in practice, because screenwriting is not a linear exercise. This non-linearity is intrinsic to the practice of screenwriting in Bombay (Grimaud, 2003: 77–97) or in Dhaka (Hoek, 2014: 33–58), where the screenplay is constantly subverted in preproduction, shooting, postproduction, and even movie theaters. Still, there is a sense in which the screenplay acts as a guiding mediator to the production process in Egypt.

Adjustments to the screenplay regularly go on into preparations and shooting. Preparations were well under way in *Décor* when Ahmad Abdalla and the screenwriters Mohamed and Shireen Diab agreed on setting the closing scene in a movie theater, where we would discover that the whole film was inside a film. The direction team was then expected to incorporate the new logistical elements needed to shoot the scene into their previous script breakdowns. The production team was expected to find a movie theater to shoot this additional scene, which was ultimately shot in one of New Century's own theaters. The assistant director Zohairy was expected to cast all the theater audience extras, which happened in collaboration with his casting agent while we were filming in a restaurant some weeks prior to the designated shooting day. The stylist Salma Sami was expected to give instructions in order to dress all these extras appropriately once they were cast. The key grip Mohammed el-Toukhy, lastly, had to find a large crane to shoot the master shot in the theater: a one-shot sequence going out of the movie screen into the crowd, thereby showing that *Décor* was a film inside a film. These kinds of imbricated adjustments show how the imponderable "film" breaks into a series of contingent tasks in preparations, but it also shows how the passage between screenwriting and preparations is not strictly linear.

Moreover, the act of screenwriting itself is iterative. The screenwriter goes over each scene several times to make sure that it communicates the meaning *(ma'na)* that s/he wants, scrapping certain sentences, putting them back, writing additional dialogue for characters, canceling entire scenes, writing several drafts, and so on. Consider the following scene in *Poisonous Roses*:

EXT. SHOE WORKSHOP. TANNERY STREETS. DAY

The NOISE of TANNERY MACHINES is mixed with RADIO SOUNDS.

TAHIYA stands in front of a middle-aged SHOE-MAKER, who is sewing a leather shoe on a small table with a flaming gas lamp. A small light falling from the ceiling lights his face, while behind him lie disorganized piles of leather with both finished and unfinished shoes.

TAHIYA gives the SHOEMAKER a sheet with the outline of Saqr's foot.

```
TAHIYA
I want a nice shoe, this size.
Something chic, imported leather.

The SHOEMAKER nods in approval and takes the
sheet.

TAHIYA gets out of the workshop and sees UMM
SAQR carrying some finished leather jackets on
her back.

   CUT
```

This scene occurs at a moment where the protagonist, Tahiya, orders new shoes to give to her brother Saqr, whom she wants to keep by her side against his will. This scene did not exist in the versions of the screenplay I saw in 2013. When the screenwriter-director Ahmad Fawzi Saleh initially thought about this scene, it was supposed to take place in front of a high-end lingerie boutique in downtown Cairo. He had three reasons to include this boutique in the screenplay: to explain to the viewer that Tahiya cares enough about her brother to spend money on him; to show underwear shop windows, whose visual provocation was stimulating to him; and to show class inequality between the poor Tahiya and the rich boutiques in downtown Cairo. The scene was originally silent, and it simply involved Tahiya walking by neon-lit shops before finding a suitable one, out of which she walked with a yellow plastic bag.

The scene above is admittedly different, yet it emerged out of the same text in word-processed format, in the same position within the narrative. The last version was written in Arabic in the summer of 2015, and I translated it as above for a grant application to the Doha Film Institute. After an initial shooting bout in which the downtown scene was not shot, and with the understanding that Tahiya had become the protagonist after the earlier screenplay was scripted to follow Saqr's story, Fawzi decided that it no longer made sense to have the home-to-work Tahiya suddenly visiting a new neighborhood just to show class inequality to the viewer. In our three-way conversations with his assistant director Yousef Abodan, Fawzi thought it more powerful to show a new location in the tanning district, where the whole film is situated, while sticking to the intended meaning of showing

Tahiya's care for her brother. This new scene had the additional advantage of being less costly in shooting, which was a constant concern on Fawzi's mind while rewriting his screenplay.

Starting with the text of the downtown scene in a shared Google Docs document, Fawzi rewrote the scene with Abodan and me to include a detailed description of the workshop, some dialogue between Tahiya and the shoemaker, as well as what Fawzi sensed was a greater token of care for Saqr: an outline of his foot for sizing the shoes. The line at the very end of the scene, where Tahiya sees her mother Umm Saqr passing by with a pile of leather on her back, was added even later, in the summer of 2015. When Fawzi and I reviewed the sequential outline of each character's appearances throughout the screenplay, which was on a separate handwritten sheet, it seemed that Umm Saqr's character was absent too long in between two major points in the plotline. I therefore proposed (and Fawzi agreed) to include her character in this scene, so that the viewer could see her in a new setting without burdening other scenes with too much action—a recurrent concern in our screenwriting talks.

The iterative exercise involved in writing and rewriting this scene shows the kinds of contingent decisions mulled over by the screenwriter and his/her collaborators. These decisions relied on various considerations that were unpredictable at the time of writing, yet would shape Fawzi's eventual film: what the image should look like; whether the plotline "makes sense" *(mantiqi)*; whether it enacts Fawzi's ideas about class struggle in Cairo; whether it gives sufficient attention to Tahiya's character; whether it would cost more or less; and so on. Decisions on these issues did not occur at the whim of our conversations; they relied on various mediating writings and images. As Strandvad notes, "as long as an idea is presented verbally, it may be easily changed. To carry an idea further, it is essential to write" (2011: 289). Our screenwriting decisions anticipated the process of film production: they assumed a sense of the sequence that would lead to the actualization of "the film." This sequence was not linear in practice, insofar as screenwriting was iterative and mixed with bouts of shooting in *Poisonous Roses*, but it was oriented toward the series of operations that would eventually lead to shooting and postproduction.

These latter stages are iterative and directional in the same manner. Shooting is a repetitive sequence of takes that are destined to become the audiovisual film material; postproduction is a repetitive adding/subtracting/cutting/pasting of images, sounds, and effects destined to become "the film."

In a sense, all these stages are linked by written, visual, or aural mediators. I have described how the screenplay and script breakdowns bridge between screenwriting and preparations, but it is not difficult to see that preparations extend into the components of the shooting day: camera movement is drawn out in a shooting script; the actor is cast and fitted with a given look based on mediating videos and photographs; the set is designed and built on paper or on computer; the lighting is planned on paper and on set; and so on. These operations are assumed to have taken place prior to the shoot. Every take, however ephemeral, presupposes a previous sequence of preparations, while anticipating the eventual sequence of postproduction. This middling situation remains intact no matter the measurable time taken between preparations, shooting, and postproduction. Whether an item has been noted down on a production list and acquired well in advance of shooting or serendipitously shot on location, this does not modify the shot's position within a sequence where it enacts previous operations and anticipates subsequent ones.

The first shooting day in *Décor* offers some concrete grounds to illustrate this sequential awareness. When I arrived at Studio Misr at around seven twenty in the morning, the set was still warming up: the line producer Farghalli had a briefing with his crew members; prop assistants were moving items into the studio; set builders and the art direction crew hung out nearby; the generator was connected to the set; and tea was being served by buffet workers. Around eight thirty, lighting equipment trucks arrived and ten or so technicians started unloading spots, tripods, condensers, foam boards, and metal poles into the studio. While the set was slowly being furnished by prop assistants, the lighting technicians were setting up the lights. They made triangular and cubic foam boxes to reflect spotlights that would be used to create an impression of daylight in studio. They hung some Chinese lanterns above the walls to light the dining room, and lit the balcony with neon and the kitchen with a light-box.[3] The video-assist crew arrived next, and Farghalli checked whether they had brought the right equipment. The video-assist operators started plugging their screens into the camera, until the artistic crew arrived around ten o'clock.

The whole scene gave an impression of "business as usual," manifesting an unspoken habitus and know-how, which was implicit to the awareness of the operations ahead: the set is furnished and lit to anticipate the shoot; the video-assist is plugged in to anticipate the artistic crew's visualization. These anticipations are built on short- and long-term preparation, extending from the beginnings of set building two weeks earlier, to the selection of lighting equipment and the lighting plan, to the tea prepared on the very same morning. This sequence is not without hurdles on the ground: for instance, while the focus puller was adjusting the camera's settings in black-and-white to approximate *Décor*'s final look, the whole set was brought to a halt because there was a problem with the monitor. Still, the shooting could continue after this brief delay, and it was again in a middling awareness between preparations and postproduction that each shot was taken.

Around eleven thirty, the crew took the very first shot in the film: a close-up on a plank of wood being cut on a table saw. Once Farghalli and Zohairy had ordered the noise to calm down, the clapper Abdelsalam Radwan went in with the scene number, the boom operator Ahmad Abdel Nasser held the boom above the saw, the sound engineer Ahmad Saleh rolled the recorder, Hefny rolled the camera, and Zohairy yelled out "Movement!" to get workers to pass by in the shot's background, then "Action!" to indicate to the carpenter Mohammed Nabil to saw the plank. They took two quick takes before Zohairy said that they would film a "*high-speed*" shot at a hundred and twenty frames per second (which is five times the normal frame rate of twenty-four). When Hossam Mohammed adjusted the camera settings, it went down again, and the set was once more brought to a halt. Since filming at a hundred and twenty frames was apparently impossible, Zohairy, Hefny, and Ahmad Abdalla settled for sixty frames. Later, they shot the carpenter Sharkas while he sanded some wood with a machine. Ahmad Abdalla was not satisfied with the sawing table's look on screen, so he added a hammer and my own teacup, picked up on the fly among other props. This was still not enough, because the sanding did not produce the anticipated sparks, so the carpenters hammered extra nails into the wood to produce more sparks. Ahmad Abdalla asked Sharkas to incline his sanding machine toward the camera so that the nails would remain invisible. The shot was retaken several times, with two different frame rates again, as well as two different lenses and different camera movements.

These shots totaled less than ten seconds in *Décor*, but again they concentrated a mixture of short- and long-term preparation that anticipated the film's postproduction. The troublesome change in camera settings between twenty-four and sixty frames per second was meant to give Ahmad Abdalla the option to either show the saw movement in real-time or in slow motion in editing. Likewise, Abdalla's adjustments on the fly were meant to create more visual options: one where Sharkas works on a barren table, another where a hammer and a hot cup of tea sit next to him, and another with added sparks generated by the hidden nails (which ended up in the final film). These short-term adjustments ought not to obscure the logistical preparations ensuring that all workers, equipment, sets, props, and lights would be gathered on this day to distill the audiovisual material that would eventually constitute "the film," without counting the prior screenwriting, scouting, casting, fitting, or image testing. These operations will be explored in deeper detail in Chapters 4 and 5.

Every day during a shoot, a similar cycle of operations is repeated until all the material needed according to the director and his/her assistant has been recorded. The material is copied onto a laptop, backed up on a hard drive, and sent to the editing office, accompanied by a list of all the takes in the clapper's daily report *(rabur)*. These mediators—the audiovisual material and the report—are the thin link between the total work invested in the project until then and postproduction, where the material circulates across hard drives and computers, being tweaked to the tune of editing, coloring, graphics, and mixing software. Each postproduction operation anticipates the next in its unfolding, just as it was anticipated in shooting. When I asked the young colorist David Maher whether video effects are common in Egypt, he immediately answered, "It depends on what has been filmed. One has to shoot with an eye to the video effects to be added." This was indeed my experience in *Décor* and *Poisonous Roses*, where all television screens were shut off during the shoot because their audiovisual content would be added with video effects. More broadly, the directors Ahmad Abdalla and Ahmad Fawzi Saleh would constantly be talking about what they could and could not later add to the material they were filming, in postproduction.

This kind of anticipation is integral to the way in which the imponderable film becomes a series of contingent tasks throughout the sequence starting with screenwriting, going on to preparations, shooting, and postproduction. The film reaches a de facto resolution after it is printed, although it retains an unfinished quality: the editor will still have a note that she has not considered; the cinematographer will want to modify a color that he did not want; the mixer will leave a noise that he would have liked to remove. Still, the film can be said to emerge once the final mix is conformed to the raw material and printed, distributed, and exhibited. Although its form and content might still change, as Hoek has demonstrated with "cut-pieces" in Bangladesh (2014), there is a sense in which "the film" is conceived as a unified product; assembled through a complex process of coordination and visualization; and destined to confront an audience whose reactions are preempted throughout the filmmaking process. All these anticipations, again, assume that the worker exists in a certain labor hierarchy, has acquired a certain habitus and know-how, and has a sense of the operational sequence in which s/he is engaged.

Ways of Making Films

When I asked whether there was a particular way of making films in Egypt (*tari'at sina'at al-aflam fi Masr*), I generally received two kinds of answers. One was exemplified by the young script supervisor Sandy Samuel, who throughout our conversation on the Egyptian film industry insisted that "there are no *rules*." When I mentioned this opinion to the assistant director and producer Safiy el-Din Mahmoud, he exclaimed, "On the contrary! The problem is that there is a very specific *system*, and people have issues when they don't follow the *system*." This sharp contrast can be traced to the ambiguous meaning of the term "making" (*sina'a*) in Arabic, which I had been using unwittingly until then. Samuel talked about *sina'a* as a process of production whose outcome is unpredictable, which can take several directions with no clear rules in its unfolding. Yet *sina'a* can also mean "industry," a self-contained entity with a political economy as described in Chapter 1, which is what Mahmoud thought about when he decried the system of production.

This distinction is interesting on its own, but its occurrence in interview settings highlights a more important notion: that there is great disparity in individual understandings of the way of making films among industry insiders. One cannot assume that every single filmmaker has a coherent model of the hierarchy, the habitus, the know-how, or even the operational sequence that characterizes the process of film production in Egypt. This disparity explains why Samuel and Mahmoud had different intuitions when I asked them about the way of making films in Egypt. This could also explain why the second assistant director in *Décor*, Renad Tarek, would regularly ask me—another novice—about the film production process, even though she was the one employed on set. Although it is tempting to ascribe uneven knowledge to the gap between a novice and a seasoned worker, it is important to bear in mind that this unevenness is equally related to the very hierarchy and sequence in which workers are situated.

Thus, when the line producer Ahmed Farghalli states that one just needs to be curious and constantly seek to learn more to "advance" *(yit'addim)* in the industry, it is important to qualify his perspective in two respects.

First, what counts as valuable information about the industry varies according to one's position within the hierarchical division of labor. Once, I was conversing with the master carpenter Hosny while watching the ongoing shooting in *Décor*. "What's this film about?" he asked. I was a little startled by the question, because it was still early in my fieldwork and I naively thought that everyone on set had read the screenplay. I summarized the story to Hosny, but he remained unconvinced. "What's the bottom line *(eih al-madmun)*?" "It turns out [Maha, the protagonist,] lives in Mustafa's world, according to the version I've read . . . she's just imagining Sharif's world." Hosny still looks unconvinced. "[The star] Khaled Abol Naga is boring *(bidan)* . . . he's too smug *(ti'il)*." Hosny adds that he liked neither *Agamista* (2007) nor *Heliopolis* (2009) because both movies featured Abol Naga. "What has this director made before?" he asks later. "*Heliopolis*," I answered with a smile. "That too!" he exclaimed.

Hosny seemed displeased by *Décor*. Perhaps I did not sell it well enough. Still, this interaction illustrates how the hierarchical division of labor constrains each worker's knowledge of the filmmaking process—and, by extension, of the film's narrative. Executive workers with no say in the narrative tend not to know the screenplay's details. Likewise, while Farghalli (as an individual) may know a lot about the industry in general, he would not be interested (as a line producer) in learning about screenwriting or mixing— two crafts with no direct relation to his work. As the mixer Mohammed Fawzi confidently put it, all production crew members in Egypt have little to no idea about the intricacies of postproduction, which creates several misunderstandings over the time and work necessary to do postproduction on a given project. In a similar vein, it is important to remember that not all cast and crew members know each other, either because they intervene in the project at different stages or because they are restricted by their position to interacting with certain workers only. If Farghalli can unequivocally state that he *never* finishes a film project without knowing every single crew member, it is likely because he is a line producer and, as such, he is professionally bound to interact with the whole crew. Lower-end workers, however, might have a harder time making contacts in the same way.

An important corollary to this point is that the unit of reckoning with the project's time varies within the division of labor. Artistic workers tend to think about the film's time in terms of shots and scenes, while on-set technicians think about takes and adjustments between takes. This disparity is illustrated in Farghalli's lament about one of the prominent vehicle-hire specialists in the industry, Sharif "MacGyver." When Sharif was young, he would stay all day on location with his cars to be available whenever called upon. Once he got to "know the job," in Farghalli's words, he would hire his cars for half-days only. "Sometimes, they rent the same car to many people on the same day," complained Farghalli. From a vehicle-hire standpoint, "the film" is not a set of shots or takes but a series of locations between which vehicles can circulate. Ironically, Farghalli's complaint contradicted his earlier, well-intentioned views on curiosity and advancement in the industry: once vehicle-hire specialists learned about the industry, they became more difficult to control.

This leads to the second caveat, which is that gaps in individual knowledge do not just result from ignorance or lack of interest, as Farghalli seems to imply, but also from an active resistance to the transmission of knowledge. This resistance is sometimes felt in the superiors' unwillingness to communicate the "secrets of the trade" to their novices. The editor Heba Othman recounted that she was not allowed to work with the editing software Lightworks because, in her view, editors in the company that owned the software wanted to avoid competition. The young colorist David Maher told me a similar story about the graphics software Smoke. Even the clapper Abdelsalam Radwan held similar suspicions about the clapper who taught him the job. In this context, I am grateful to Farghalli for having answered all my queries as transparently as possible, yet I am now unsurprised to remember one of his assistants jokingly saying, once, that Farghalli should not tell me too much or else I would "steal his job." Likewise, when I started working as an assistant to Ahmad Fawzi Saleh in *Poisonous Roses*, the assistant director Omar el-Zohairy joked that I should pay him because he taught me everything while I was observing his work in *Décor*. This association between knowledge of the production process and professional advancement indicates that my interest in film production was not always perceived as an innocent one. I was often asked whether I would work in the film industry once I was done with my doctorate, and some regular interlocutors assumed that I really just wanted to become a director. Working on *Poisonous Roses* did not alleviate their suspicions.

The core assumptions described in this chapter are well established in the industry, but they are not evenly distributed. This is not to say that

I, the anthropologist, know more about the "way of making films" than my interlocutors, or that there is such a unique (or uniquely Egyptian) way to begin with; it is to say that I struggled just as much as my variously positioned interlocutors to get a grasp on the industry's overall workings. All in all, it is not necessary to hold a concrete picture of the entire labor hierarchy and operational sequence in mind to work on a film project. One simply remains aware that, here and now, some eventual operations specific to one's position will have to serially unfold so that "the film" can be made. Each operation anticipates subsequent ones through various mediators—the screenplay, the audiovisual material, the postproduction effects—whose presence conditions the individual agent's apprehension of the filmmaking process and the film's imponderable future. This is crucial because the very concept of an imponderable outcome is based on the filmmaker's situation between his/her current activity and his/her expectations about the operational sequence in which s/he is engaged. To understand how this mediation between the present and the future works, one needs to pay heed *both* to the teleological character of filmmaking *and* to its daily practice.

Paper, Phone, Laptop

I sit next to Ezzat while he inputs an ink drawing of a floorplan on his Lenovo laptop in early December 2013. "What is that?" I ask. "It's the apartment on the fifth floor in our building." I had heard that the apartment was recently booked to become Sharif and Maha's apartment. The three-dimensional software plan is much more detailed than the printed floorplan. "Will you plug furniture into that plan?" I ask while pointing to the computer screen. "I will, once we decide on it."

Ezzat leaves around four thirty in the afternoon. Setohy, Farghalli, and I order shawarma sandwiches. The production assistant Adham walks into the office while we eat. He shows Farghalli some new scouting pictures on his iPhone. "It looks good," says Farghalli. He asks Adham to transfer the pictures onto his computer. After we are done eating, an office assistant sets up an Excel sheet for Setohy, who inputs each crew member's name, role, type of contract, wage, and phone number into it. Setohy gives Farghalli the Excel file on a USB key once he is done inputting all the information. Farghalli adjusts the budget on his MacBook in the meantime, while asking Setohy about wage numbers.

Some days later, I arrive at New Century around three fifteen in the afternoon. Ezzat sits with Farghalli and Setohy, while Asem sits in another room. I have grown accustomed to noticing the gadgets without which filmmakers seem unable to work. Everyone has their eyes fixed on their laptops, but while Ezzat and Asem work on set designs, Farghalli and Setohy are playing Candy Crush. I can trace some sequences of action within the office: (1) Farghalli briefly calls the assistant director Zohairy to ask him about the star Khaled Abol Naga's schedule; (2) Setohy follows up with Zohairy by phone a little later; (3) Farghalli receives all required schedules by email; (4) Farghalli sends the schedule to Setohy to print out; (5) Setohy borrows my USB key to bring the document to the printer upstairs, because his own key is apparently malfunctioning; and (6) when Khaled Abol Naga's assistant walks into the office a little later, Setohy gives her the actor's printed shooting schedule.

Ezzat sits right next to me on his computer. He is creating a digital drawing of a library and a desk on SketchUp. The designs look like a 3D outline filled with plain colors and measurements to the side of the objects. Ezzat turns the 3D drawing around with his mouse to get different angles. He goes back to straight views using keyboard shortcuts: from above, from the front, from the side. "I'm still amazed by your software," I tell Ezzat while marveling at his dexterity in manipulating what looks like a difficult piece of computer engineering. He smiles without losing his concentration.

Asem walks in and out of the room, regularly asking Ezzat whether he is done yet. "Have you inputted measurements in Maha and Mustafa's apartment? . . . Have you finished my designs?" "Not yet," answers Ezzat while staring at his screen, clicking away in focused silence. "When you're done, open the full apartment file," orders Asem. Opening the file takes some time. After five minutes or so, Asem loses patience: "Isn't there a way to compress the file?" "It won't happen, it's full of details," answers Ezzat. Asem asks about another file he had created and whether it would be as heavy. "No," answers Ezzat, "it doesn't have as many curvy lines as in Sharif and Maha's apartment." "Does that matter?" Asem asks with irritation. "Yes," asserts Ezzat while the file is still loading.

Ezzat and Asem are done around six fifteen in the evening. "We'll come back tomorrow with Nihal to work on props in Sharif and Maha's apartment. Will there be a production worker to open the door?" asks Asem while packing up his computer. "We'll be there tomorrow," answers Farghalli. I would like to think that his nonchalant answer includes me as well as his production team. I will be there tomorrow no matter what.

3

Reserves

S o far, I have given a faint impression of the presence of technological devices in Egyptian film production. Paper, phones, cameras,
monitors, laptops—all these devices populate the everyday ecology
of the industry, but in what ways are they involved in the *activity* of film
production? The issue at stake is whether it is possible to describe filmmaking as an abstractly "sociotechnical" phenomenon without examining the
actual devices through which this phenomenon occurs. I partly hinted at
this issue in Chapter 2, where I argued that technical actions hold, in their
very execution, an orientation to the unpredictable yet expected future of
a sociotechnical process, which gives meaning to individual working practices. I hope I sufficiently evidenced this claim, by highlighting how each
operation in filmmaking leads to subsequent ones thanks to mediators like
the screenplay, the scouting picture, the video-assist monitor, and the mixer's reference image.

This chapter describes in more detail how technological objects are
physically present in the Egyptian film industry. I begin by examining the
emic conception of technology in Cairo, which provides a useful background
to the description of "commodity-objects" in the subsequent section. What
I call an object is, in a narrow sense, a physical entity no matter its use. It
corresponds to the Egyptian worker's ordinary concept of a smartphone, a
laptop, or a spotlight as "things" (*ashya'* or *hagat*). This notion is a consequence of "the progressive disembedding or 'cutting out' of the technical
from the social that . . . lies behind the institutionalized separation between
technology and society that is such a pronounced feature of modernity"
(Ingold, 1997: 129). This disembedding, this "purification" to use Latour's
term (1993), establishes a clear-cut separation between physical objects and
physical subjects, where subjects are set in inexorable motion by technology

toward a better future. This point will be made evident in my description of the Egyptian category of *tiknulujya*.

While suggesting a deterministic drive toward social progress in a broad sense, the term *tiknulujya* has come more specifically to designate digital devices in Egypt. Keeping in line with a social science tradition extending to Veblen (1899) and Bourdieu (1986) before Miller (1987), I suggest that the consumption of digital devices is a way of showcasing one's status, both in terms of the Egyptian film industry's hierarchy and the wider society's class system. These devices may be nonhuman, therefore, but they are not asocial. As Miller convincingly argues (1987), material culture is always entangled in a wider web of social relations. In today's Egypt, it is inevitably entangled with mass commoditization and mass consumption. Just as smartphones and laptops are conceived as technological devices, their proximate origin is conceived as a concrete market—the local tech store, the local bookstore, Souq.com—without attention to these commodities' biography—in a Silicon Valley research and development room, in Indonesian factories, or in an Egyptian port. Thus, digital devices are made present to my interlocutors in Cairo as commodity-objects.

Given this conception, the concrete use of commodity-objects rarely comes under reflexive scrutiny. This is in fulfillment of Bolter and Grusin's remark that "our culture wants both to multiply its media and to erase all traces of mediation: ideally, it wants to erase its media in the very act of multiplying them" (2000: 5). In consequence, to use the metaphor of a blind man's stick, the technological object "becomes, through time and practice, incorporated and thus transparent. It is itself forgotten" (Malafouris, 2013: 7). In other words, there is a discrepancy between what people *say* about commodity-objects and how they are *used* in everyday practice, especially in processes such as filmmaking. I engage with objects as they are used in everyday filmmaking practices by attending to what I have called technological "reserves." The reserve is an object that makes constant demands on the worker's attention to engage in a situated, future-oriented task, transforming him/her in turn into a human reserve. The reserve is not a substitute to the "real" object in this sense; rather, it is a stock of energy, a resource, ready to be marshalled at any moment to face an imponderable outcome.

For instance, the production assistant Mahmoud Abdallah used his Samsung smartphone in multiple ways while working on *Décor*: he would visit his Facebook page, play the popular Facebook game Candy Crush, take personal pictures, send text messages, and call various people at work and at home. The smartphone, here, is better conceived as a multifunctional object. Yet, when he was sent by the line producer Farghalli to accomplish a scouting mission, Abdallah's smartphone became a "picture-reserve," channeling his efforts toward the production of a specific set of visual mediators (in this case, scouting pictures) in the wider process of *Décor*'s production. The object and the reserve are not strictly speaking two different things, but two different moments in the apprehension of things. At one moment, Abdallah considers his smartphone as a multifunctional object with a set of inert technical specifications. At another, it becomes a reserve that compels him to take scouting pictures.

The description centers on my experience in Egyptian film production, but I do not expect to highlight a specifically Egyptian way of using technological devices. Rather, I wish to show the way in which these objects, by becoming reserves through their use, compel the filmmaker's attention to specific tasks to come within a long-term production process. On a theoretical level, the distinction between objects and reserves moves beyond consumption-centered approaches to the study of material culture (see Appadurai, 1986; Miller, 1987). These approaches examine how objects are embedded in synchronic social relations with a contingent past without examining how, in some cases, these objects come to mediate between the present and the future of a production process. This distinction is crucial to understanding the ways in which Egyptian filmmakers mediate imponderable outcomes. These outcomes are never simply imagined inside their heads, but always "delegated" (Latour, 1988) among a set of human and nonhuman reserves.

On *Tiknulujya*

The technological devices used in today's Egyptian film industry correspond to the local category of *tiknulujya* or *al-tiknuluji*. The category designates digital technologies like mobile phones (including smartphones), laptops, tablets, liquid crystal display (LCD) screens, cameras, storage units (including USB keys, hard drives, secure digital cards), and attending digital accessories (Wi-Fi routers, Internet cables, USB cables). *Tiknulujya* has become a distinctively digital term, contrasting with "predigital" objects like paper, analog electronics, and heavy machinery. Furthermore, the digital devices denoted by the term are associated with abstract notions of modernity *(hadatha)* and progress *(taqaddum)*. *Tiknulujya* has therefore become a general category that connotes a "unilinear progression from simple tools to complex machines," a major assumption in the "standard view of technology," in Pfaffenberger's terms (1992: 507).

I will come back to the digital devices denoted by the term *tiknulujya*, but, first, I wish to illustrate the term's wider connotations in contemporary Cairo, starting with an impromptu remark I heard at a conference organized by the Supreme Council of Culture in October 2013. The conference was titled "Egypt's Culture in Confrontation" *(Thaqafat Misr fi-l-muwajaha)*. As I was told by the journalist and writer Hesham Aslan, it was a customary exercise in getting intellectuals to recommend changes to the Ministry of Culture's administration. The conference's overtly postrevolutionary rhetoric did nothing to convince my skeptical companion of its political efficacy, as he thought the conference was an umpteenth attempt to reinstate "serious culture" *(thaqafa bigad)* in a ministry run by bureaucrats uninterested in art or culture.[1] I was struck by a particular remark made in the closing session, when recommendations to the ministry were read out in a crowded press conference. Various speakers intervened in support of the recommendations, including the well-known writer Bahaa Taher, the director Magdy Ahmad Ali, and the publisher Mohammed Hashem. What caught my attention, however, was a comment made by a certain Mohammed Awad, a young man invited to speak as a demographic representative of "the Egyptian youth." This was a tantalizing task when one knew that a large part of the postrevolutionary public targeted by the conference was, at least rhetorically, the "youth of the Revolution" *(shabab al-thawra)*.

Awad said that "the youth" feel like they are going "so much faster" than their elders because they live in an era of *tiknulujya*, implying that they need political change in the ministry to match their swifter pace. This remark seemed to be barely noticed by the audience or the speakers, yet the very fact that it was unremarkable struck me at the time, because the substance of Awad's argument crystallizes several assumptions about the power of *tiknulujya* in Egyptian society. Awad's remark implied, first, that there is a generational divide between the tech-savvy youth and their unsavvy elders; second, that this divide is alienating to the youth because they "go faster"; and, lastly, that they go faster because technology is advancing fast as well, and only the youth are in tune with this pace, as opposed to their elders. This is a clear expression of mutually articulated, technologically deterministic assumptions: *tiknulujya* is a motor of progress, specifically in the youth's eyes, who are "naturally" more in tune with the inexorable political/economic/societal progress driven by technology.

This idea of inexorable progress has become naturalized in today's digitized film industry as well. During our interview, the script supervisor Jaylan Auf indicated that there were many new computer programs designed to create automatic lists of props, locations, costumes, and so on using a word-processed screenplay. The software might not have become widely used in Egypt "because it's all in English," as she said, but when this *tiknuluji* settles in Egypt, "it'll be easy to do script breakdowns." In consequence, some positions would become redundant, presumably because the labor invested by direction assistants in going over breakdowns would be reduced. "It's just a question of time," she concluded. Auf's comment perfectly toes Awad's technologically deterministic line, even though there was—and still is—no evidence to suggest that this software will be spreading in the industry or, even more unlikely, that the software would automatically make certain positions redundant.

This supposed power of technological devices was again highlighted, albeit in a different way, by the editor Mostafa Nour. He worked with the director Ahmad Fawzi Saleh on his documentary about the 2012 Port Said stadium massacre, where seventy-two football supporters were killed in a melee after a game. I asked Nour how the editing was going and he replied that things were fine, adding that "as usual," Fawzi was undecided about the movie's cut. He was especially tired of Fawzi's constant requests to bring some technical modification or other to the image. In some cases, as in cropping or rotating an image, the operation was not too difficult for Nour, yet Fawzi would be "dazzled" *(mabhur)* by these technical feats. In other cases, Nour intimated that Fawzi asked too much, because "he thinks that anything is possible with technology."

The idea that one can do "anything" *(ayy haga)* with technology is indeed very common in Cairo. "With a Samsung, you can do everything: sending emails, texting, and calling. You can also take hand notes!" This is how Hesham Aslan, the journalist who accompanied me at the Ministry of Culture, heaped praise on his new Samsung phone:

> At first, I had a BlackBerry. I thought it was very good, because I could send emails, texts, et cetera. When I decided to buy a new phone, I wanted a BlackBerry. But everyone tried to convince me to

buy a Samsung. So . . . I bought this one [he points to his Samsung phone]. The Samsung has everything you want. Everything. The crazy thing is that you can download all you want on Android, for free. All applications are for free. Whatever you want. Imagine: you can call anywhere for free! This Viber thing is a work of genius! . . . With Samsung, I realized, BlackBerry is very primitive. . . . You know what, I think after this [he holds up his phone] there's nothing else. Nothing!

These stories illustrate a naive enchantment with the power of technology and the notion that technology allows unlimited liberty to the mind of the user. Although Nour exaggerated Fawzi's naivety, notions of enchantment and indefinite potency are certainly part of the cluster of meanings associated with *tiknulujya* in Cairo, as elsewhere. In fulfillment of Gell's remark, perhaps, "if we no longer recognize magic explicitly, it is because technology and magic, for us, are one and the same" (1988: 9).

One last story serves to confirm the existence of all these assumptions at once. When I told the well-known cinematographer Marwan Saber that I was interested in the influence of technology on the Egyptian film industry, he immediately launched into a monologue on the fast-paced evolution of digital cinema technologies. "It's not just sensors that are evolving, but also lenses, filters, lighting equipment, editing units. . . . The whole *workflow* is changing." Ultimately, he continued, the cinematographer wants to be able to "create" without limits *(yibda')*. He needs to understand his technology in order to know what image he can get, and he needs to understand the whole workflow between shooting and postproduction. Being a cinematographer, in his view, is about "knowledge" *('ilm)*, especially in a rapidly advancing technological world where it is hard to keep up to date.

Saber compared technological innovation in digital cinema with innovation in smartphones, where new software is released every day to improve on older software. A new iPhone version might be faster than a preceding version, but it will have many more bugs, such that another version is needed to fix the bugs, and so forth. When I asked Saber whether older cinematographers have a harder time adapting to the new technology, he answered that this goes beyond the specific case of cinematographers. Older people in general have a hard time learning to use new technology, and he mentioned his father's inability to understand how smartphones work to support his claim. His generation, in turn, has an easier time adapting because they lived through both phases of technology (analog and digital). He himself was a contemporary of the entry of the Internet, mobile phones, and all this *tiknuluji* in Egypt, such that he was predisposed to interact with digital cinema technologies when they took over the film industry.

In addition to reiterating the assumptions that technology propels fast-paced societal change and that it remains ungraspable for older generations, Saber introduced the idea that technology allows unlimited creativity (*ibda'*). To the artistic worker, this idea of technology's infinite potential is appealing insofar as it seems to open a realm of indefinite creation, as was apparent in Fawzi's enchantment with technology. This assumption is disputed by some workers in the industry. When I told the star Mahmoud Hemida that I am interested in studying the impact of technology on the Egyptian film industry, he immediately replied that technology has nothing to do with cinema, adding that the great director Youssef Chahine said that movies needed to be made without artifice—if necessary, without a camera. The sociotechnical description presented in Chapter 2 ought to put this position in doubt, but it is evident that Hemida's statement is directed against the opposite extreme view—the kind of pervading technological determinism evoked by Saber, whereby *tiknulujya* seems to become the end-all-be-all of artistic creation.

What is fascinating, in my view, is the way in which these assumptions permeate levels of analysis ranging from the micro-interaction with the iPhone update to the macro-social dynamics of generational divide, artistic creation, or, as the case may be, political struggle. The basic idea is that technology deterministically drives "progress" in these social arenas, and whether one owns an iPhone or works with a digital cinema camera, *tiknulujya* can be seen to do its modernizing wonder work. To some extent, this work is deemed to occur thanks to the physical properties of the technology at hand.[2] Indeed, if these vignettes are any indication, the digital devices called *tiknulujya* contribute to making present the modernist assumptions attributed to the notion of *tiknulujya* in everyday life. Progress is, after all, just like regular iPhone updates.

This notion of "progress" needs to be taken in a morally neutral sense: while the examples that I have given emphasize a positive valuation, the progress forced by technology is deemed undesirable by some Egyptian filmmakers. When I asked Ahmed Farghalli whether digital technologies make a difference compared to analog technologies, he replied that *tiknulujya* only made things worse. He used a particular example to sustain his claim. When film material was on film negative, he knew exactly that it was "there" whenever stored in correct archival conditions. With digital technologies, however, the files harboring the material can be corrupted, and the material can be indefinitely copied, which makes it easy to steal film material (as had happened at New Century at the time). Farghalli did not dispute the idea that *tiknulujya* drives progress in inexorable fashion; he was resigned to the fact that he had to adapt to it. However, he did not agree that it was necessarily a positive development, evoking the respective affordances of film negative and hard drives, in this case.

Commodity-Objects

When they talk about *tiknulujya*, Egyptian filmmakers distinguish between personally owned digital devices and specialized cinema equipment (*mu'iddat* such as cinema cameras, dolly tracks, lighting spots, editing software). When I declared my interest in technology, my interlocutors would assume that I was interested in cinema equipment specifically. Personal devices are in some ways so infused with the everyday that their impact on the work of film production seems negligible. I will dispute this assumption below, but it is useful to dwell on cinema equipment insofar as it is the locus of the industry's recent transition to digital technology.

In Egypt, equipment rentals tend to be managed by specialist companies, but the equipment itself is owned by production companies or the very workers using it. Cinematographers own cameras; gaffers own spotlights and gels; key grips own at least one dolly with a set of tracks; set builders own mechanical saws and sanding equipment; and sound engineers own mixers and microphones. As renting equipment counts as a separate production cost, workers who own equipment tend to work with it or rent it out.[3] This way, as the manager in Egypt's largest equipment-rental company once put it, one can "benefit others and benefit oneself with the equipment."

Until the early 2010s, cinema equipment was analog. The standard cinema cameras worked with thirty-five millimeter negatives, Moviola editing suites were the standard editing equipment, and local postproduction was exclusively conducted in Studio Misr or the EMPC, which were equipped with laboratories treating the negative through coloring, special effects, mixing, and printing. When I started fieldwork in 2013, the advent of digital cinema had obsolesced analog equipment. The largest equipment company in Egypt, Focus, no longer rented out analog ARRI 535 cameras, which had ceded to the Red Epic and the ARRI Alexa.[4] Moviola editing suites had been out of use for some years, having ceded to Mac desktops with Final Cut Pro software by the mid-2000s.[5] Even the Studio Misr and EMPC laboratories had ceded (except in printing) to private postproduction companies like TimeCode and Aroma, which own stations equipped with digital coloring suites (Base Light), graphics software (Smoke), and sound design software (Pro Tools).

The passage to digital cinema did not radically change the totality of equipment used in the Egyptian film industry, except in areas like camera capture, the transportation of (digital) audiovisual material, and the computerization of postproduction. Still, there have been wider changes in working practices, according to many interlocutors. When I asked the director Akram Farid about the changes in film production brought by digital technologies, he shrugged and said, "Nothing much. . . . There's just more gluttony *(tafasa)*." He elaborated by saying that there is freedom to "shoot more," as all rehearsals can now be shot and reviewed on the spot, which was impossible prior to the digital era. Likewise, the now prevalent habit of shooting "*one more for safety*" was not widespread. The experienced assistant director Wael Mandour added that the difference between analog and digital cinema lies in "*discipline*." In the analog era, filmmakers would rehearse a great deal prior to shooting; technicians would come on time; and editing decisions became final once the negative was literally cut. Nowadays, rehearsals are filmed on set; punctuality has become an issue; and editors can in no time remove frames and put them back in the final cut. "The idea of organization on location makes a big difference," the cinematographer Abdelsalam Moussa summarized. "It's not like anybody can shoot, or anybody can assist in shooting. No assistant director [talked] during the shot, no one [went] in front of the camera . . . there [was] a sacredness to the location." These perceptions might be overstated, but they are representative of the opinions held by higher-end crew members about the transition to the digital era in Egypt.

This transition has been so complete, in fact, that the era of film negatives is spoken about in a nostalgic mood. Mustafa Msallem, an assistant camera worker who had followed in his father's footsteps, spoke of the gigantic cameras on which his father worked as though they were fabulous beasts. One camera "wouldn't work on batteries," he exclaimed, because it was so big and needed so much energy that it had to be plugged directly into the electric current. This camera, as he described it, was about three times the size of an ARRI Alexa, and its accessories were so big and numerous that they needed forty-seven boxes to be carried around (compared to the four to five boxes needed with an Alexa). "Cameras aren't what they used to be," he sighed, with the possible implication that his own work as a camera assistant has been devalued to the same extent as cameras shrank in size.

Smaller cameras were more favorably regarded by the sound engineer and mixer Abdelrahman "Mana" Mahmoud, who argued that the size difference lessened the "great neuroses" *('u'ad)* among ego-driven camera crews. The ten people who worked on analog cameras—including the camera supervisor, his/her assistants, the loader, the lighting script, the focus puller, and the cinematographer—treated the camera "as a kind of sacred idol" and would not let a single worker come close to it. This is not really the case anymore in his view, because cameras are now portable and easily accessible. While Mana perceived digital cameras as a positive development, he could not but associate its positive impact with the same change in labor dynamics that was interpreted in a negative light by Msallem.

Considering the speed at which the transition to digital cinema took place, it is understandable that nostalgia sometimes meets disbelief.[6] Witness the editor Heba Othman, who was among the last graduates of the High Cinema Institute to start and finish her editing course on a Moviola: "The first time I heard that editing can happen on a computer, I didn't believe it." The person who told her about it was a professor who was known to be overly theatrical at the Institute. Some time later, some members in her cohort went online (which, at the time, could not be afforded by everybody) and learned that this possibility was indeed serious. Still, in her mind, it was shocking to know that the work done on a Moviola could now be done on a computer. The Moviola consists of two rolls *(nwayo)* through which the film passes, with a little light projecting the positive image on a paper screen. The film was cut with an instrument akin to a paper-cutter; cuts were scotched with tape; markings were made with a white wax pencil on the film's perforated strip; discarded cuts *(dishay)* sprawled all over editing rooms. Mimicking the feeling of grease and hair stuck in the machinery, Othman concluded with yet another baffled remark, "I just could not believe it could be done."

Nostalgia and disbelief are not shared by all. Those filmmakers who are skeptical about the powers of *tiknulujya* resist these attitudes. Wael Mandour stated that he is "not a nostalgic for the thirty-five millimeter," because ultimately cinema is about "a subject" *(mawdu')* and not the technicalities of its making. Still, digital cinema is perceived as a genuine revolution in the history of Egyptian cinema. The sound engineer Abdelrahman Mana told me that recent technological shifts had changed the medium to the same extent as "the invention of montage; the advent of sound; the advent of color . . . it opens brand new possibilities." Mana is of the generation that saw the last days of analog sound equipment. Until the mid-2000s, sound was recorded on Nagra *(nagara)* machines using quarter-inch magnetic tapes, but these tapes rapidly disappeared when digital audio tape cassettes started to become popular. "But the miracle happened around 2009, 2010," he recalled. This miracle was the four-track digital recorder. Contrary to the mono tracks recorded on Nagras, which indistinctly captured all sounds on set, the digital recorder made it possible, for the first time in Egypt, to record tracks separating each microphone on set (including the microphones capturing the character's dialogue and the boom mic). When the four-track recorder came out, sound engineers were initially reticent to use it, according to Mana, because it did not look like a sophisticated machine (and, by extension, it did not seem to warrant enough prestige to the sound engineers on set, a profession that already lacks luster in Egypt). So when he started working without a mixer, using his smaller four-track recorder, "no one could really believe that I recorded everything digitally."

One should note that Egypt has followed a global trend toward digitization in commercial film industries (on parallel transitions to digital technology, see Ganz and Khatib, 2006; Kiwitt, 2012; Mateer, 2014, in the United States; Stephanie, Sharma and Ramasubbu 2012, in India; Messuti, 2014, in Argentina). According to Marwan Saber, who is the technical director at Focus, there is little difference between the equipment in Egypt and in the United States today, in contrast to the way outdated analog equipment survived with minimal maintenance between the 1970s and the 2000s. This does not mean, however, that the exact same models are used in Egypt as abroad.[7] Moreover, since Egyptian productions have a more limited budget than, say, major American productions, they are likely to use less expensive equipment or second-hand items. For instance, the cinematographer Mahmoud Lotfy swears that, until the 2010s, there were still Strand lamps being used in the industry, when they had been obsolete for the previous twenty years outside Egypt. This situation represents a creative challenge in Lotfy's eyes: "Outside Egypt, all the *DOPs* [directors of photography] know what every single lamp is for, and they have access to all these lamps all the time. In Egypt, you have to work with what you have, so you have to be more *creative*."

It is important to remember that this equipment works thanks to a constant supply of electrical current—a precarious commodity in a context where power cuts are regular occurrences. Once, I entered the colorist David Maher's office while he sat in darkness. "What's up with the electricity?" I asked with a little smirk, expecting the usual litany about the state's inability to provide a regular supply of electrical current. Maher was rather terse in his answer: "Without electricity, I can't work." Spoken by a worker whose work is entirely conducted on a computer, this truism serves as a reminder that the electrical infrastructure should not be taken for granted in Egypt, even though it is vital to the work of filmmaking. On set, the provision of electricity is made mobile: generator trucks supply current through large cables to the lighting equipment as well as the numerous power bars *(mushtarakat)*. These bars are important to charge the numerous batteries used to power equipment (such as the camera, the video-assist), and they can become important points of congregation on set. For instance, when the art directors Asem Ali and Nihal Farouk first entered the studio in *Décor*, they immediately asked the production team to extend an additional power bar so that they could plug in their computers and engage in discussion with the artistic crew. The power bar charges both technological devices and conversations.

Digital cinema equipment—like personally owned digital devices—is conceived as a set of black-boxed commodities in Egypt. The "black-box" metaphor was proposed by Latour, who used the term to describe scientific facts whose internal workings are mysterious, yet whose inputs and outputs are known and fairly predictable (1987: 2–3). Ordinary digital devices are also seen as a black box by Egyptian filmmakers. Everyone has a different level of knowledge and insight into the object's workings, but all filmmakers use these objects nonetheless. As Sigaut remarked, "millions of people around the world listen to the radio and watch television without having the least idea about the way in which these apparatuses work (and I am one of them)" (2003: 5). Some crew members, such as the production assistant Mahmoud Abdallah, are said to be more skilled with digital objects *(shatir fi-l-tiknulujya)*. Abdallah therefore received regular troubleshooting requests from all production crew members at New Century whenever a device was not working well, or whenever software needed to be installed on a computer, or whenever an app needed to be downloaded. This is the kind of technical knowledge that the cinematographer Marwan Saber hinted at earlier: it is a specialized skill with digital objects, which is to be distinguished from the ordinary know-how through which filmmakers input and output information on these objects.

Digital devices are not simply black-boxed because their technical functioning is unknown, but even more so because the relations of production invested in their making are occulted. Many technological objects, including cinema equipment, have become vital tools in the everyday work of film production, yet no one manufactures them in Egypt. As Focus' manager Reda Zanita once joked, the manufacture of specialized equipment is not only nonexistent in Egypt, it is "an insult to nonexistence" *(ihana li-l-sifr)*. The same could be said about ordinary technological devices like smartphones or laptops: all these products are acquired via international imports, including as second-hand goods. Cinema equipment, in particular, is known to be manufactured in a few Euro-American locations. As Marwan Saber told me, the ARRI Alexa is made in Germany, and all major repairs to the camera are referred to the German headquarters when local expertise is insufficient to deal with them.[8] Even if Saber is well-attuned to the camera's technical functioning, his interactions with the camera as an object do not just rely on his own technical knowledge, but also on the knowledge made available through instruction manuals, Internet forums, and major international corporations such as ARRI.

With mass consumption goods like smartphones or laptops, the understanding of the object's inner workings can be less important to the filmmaker than the object's commodity status. The possession of technological devices serves as a class marker in contemporary Cairo, in a manner reminiscent of color televisions in 1990s Egypt (Abu-Lughod, 2005: 220). In one backstage conversation in *Décor*, I overheard production assistants and technicians talking about the new iPhone. Someone mentioned that it would cost the hefty sum of seven to eight thousand Egyptian pounds. "Why buy a phone when you're not using it to its full capacity?" exclaimed one worker, adding that a phone should just have the right options to be useful at work. The others answered, "Yeah . . . but nobody buys a phone with this logic." The logic they were likely invoking was summarized by a cinema journalist: "People just buy what they know. . . . I'm a journalist, so I maybe need a phone with Internet, a large enough screen to read, . . . and a good enough camera to take pictures. But if I'm someone in Upper Egypt, and I just use my phone to manage a couple of employees in a local company, why would I need an iPhone?" To which he added, "But there you go, everyone wants an iPhone. . . . It's *prestige*."

The journalist's narrative plainly illustrates the association between smartphone and class, and how the privilege of owning a smartphone is afforded to the (superior) metropolitan journalist, not the (inferior) Upper Egyptian. In the film industry, any crew member who can afford it is likely to own a smartphone, because it is a way of claiming a superior status no matter one's position in the industry's hierarchy. To give another example, the assistant director Habi Seoud once told me that he was offered a "worthless" work phone by his previous company. "Like mine?" I interjected. "No. Well . . . show me your phone." I took out my cheap Nokia phone, which surprised many filmmakers precisely because it is atypical of my class background. "No, yours is much nicer. Yours is like the work phone of the company's director." We both laughed. Seoud's joke reinforced the hierarchical association between mobile phone and class. My Nokia phone was a running gag for this very reason: the director Ahmad Fawzi Saleh once joked that he could never touch my pay-as-you-go phone because he had reached a higher class position as a director and, as he put it humorously, "one cannot regress in the class struggle."

The heads of all artistic teams in *Décor* and *Poisonous Roses* carried smartphones (usually iPhone or Samsung Galaxy), while many crew members who were not independently wealthy carried the much cheaper Nokia phones. Farghalli was regularly teased by his production team because he owned a MacBook laptop and a tablet—two expensive pieces of equipment contrasting with the crew members' older, sometimes refurbished PC laptops. The running gag was that since Farghalli had become a line producer (and had therefore upgraded in the team's hierarchy), his pockets were suddenly filled. He could spend as he pleased on glitzy technological commodities. In addition to their technical specifications, these commodities are valued by workers according to their price in the local market and their "*quality*" within an implicit hierarchy of manufacturing nations. Thus, Korean manufacturing companies are deemed to be better than Chinese ones, which is why the Samsung Galaxy smartphone is deemed superior to "Chinese" smartphones (*Sini*, meaning "counterfeit" as well). The categories "Korean" and "Chinese" do not stand for the factories where actual workers make these objects; they become, rather, quality signifiers ascribed to the black-boxed commodity.

The digital devices included in the local category of *tiknulujya* are not necessarily experienced as objects in the Egyptian film industry. They can be, in equal measure, a technical device accessed through specialized technical knowledge, commodities evaluated according to class hierarchies and "*quality*" signifiers, and reserves in filmmaking. It would be reductive, then, to associate the acquisition of digital devices with a purely technical imperative, or a purely class-based exercise in distinction, or even a purely cinematic activity (just as my interlocutors expected my interest in *tiknulujya* to mean interest in cinema equipment specifically). On their own, each of these views reduces the object's importance in the filmmaker's everyday activity. Nevertheless, when I asked direct questions about these technological objects to my interlocutors, I would most likely receive some "purely technical" answer in line with the subject/object dualism current among Egyptian filmmakers. In some respects, this dualism makes them impervious to the observable uses to which these objects are put. These uses, I contend, are better described through the category of "reserve."

Reserves

Actions ordinarily understood as "technical" are embedded in a wider sociotechnical process in the Egyptian film industry. Thus, taking scouting pictures is not just about pressing a button on a camera; it is conducted with a specific know-how by production workers at the behest of their superiors, an exercise which involves specific aesthetic and logistical decisions at successive stages in production. The interaction between a production worker such as Mahmoud Abdallah and his smartphone occurs in this sociotechnical context, where it is possible to describe technological devices as "reserves" or resources summoning the filmmaker's attention to incoming junctures in the filmmaking process, following the operational sequence of filmmaking within a digitized industry. This summoning anticipates the film's imponderable outcome, while becoming ever more contingent on previous operations in the filmmaking process.

Screenwriting is a good starting point to explain how reserves work. Egyptian screenwriters use pen, paper, and word-processing software to write screenplays and script breakdowns. Given that the practice of screenwriting is restricted to the screenwriter, the director, and their close interlocutors, all other crew members have no access to screenwriting except via printed copies distributed by the production team. I did not participate in any screenwriting sessions in *Décor*, but my involvement with the film began when I was given a printed screenplay by the line producer Ahmed

Farghalli. In *Poisonous Roses*, where I directly contributed to screenwriting, the main texts constituting the screenplay were written on a computer, but the director Ahmad Fawzi Saleh still used a wide variety of notebooks, spare paper, Post-it notes, and printed screenplays while reading, writing, and rewriting his text.

The various forms taken by the screenplay and its ancillary inscriptions offer significant material to the screenwriter and the director to develop their ideas. What counted as an "idea" in our screenwriting sessions in *Poisonous Roses* was situated between oral conversation and the various notes we made on paper while thinking about the screenplay. Some fleeting suggestion made by Fawzi could be brought into the conversation some days later, if he or I had any memory of it, or if it was written down in our notes. The modifications undertaken in the scene described in Chapter 2 serve as a good example. A scene where Tahiya was originally going to walk by lingerie stores in downtown Cairo became, on one night in the summer of 2015, a scene where she ordered new shoes for Saqr from a tanning workshop. Some days later, an additional detail was added to the scene. When it appeared that Saqr's mother's character had been absent too long in the screenplay upon reading a handwritten breakdown of her scenes, we decided to include her in the background of the scene where Tahiya goes to the shoemaker.

Once we had agreed on including new ideas, what was written on paper was used to rewrite scenes on computer. For instance, the extensive profiles written for each character in *Poisonous Roses* were later transformed into word-processed scenes. These scenes were read and criticized by our trusted interlocutors, which led to more rewriting. All these versions, combined with our live discussions, were transformed in every screenwriting session, but the transformation did not occur at the whim of our interlocutions. Rather, it evolved through the manipulation of large blocks of word-processed text, allowing us to think through the writing of a screenplay that conveyed Fawzi's desires. This practice is more accurately grasped by saying that the various technological devices we used in inscribing written mediators were reserves that contained a potential to summon past or present ideas while summoning our attention to creating the film ahead.

This mutual summoning flattened interactions between Fawzi, his assistant director Yousef Abodan, me, and various written mediators, transforming our materially extended imaginations into reserves set on creating *Poisonous Roses*. On his own account, Fawzi did not know "what [he wanted] to say in the film" until he underwent this discussion/inscription process. This statement, I would argue, means that he could not exactly determine the movie's plot, let alone its visual appearance, without interacting with a variety of reserves—printed copies, Post-its, smartphones, laptops, interlocutors—all of which were summoned to the task of screenwriting. This iterative practice is made possible by the becoming-reserve of these humans and nonhumans. Iteration presupposes, indeed, dedicated surfaces upon which the screenplay's text can be inscribed and reinscribed, whether the blank paper, the computer screen, or Fawzi's interlocutors. These reserves preserve the screenplay's content as an evolving potential, slowly but surely materialized as we were summoned to create the screenplay.

The use of technological devices in preproduction illustrates this summoning in a different context. In the production (and direction) team, personal mobile phones, computers, and paperwork are used to coordinate logistics. All members of *Décor*'s crew carried a mobile phone, but Farghalli was exceptional among hierarchically superior workers in that he carried an old Nokia phone. Although he owned a MacBook laptop and a tablet, he thought a Nokia was more reliable than a smartphone because it has an extensive battery life. Likewise, Setohy told me that he bought a scouting camera with rechargeable batteries because cameras with AA batteries cannot bear long working hours. This technical interest in battery life is bound with a more general concern with "being available," as I explain in Chapter 4. Farghalli, Setohy, and their crew members at New Century were never entirely relaxing, whether at work or outside of work, because they were under the pressure of a strong expectation to remain available by phone. If Farghalli's or Setohy's phone died, they could not be reached except in person, which is inconvenient, if not damaging, in urgent time strains. The strong expectation that one will answer the phone is reinforced by a general preference for calling in person over sending text messages or emails. "I only [send messages] when [the phone] is busy or closed," said Farghalli, who argued that live contact is best for communicating his directives. "People can make excuses about how they didn't see a message, or they were sleeping, or they didn't check," but they cannot pretend they did not hear his voice. In fact, Farghalli preferred that his production crew remain in the office or on location with him, in person, even when their jobs did not require their physical presence.

This expectation of "being available" depends on one's position on the crew. Although the director Ahmad Abdalla had license not to answer his assistants or the line producer, a production worker would get scolded by Farghalli were he not to pick up the phone. On countless occasions, I saw Farghalli irritated by the fact that a crew member did not pick up the phone after a few calls. If the crew member called back any time thereafter, Farghalli's first question would be, "Why don't you answer?" In the film industry, not answering is rarely interpreted as an ordinary occurrence (the phone was elsewhere) or technical fault (the battery died). Rather, it is perceived as a conscious decision not to answer, which begs the question as to *why* the worker is not answering. The question implies that the worker sought to avoid work or, at least, that s/he was not doing his/her job properly, which in practice elicited impassioned denials or profuse apologies by production crew members. Workers are well aware that they will get scolded if they do not answer their phones or if they do not keep them on, and they act accordingly.

An anecdote relayed by Farghalli illustrates the importance of answering calls. Once, he was on location with an assistant who was later fired. He called him on the phone several times, but the assistant would not answer. "If I'm on location with someone, and I'm calling on the phone, it means that it's *urgent*," he told him. If it were not urgent, he would either wait to see the assistant in person or get someone to get him, but there is a reason why he is phoning him on location. Fifteen minutes later, Farghalli saw the assistant. "Why aren't you answering?" he yelled out, to which the assistant answered that he was talking to his mom on the phone. Farghalli told him that next time, he needed to hang up on his mom and talk to his boss, because a phone call on location is urgent. The assistant apparently could not understand why Farghalli was frustrated, and he could not believe that he would have to hang up on his mother to answer a phone call on location. The assistant could not bear the idea of cutting his social ties, which is what eventually got him fired, according to Farghalli: because production requires workers to remain committed to their work over and above their contact with family and friends.

The expectation to remain available by phone extends over all stages in production, such that the phone becomes a reserve of calls to communicate working commands while disciplining the production worker into becoming a reserve of attention and labor. This discipline is not just a bodily one; it emerges out of a specific configuration of hierarchical positioning, operational awareness, and technological use. The phone-reserve is a constant physically present potential to summon the worker's attention to tasks that are most often assigned by hierarchical superiors, and the worker is compelled to answer the phone.[9] Even if Farghalli perceived the Nokia phone itself as an object working on a minimal technical level—"it says hello," as he would say—the phone-reserve channels his concentration to future tasks in the everyday work of film production. The reserve of calls has no end in sight: a crew member might want to report back to him; the director might want to ask about the scouting operation; the assistant director might want to follow up on the director's demands; the art director might want additional funds *('uhda)* to buy a new prop; or Farghalli himself might want to report to the producer concerning the budget, or to change the scouting journey of a production worker. What matters to the argument, much as in screenwriting, is the way in which the phone and the worker become reserves summoned to a specific future task—in this case, mediating the imponderable logistics of film production.

The immediate summoning afforded by mobile phones is akin to the longer-term summoning afforded by computer printouts in preproduction, including script breakdowns, handwritten to-do lists, and accounting paperwork. For example, the script breakdown—and, subsequently, the shooting schedule design—is created by the assistant director with the help of his/her assistants and some technological devices. In *Décor*, the assistant director Omar el-Zohairy worked with a screenplay copy annotated by hand, scribbled notes, and tabularized lists of logistical elements constituting, after extensive review by his assistants and him, a final script breakdown. From the screenplay's pre-inscribed matter, Zohairy molded a breakdown through iterative inscriptions and transcriptions, in such a way that he could, as he said, "learn the film by heart" *(yihfaz al-film)*. This highlights the expectations set on the assistant director as a record-keeper of artistic work, and it explains why the breakdown holds an important mnemonic weight in the execution of shooting days. The breakdown, whether inscribed on paper or on a phone, mediates the artistic demands to be executed and verified on set by the direction team.

Not unlike paper and phones in this context, digital cameras summon artistic workers' attention to the film's eventual appearance when they are used to take scouting pictures, casting videos, or fitting pictures. In *Décor* and *Poisonous Roses*, these pictures were shown in person or via email to artistic crew members, who would in turn show each other "*reference*" pictures in person, via USB, email, or social media like Instagram. Prior to shooting in *Poisonous Roses*, Fawzi once confessed that he was "no longer afraid of the film," because he had "watched twenty thousand images," which made him feel more secure about his cinematic style. These images include a great number of movies, paintings, photographs, and innumerable scouting pictures of the tanneries district. Such visual capital is integral to the artistic worker's imagination and is indicative of the importance of technological devices in anticipating film creation. Again, the workers' laptops, tablets, or smartphones became reserves, in this case summoning their attention to what the film would eventually look like (see Chapter 5).

The potential inherent in mobile phones, computers, or paper to summon a scouting picture, a prop picture, or a casting video is matched by the artistic worker's anguish over what "the film" will be like when it is made. This was especially evident with visual mediators circulated among artistic crew members in *Décor*: when the art director Asem Ali sent prop "*references*" to Nihal Farouk to decide if it "looks good" *(hilw)*; when the stylist Salma Sami sent an email with the star's latest fitting pictures to discuss her look with the director; when Zohairy scrolled through casting choices on a picture/video database to select extras for *Décor*'s final scene; and so on. The digital device in each case has a potential to summon visual mediators, which summons the worker's attention to the future of his/her creation. Here, the analytical difference between the laptop and the smartphone—or between the artist's relation to the laptop as opposed to the smartphone—is eroded. It becomes more economical to describe workers and objects as "reserves" engaged in a relation of mutual summoning toward an eventual end—in this case, visualizing what the film will look like. This summoning goes beyond the subject/object distinction while underscoring the necessity of seeing technological devices as more than "actants" (Latour, 1996), because reserves anticipate the film's future more than they translate its past.

Reserves can work across different stages of film production. For example, printouts and mobile phones serve to coordinate the production team's logistics, whether in preparations or in shooting. The script supervisors Jaylan Auf and Mariam el-Bagoury would use an annotated screenplay copy (made in preparations) and continuity videos (made on set) to ensure the continuity of dialogue, movement, or costumes while shooting *Décor*. The assistant director Zohairy would make his daily call sheets in a Word document by copying and pasting rows of his sequential table (made in preparations) into a separate call sheet document distributed as a printout on set (see Figure 2). Thus, talking about "reserves" eschews the boundaries between preparations, shooting, and postproduction, because what

فيلم ديكور

Call sheet no : 2

الإخراج : أحمد عبدالله السيد	الطلائع : ٢ ديسمبر ٢٠١٢ – ستوديو مصر – بلاتوه ١
مدير التصوير : طارق حفني	حضور فريق التصوير : ٧ صباحا
منتج فني : احمد فرغلي	
الديكور : عاصم علي / نيبال فاروق	ملابس : سلمى سامي
	Camera roll : ٨ صباحا

م	المشهد	زمن ن/خ	الديكور	ملخص المشهد	الشخصيات	التشخيص
1	Avant titre	ن / د	الصالة	Track out . شريط شخصية مكان عامود النور .. شريف من ظهره و يشعل سيجارة في الخلفية العمال يحملون باقو .. لقطة ثابتة تشعل فيلم داخل شريط شباب النيكوزة عند الصالة العمال يرفعون النيكة إحدى الجوانب	مها \ شريف \ عمال الديكور
2	٢ + ٣ + ٤ + ٥	ن / د	كل الديكور	التشخيص و التصوير يضافون البلاتوه . جميع فريق التصوير حاضرين . صحورين و صحفيين في كل مكان حسين .. منتفخ حول المطفئ .. الديكان . صحورين يضافون شريط حذاءه و ملطخ بالطلاء .. مساعدو الفريق التصوير و المساعد الصحفين و مسك بالنوتة البيلوج . مها تناديه كي يساعدها . هيا تنويه تناديه تركيب الكتبة . بينما عمرو و طارق عامل الديكور .. هيا يحرجان مع عمرو	مها + شريف + عمرو سلامة + الطفلة + مساعد الصحفين و طارق عامل الديكور
3	١٤	ن / د	الصالة	هيا تنويد تظهر في كبدة ديكيونيات وشريط ما تنفي من الديكور حيث ناشر في الكتبة .. يظهر عمرو سلامة . يذكرهم بأن الفيلم سريع و يجب عدم الدقة في التنكيد . مها تنفي لشريط في لوح على ذلك الوضح . هيا و شريف يحتضان ان ما تنفي من خطوات التنكيد لانجدار لانجدار النيكور	مها + شريف + عمرو سلامة + فريق التصوير +
4	٤٧	ن / د	ديكور تصوير الفيلم جزء من المطبخ	يوسف نحمل الديكور . يوم تحضير ديكور . نذهب لنشاال شريط هيا نحمل الديكور . اكل يخلخل من وجودها . يراقب السيكي و يلين منبسطا و الديكور السيكي	مها + شريف + طارق عامل الديكور + السيكي + مساعد

2. First page of the call sheet for *Décor*'s second shooting day, made by Omar el-Zohairy. Photograph © New Century Film Production.

matters most is the way in which workers and technological devices are both summoned toward future tasks. This is not just the case with personally owned digital devices, but equally with specialized cinema equipment like cinema cameras, video-assist monitors, postproduction computers, and on-set microphones.

The camera and the video-assist monitor are central congregating points on set, as artistic workers tend to gather around these screens to comment on the film's image. While the cinematographer and the cameraman tend to check the recorded action on their viewfinder, it has become standard practice to add a monitor over the camera's body to help the focus puller with adjusting the image's blurriness and, when a video-assist is impracticable,[10] to allow the director to check the action. Any adjustment to the image during a take is communicated by reference to the camera or video-assist monitors on location. This desire to watch what will become "the film" as it is unfolding is apparent in postproduction as well, where all work extends between the postproduction worker, the director, and computer monitors acting as a common visual reference. The relations among all these screens and artistic workers is better described as relations among reserves: screens are summoned to reveal the film's image, while the artistic crew is summoned to adjust this very image. So much more is happening on set or in postproduction, not least the logistical groundwork necessary to both activities, but the mutual summoning of reserves is integral to the way in which the imponderable "film" gradually becomes actualized.

Watching higher-end crew members congregate around the camera and the video-assist exposes, in a way, the extent to which the image is valued over sound in the Egyptian film industry. Yet the undervaluation of sound should not overshadow how microphones are not just sound-recording machines, because they also act as reserves in much the same way as visual devices. Microphones summon the sound engineer's attention to the quality of the sound material prior to postproduction, while being summoned to record all dialogue and ambient sounds on set. When I asked the sound engineer Ahmad Saleh why he did not call for a retake when the recorded sound was imperfect, Saleh answered that he would avoid retaking because he could anticipate, while listening to his on-set sound, how he will eventually repair errors in postproduction. Thus, his attention to the film's sound environment is not prior to the recorded sound itself; it is summoned by the microphone-reserve, which in turn summons on-set sounds through recording.

The sound example highlights, perhaps better than a visual one, the importance of thinking about technological devices as reserves and not just as objects. Throughout the filmmaking process, many devices can materialize images or sounds that would otherwise be invisible or inaudible. In a trivial sense, the director cannot "see" the film unless it is shot, just as the sound engineer cannot "hear" the shot unless it is recorded, because movements and noises on location overshadow the specific audiovisual content within the shot. To understand how this otherwise inaudible or invisible content becomes summoned to anticipate an imponderable future, we cannot simply attend to technological devices as objects materializing the invisible or the inaudible—as though they were a material substratum to the "cultural" work invested in sound and image work. The microphone—just like the laptop, the mobile phone, the camera, the video-assist monitor—acts as a reserve in film production. These reserves summon otherwise unactualized potentials, whether screenplay ideas, logistical actions, images, or sounds, to mediate the incoming future of "the film."

Worktime and Technology

This chapter has described the emic conception of *tiknulujya* in contemporary Egypt, moving on to the way in which digital technologies are perceived in commercial film production, how they are conceived as commodity-objects, and how they act as reserves within the production process. Reserves, in addition to the labor hierarchies and processes described in Chapter 2, are vital to understanding how imponderable outcomes are mediated throughout the course of film production. The way in which reserves act as proxies between the near and the far future is unique neither to Egypt nor to the film industry. Throughout my stay in Cairo, I felt a certain kinship between my research activity and the concrete labor of making a film, in a manner reminiscent of Boyer's sense of familiarity with "screenwork" among digital journalists in Germany (2013). Both research and cinema are oriented toward an imponderable future: in one case, toward the writing of an academic piece; in the other, toward the creation of "the film."

These affinities are not unique to the digital era. Digital devices do not necessarily make filmmaking "better" or "faster," yet this idea remains a common representation in Egypt.[11] A case in point is a brief exchange I had with the production manager in *Décor*, Mohammed Setohy, who had been complaining about his computer's constant failures while we were in preproduction. "What's wrong with pen and paper?" he once joked. I answered nonchalantly that his work is probably much faster now. "Of course! I was just joking." He did not challenge the technical statement I made, nor did he historicize the claim according to which production work is "faster" now, which is surprising given that Setohy would not have had the same time-consuming problem with paper as he had with his fledgling laptop. This exchange testifies to the ingrained way in which computers are inserted in a narrative of technological progress beyond the concrete socio-technical activity in which these devices participate. What I have argued is that, no matter this representation's persistence, there is still a way in which technological devices, whether digital or analog, work differently in their everyday use. Within a given operational sequence, these technologies can act as reserves to help certain workers mediate between the present and the imponderable future of their activity.

This specific argument ties into a broader issue concerning the relation between technological devices and the experience of worktime in capital-ist societies. This link has been noted since E.P. Thompson's classic essay tracing the emergence of machine-driven time in the early days of indus-trial capitalism in England (2009 [1964]). Thompson convincingly argues that early industrial workers became gradually used to a new experience of work thanks, in part, to new timing technologies. Contrary to task-oriented time, which is concomitant to "natural" cycles like the harvest or the tides, machine-time gives accurate objective measurements to synchro-nize manufacturing work and to determine wages. Of course, one should not assume that modern technology inevitably leads to identical changes in time-concepts across capitalist settings.[12] One might still note, in line with Thompson, that sociotechnical change—like the one that brought digi-tal technologies to be ubiquitous in contemporary Cairo—still affects the experience of worktime.

This experience has been described in terms of a broad distinction between "home" and "work" in cultural studies. In his pioneering book on television, Raymond Williams notes that broadcasting technologies have emerged in a context where "modern urban industrial living" was governed by "two apparently paradoxical yet deeply connected tendencies . . . on the one hand mobility [to work], on the other hand the more apparently self-sufficient family home" (2005: 18). In Nippert-Eng's words, "The normative expectations of a segmented home and work experience have resulted from the separation of the values, activities, social functions, and people of home and work into separate spatiotemporal locations" (2010: 18). This is not a productive way of analyzing the daily experience of Egyptian filmmakers, or indeed any worker in a flexible industry, where home and work are not opposites in a continuum as Nippert-Eng contends (2010: 5). Instead, digital devices inform the worker's experience of time in a way that is most closely articulated by Ladner in a short study of the use of mobile technologies in a Canadian interactive agency (2008). As she puts it,

> Mobile technologies present a confounding development in one of the defining debates in the study of work: the division between work time and private time. The use of immobile technologies, from factory machines to desktop computers, has contributed to the spatial centralization of work on the one hand and to firm divisions between work and home on the other. But with the widespread adoption of cellular phones, laptop computers, wireless Internet, and mobile email devices, this spatial rigidity has broken down, complicating a central tenet implicit in most employment relationships: the right of workers to restrict workplace or management access during private time. (Ladner, 2008: 466)

Through numerous interviews with agency workers, Ladner shows how mobile digital technologies mark an interpenetration of "home" and "work" as experiential realms. Without adhering to Ladner's linear narrative of passage between immobile and mobile technologies, I would argue that, in the case of Egyptian film production, technological devices shape everyday working experience by summoning, in the present, both near and far futures, giving a distinct feeling to the labor of filmmaking. Technological devices acting as reserves modify the filmmaker's conception of his/her work to the extent that they involve, in practice, this capacity to project oneself into an unpredictable yet expected future.

Again, this future-orientation is not unique to Egyptian film production. A reflexive note about my research illustrates the point, taking inspiration in Pandian's thoughts about "the temporal horizons of our own work and thought, as they unfurl in our relations with others and in the distance we assume to ourselves" (2010: 549). In one of the notebooks constituting the basis of the next chapter, I wrote the following remark, "If it is not evident enough, the *tagammu'* [meeting point] at the beginning of the day is a clear example of the work of coordination accomplished by phone." When I wrote it down, I had in mind a dissertation chapter about coordinating the logistics of a shooting day, and I wanted to highlight to my (future) self how these notes could be relevant to this chapter. When I started writing the dissertation six months later, I was copying the notes on my computer when I saw this little "note to self" in the margins. While in the field, this note instantiated a present record of what I had witnessed on that day geared toward a future task: writing the next chapter. Throughout the sociotechnical process of writing a book, I have resorted to various technological contraptions to summon written notes, while being summoned to write this book in turn (without forgetting that the process occurs in a specific institutional context located in a late capitalist society).

Writing a book in Oxford involves a vastly different process to making commercial films in Egypt, but without spending too long on obvious discrepancies, I am struck by the way in which my notebook/computer acts as a reserve in much the same way as script breakdowns, digital cameras, and video-assist monitors do in Egyptian film production. While I work with different assumptions and mediators than my interlocutors—handwritten "notes to self" as opposed to phone calls and cameras—the situation whereby we are made to think about the future of our respective projects via various reserves is common to our working experiences. This commonality, I would argue, is central to the way in which digital technologies affect the experience of worktime in late capitalist societies. Without announcing a grand historical passage between immobile and mobile technologies, it is precisely the ability of digital technologies to summon the worker toward specific futures that captures, to my mind, the way in which we experience our day-to-day work. What is comparable, in this sense, is the way in which reserves inform everyday working experience, whether in writing a book or making a movie.

Time and Budget

A week before shooting, I sit in front of studio number one with the production assistant Ahmad Abdallah Abdel Halim. The set is being built inside: mechanical saws churn, hammers hit nails, sand and dust hover in the air. Although I am curious about what is happening on set, the general cacophony and my relative unfamiliarity with set builders make me sit next to the production workers, who have become much closer acquaintances by now. A carpenter emerges from the noisy and dusty studio once in a while to ask Abdel Halim for more sanding paper or more nails. Each time, Abdel Halim sends an assistant to the nearby construction shops in Mariyutiya to buy the needed materials. This was, I thought, logistics in action.

Farghalli comes in and out of the studio office. He asks Abdel Halim to prepare a list of all the craftsmen who worked on set this week. He did not say it explicitly, but I understood that he wanted to determine how much would be spent on how many workers. After some calculations, Abdel Halim comes back to Farghalli: "I couldn't calculate exact numbers because I'm not sure about December 18 and 19." "No big deal . . . it's not the final receipt," answers Farghalli. From his reaction, I understood that he just needed a ballpark figure to estimate the budget for now.

After sitting outside for too long, I decide to brave the dust and venture inside studio number one. The craftsmen are starting to build the library, which was supposed to be built on the previous day but the materials had not yet arrived. The master carpenter cuts out the main wood planks. The planks would be assembled on the next day, then the painters would sand it, fix it with latex, and add a layer of primer on it. All the studio walls are painted in the yellow shade chosen by Asem and Nihal, while carpenters are busy finishing the studio's parquet. "Will you be done with everything today?" I ask Ezzat. "Insha'allah," he answers.

I go out to sit with the production team once again. Farghalli seems much tenser than usual. When Ezzat comes out asking for more ceramic tiles, he chides Abdel Halim with excessive irritation: "Why haven't you bought the ceramic yet?" The location manager mumbles an answer about it being too late to send a worker to buy it the previous day. Farghalli is almost screaming: "Buy it right away!" Abdel Halim checks with Asem and Ezzat what kind of tiles they want. "Just plain white fifteen by fifteen [centimeter] tiles." "How many meters do you need?" "About eight." Abdel Halim dispatches the runner Mohammed Fathallah to get the materials. I tell myself that these logistical miscues must happen all the time.

Later in the day, the production assistant Mahmoud Abdallah arrives with a bale of paper. These are the first call sheets in the shooting schedule. While I am reading the sheets, I ask the production assistants Hany and Mahmoud why they get them so far in advance. "It is early," agrees Mahmoud. "We'll bring most of these things the day before we start shooting anyway." Hany disagrees: "I need to make sure everything is ready on time. . . . Once we're on location, we're supposed to have everything already set. . . . Now that we've got the call sheets, we're entering a new phase in the film. Preparations are over, we're officially in shooting." Hany enounces this sentence with a smile and looking straight at me: "You must be happy to advance to a new stage of your research." I did not know that I was there yet, but I certainly felt more comfortable around the location.

Around sunset, Farghalli and Asem sit down in front of studio number one to look over the call sheets. Hany, Mahmoud, Ahmad, and Georges hover around in silence, while taking occasional notes on their own sheets. Farghalli reads out the sheet verbatim while Asem answers his questions. "Who will the workers on location be?" "I won't need any workers of my own," says Asem, but Farghalli explains that some workers will have to appear as silent extras in one scene. "All right, there will be three carpenters and an upholsterer." He seems to make things up as he goes.

I go inside the studio after the meeting breaks. The carpenters are still finishing the dining room door; the metal specialist arrives with metal window frames; the painters paint walls; the varnish specialists work on wooden furniture. When all the workers are almost done near the end of the day, the chief builder Hussein Wezza comes up to Abdel Halim to collect the week's checks. Abdel Halim gives him a stack of cash and a few empty envelopes, but Wezza seems hesitant. "What? You want me to divide it as well?" asks Abdel Halim with a hint of surprise. "I never divide it myself," answers Wezza. Abdel Halim goes away to look through his paper accounts and separate each worker's pay into white envelopes.

It had long been dark when the production runner Fathallah comes back after looking for the ceramic tiles all day. "I didn't find any," he says with an apologetic tone. Abdel Halim had contacted him a few times during the day, but each time Fathallah would answer that he had not found the right size yet. "It's an unusual size," Abdel Halim explains to me, "but it's necessary because [the studio] must have the same interior design as the apartment in Garden City." They agree to pick up the materials on Saturday morning.

When we are on our way home in the company's microbus, Fathallah still feels like he could have done more. "I can go pick the ceramics up myself on Friday," he suggests with an eager tone. Abdel Halim looks at him with a smile. He rhetorically asks him how he will transport very heavy ceramic boxes, bring them all the way up to his apartment without an elevator, all the way back down, and then deliver them to Studio Misr without even having his own car. "It would be too difficult," he states with a conclusive tone. Abdel Halim goes on to tell an anecdote about how he once transported just one ceramic box on a microbus to gain some time in set building. The box was too heavy, and he did not gain much in the end. "It was the worst day of my life."

The next day, Ezzat shows me his building checklist. Only one or two boxes are checked. "It's discouraging," he says. "We're working all day, but nothing gets finished." Meanwhile, Asem is hammering nails into some abandoned planks of wood in the studio. He comes around to Ezzat and Wezza to press them to increase the pace. "Things need to get done faster!" Another logistical conflict was brewing, so I lent an ear to the conversation.

"Could we have worked any faster?" asks Wezza. "It's okay, but it could have been a bit quicker," answers Nihal in diplomatic fashion. "How come?" counters the chief builder, adding, "This set would normally take ten days with loads of workers. I've just got six days with a few workers." "You could've organized the work better," intervenes Asem with a harsh tone, "you could've had people start on different things at the same time, so they don't waste time on every detail." Wezza disagrees in silence.

I am puzzled by what looks to me like undue pressure to accelerate the pace. "I'm constrained by time and budget to finish the set," explains Ezzat. "If they want it in less time, they need to hire more workers, so they need to increase the budget. . . . If they don't want to pay more, then workers can only work so fast, because they need to make quality work. . . . If the *finish* isn't good enough, I'll be told to redo some things." Asem presses Wezza to work faster, because they will not have any time or manpower the next day.

4
Coordination

A week prior to the start of shooting in *Décor*, the assistant director Omar el-Zohairy was running around New Century's office to make the key crew approve his schedule. The cinematographer Tarek Hefny was okay with the schedule, but disappointed that they would not be able to celebrate the New Year. "I can't do otherwise," answered Zohairy in a hurry, citing the constraints imposed by the holidays already booked by stars Horeya Farghaly and Khaled Abol Naga in the middle of the schedule. When Hefny gave him a mischievous look, Zohairy reacted in a defensive tone, "It's not my fault, I told Horeya she's the boss *(rabb al-'amal)*." The art director Asem Ali joked that he would not have enough time to finish the set on this schedule, but Zohairy ignored the growing mockery and gave his schedule to the line producer Farghalli and the production manager Setohy. Both checked that the dates matched their own requirements, then made several photocopies to be distributed to the crew.

Setohy went back to the other office, sitting across from the costume script supervisor Mariam el-Bagoury and the assistant stylist Asmaa. He asked Bagoury to send him the general costume breakdown in separate Excel sheets for every character, so that he could send each actor his/her costume list on its own. Bagoury seemed reluctant to separate the costume breakdown in this time-consuming way, so I offered to do it myself. While I parsed out each Excel sheet into a separate document on Setohy's computer, Bagoury helped Asmaa parse out piles of paper in a binder to separate each character's costumes. Meanwhile, Farghalli was making a location breakdown with his production assistant Georges, listing scene number, location name, and scene descriptions in three different colors on a blank sheet.

Later, Setohy signalled to Farghalli that they needed an actual VHS cassette of *al-Layla al-akhira* (*The Last Night*, 1964), a black-and-white melodrama to which *Décor* was broadly an homage. "We see Maha's character

113

put it inside the VHS machine in the movie," explained Setohy. "They just need some videocassette," replied Farghalli, adding that the material on screen will be taken from YouTube, but the cassette cover needs to look like it is *The Last Night.* "Where can I find this VHS?" asked Setohy. "Anywhere on Shawarbi Street," answered the production assistant Mustafa Abu Zeid, who was sitting nearby. "I know, but I don't remember the guy's name . . . ," muttered Setohy while looking through his contacts to call the salesman in question. After dinner, Farghalli asked Setohy why the hairstylist Moham-med Hafez had not arrived to attend Yara Goubran's fitting, which was taking place in another room. Setohy answered that Horeya Farghaly had not come that day. "He's supposed to be the hairstylist for the whole film, not just Horeya," grunted Farghalli. He got Hafez's number from Setohy and called him outside the office. All I heard were his initial words: "What's wrong, Hafez? You'll screw over my appointments from the start?"

Around nine o'clock that night, Farghalli discussed the next day's assignments with Setohy. With a to-do list in hand, they thought about how they could deliver the cash necessary to cover set building expenses in Stu-dio Misr the next day. When Farghalli left, Setohy organized the next day's assignments on paper. Around ten o'clock, the office was empty. Setohy and I were sitting on our own when we got a call from Farghalli. He said that Horeya Farghaly's fitting had been delayed from eleven to one o'clock the next day. Setohy rolled his eyes and contacted all concerned crew members to notify them about the change. He first called the stylist Salma Sami, then the production assistant Rasha Gawdat, the makeup artist Mustafa Awad, the hairstylist Hafez, the costume script supervisor Bagoury (who did not answer, but Setohy sent her a text message), and lastly the costume assistant Refaat. When Setohy was done with one phone call, he would ask me to mark it down on his long handwritten to-do list. I helped him with these calls until we both went home late at night.

This extended description illustrates the complexity of the logistics involved in planning a feature film like *Décor.* All these activities occurred on a single day, which is but a fraction of the total work invested in prepar-ing the shooting over six weeks. The flurry of preparations could be felt in the stench of cigarettes hovering around New Century's office, where overflowing ashtrays covered the tables next to piles of paper, laptops, smartphones, one or two CDs, a three-in-one photocopier, tea glasses, lighters, empty cigarette packs, phone chargers, and some more trail-ing paper. The logistics of *Décor* were handled amid this commotion by

Farghalli's production team in conjunction with each artistic team and their key assistants—the assistant director, the script supervisors, the assistant decorator, and the assistant stylist. While I was told by Farghalli that each team had a different "*system*" to coordinate the shoot, they all faced the same logistical issues in need of more or less urgent solutions. Hence the endless reviewing of schedules, script breakdowns, shooting items, cash flows, appointments—in short, what would sustain the next shooting day.[1]

These solutions are never exhaustive, because the overall outcome of logistical preparations *(tahdir)* is imponderable, while the steps moving toward execution *(tanfiz)* are contingent on the film's unfolding. Going back to the opening vignette in the introduction, no one knew how the first shooting day would unfold a week prior to shooting, let alone how the shooting would unfold over the entire schedule. This does not mean that crew members capitulate to uncertainty; rather, they mediate the imponderable outcome of preparations and execution. Chapter 2 laid out the executive hierarchy and operational sequence within which logistical coordination conventionally occurs. Such conventions are central to successful coordination in a temporary organization such as a film set (Bechky, 2006). Chapter 3 showed how technological objects act as "reserves" through which executive crew members summon mediators that aid their coordination tasks, while being summoned to execute these tasks eventually. This explains the overwhelming presence of paper, phones, and laptops in New Century's office.

Despite all the assumptions and mediators marshaled by executive workers, preparing and executing the shooting remains imponderable to the individual agent. S/he mediates future outcomes by breaking them down into a set of contingent tasks, assigned to specific crew members at specific junctures in the filmmaking process. To individuals like Farghalli or Setohy, the imponderability of preparing and executing a shooting day becomes, through this mediation, a series of punctual tasks to which they are assigned and assign others—say, to approve the schedule, to get the VHS of *The Last Night*, to call crew members, to set appointments. This granular account of everyday film logistics echoes recent scholarship in production studies (see Banks, Mayer and Caldwell, 2009; Szczepanik and Vonderau, 2013; Banks, Conor, and Mayer, 2015), with an ethnographic emphasis on the unpredictable environment within which my interlocutors operated day to day. Such an account brings to light a local division of labor with a different set of complexities to the ones handled by a transnational division of labor in "runaway" Hollywood productions (see Miller, 2001; Goldsmith, Ward, and O'Regan, 2010; Sanson, 2018; Steinhart, 2019).

This chapter describes how the shooting is prepared and executed in today's Egyptian film industry. I start with a description of three logistical issues in film preparations—budgeting, scheduling, and transportation—while showing how they are, to the individuals in charge, imponderable without being uncertain. I go on to illustrate how logistical planning is never perfectly executed by describing the ways in which executive crew members try to avoid recurrent failures or "*drops*" on set. In this connection, I describe the asymmetrical expectations imposed on executive workers to be available and faultless. These expectations bear important consequences for the way in which contingent tasks are executed and, ultimately, the way in which imponderable outcomes are mediated. In conclusion, I reflect on the importance of technological devices in coordinating the shooting, which act as reserves summoning crew members to execute what remains to be done at each juncture in the filmmaking process.

Budgeting

The logistical problems involved in preparing the shooting begin with budgeting. Once a project starts, a budget is made available by the producer to buy props and costumes; to rent camera equipment; to buy materials for set/prop building and pay the craftsmen's weekly salary; to pay advances on wages (*'arbun*); and to provide "gifts" (*ikramiyat*) to permit-issuing bureaucrats, police officers, or local fixers. During shooting, the initial budget is burdened with weekly payments to the cast and crew, equipment rental, on-set meals or their cash equivalent (*badal*), as well as on-set emergencies (such as buying an essential prop or costume that was forgotten). While the experienced line producer can anticipate most production costs, various contingencies can affect the actual amounts paid as opposed to the budgeted ones—most notably, unforeseen additional shooting days and last-minute demands by the artistic crew. Larger productions like *Décor* have enough liquidity to satisfy these costs, but smaller productions like *Poisonous Roses* prioritize what they pay first.[2]

Even when enough funds are available, production crew members tend to negotiate heavily before loosening the purse strings. The assistant director Habi Seoud had an interesting yet typical anecdote to tell in this vein. One of his assistants once came in a taxi to the location in October City, which cost him forty-five Egyptian pounds. Seoud asked the producer to reimburse the displacement, as is customary in work-related journeys, but the producer refused to pay. My initial instinct was that the producer did not want to pay because the assistant took a taxi, a relatively expensive means of transportation, but the producer had a different concern. "I usually take the trip for thirty-two pounds," he told Seoud, implying that the assistant was either inflating the journey's price or got conned by the driver. "I can't believe we were having a conversation over thirteen pounds!" exclaimed Seoud while I laughed, as the difference was insignificant considering the overall investment in the shooting.

Tighter purse strings are not just imposed by production workers on the crew, but in some cases by the producer in person. The line producer Khaled Adam disliked producers who are hesitant to untie the purse because he cannot then "make the production work without the right tools" (*yimashshi al-urdar min ghayr adawat*). All artistic demands require money: he might be able to cut costs by paying a gaffer six thousand Egyptian pounds per week instead of twelve thousand, but the gaffer will come with fewer assistants, not all of whom will be skilled enough, which might delay the shooting and accrue additional costs. Therefore, he would rather spend a greater amount of money up front to avoid unaccounted expenses later, such as extra shooting days, which in turn add on equipment costs, location rentals, and wages. More important, filmmakers have no idea which specific contingencies will require money on set. For instance, when the artistic crew wanted to shoot at the Demerdash hospital in *Out of the Ordinary*, where Adam was a production manager, his crew had to get special permission from the directors in each building, then refer these permits to the hospital's director of security, the director of infrastructure, and so on. In the end, they spent around twenty-five hundred Egyptian pounds for each building to ensure that they would be able to shoot on schedule. Adam lamented that producers still ask him why he gives away so much money, and his answer is adamant: "To make the production work!"

Such contingencies make budgeting into a tentative and ever-adjusted exercise, and the discrepancy between the budget and the film's expenses is unpredictable yet expected. I had the occasion to sit next to the line producer Ahmed Farghalli while he was adjusting his budget in *Décor*. The budget was in an Excel document with a dozen sheets, each related to a specific section of the budget (location rental, equipment, wages). Each item was listed in a separate row with its name, number of days or weeks needed, and daily or weekly price. Farghalli would either change the cost of certain items or change the number of days/weeks required, mostly to reduce cost and time. Farghalli gathered information on costs from his production crew. While he was adjusting the budget at the very beginnings of *Décor*'s preparations, he asked Setohy about the highest rental price he had heard while scouting apartments in Dokki. "About eighty-four hundred pounds," said Setohy, after which Farghalli changed the location estimate on his Excel sheet from fifteen thousand Egyptian pounds to ten thousand. His estimates reacted to on-the-ground market information, while leaving an additional margin for unanticipated costs.

When Farghalli started adjusting his budget that day, the total estimated budget was around 6.8 million Egyptian pounds. When he was done, he had reached a total of 6.4 million. When he saw that the overall savings stood at only four hundred thousand pounds, he cursed at his computer. I asked whether he had an upper limit to respect, and he answered that he constantly discussed the budget with the general manager but needed to reduce costs as much as possible. *Décor* ended up costing around ten million Egyptian pounds.[3] This would have seemed excessive to Farghalli at that point in time, yet budget increases were eventually negotiated between the artistic team and the production company. In retrospect, the initial budget was significantly exceeded, but this matters less retrospectively than prospectively to the production crew. Farghalli's angst about keeping budgets low is not about the unpredictable total that will have been invested once "the film" is made. It is broken down into a set of smaller, contingent decisions on equipment, location rentals, or individual wages, each with its own prospective cell on the Excel sheet, and each being priced on its own no matter the total which would have to be spent. Of course, a large production like *Décor* can stomach the accruing cost, while a smaller production would probably have to stop for lack of funding, but these "hard" economic realities are only perceived as being hard *a posteriori*. When production crew members are still planning the shooting's budget, the imponderable cost matters less than its mediation via smaller contingent decisions.

Furthermore, as all transactions in the industry are cash-based, the physical circulation of cash requires some planning of its own. In larger companies, the accountant handles all the books and the cash, which is why New Century's accountant Mohammed Hosny would frequently come on set in *Décor*. Hosny was adamant that he could not pay out production expenses on his own initiative: he always needed Farghalli's approval, who thereby controlled the flow of cash.[4] Sometimes, Hosny would go on location to deliver an advance on the budget *('uhda)*; other times, he would deliver wages. Although Hosny's visits to the set were more frequent than the weekly payment time, his mere presence elicited jokes about "getting the white envelope" *(al-zarf al-abyad)*, which conventionally contains weekly wages. The act of filling envelopes with cash *(tazrif)* is itself part of the production crew's lore. Once, the production assistant Hany Abdel Latif asked Georges to fetch envelopes to pack some craftsmen's wages. "What kind of envelopes?" asked Georges. "Nice, long, white envelopes," lingered Abdel Latif. "Does the color of the envelope matter?" I asked cheekily while Georges was away. "It's better to get long white envelopes because they look more decent *(muhtaram)*," replied Abdel Latif. He added that they have sticker seals and the money fits straight into them, unlike the smaller envelopes which need to be licked and have money folded into them.

The material relationship with cash and envelopes extends to a range of accounting paperwork, including receipts, purchase lists *(kashf masrufat)*, expenditure summaries *(hawafiz, sing. hafza)*, and accounting books. This paperwork is usually written and collected by the production crew, except when another crew member is responsible for purchases—say, when the stylist buys costumes or when the prop master buys a prop. The stylist Salma Sami and her assistant, for instance, kept expenditure summaries with receipts for all the clothes they bought for *Décor*, in addition to preparing purchase lists for the characters who were still to be clothed. Hany Abdel Latif hated writing expenditure summaries because it is a very finicky operation, but neither the line producer nor the accountant would reimburse him for an item without it being inscribed on paper and attached to a receipt—otherwise, he had to pay out of his own pocket.

The strict regime maintained by the line producer and the accountant in *Décor* is not necessarily the norm in the industry. Suspicions of theft still abound in a context where transactions are likely to leave no paper trail or, better yet, leave a paper trail that is different from the transacted amount. Outside supervision by superiors in the hierarchy, there is no guarantee in practice that cash transactions will be inscribed faithfully on paper. In Bollywood, where cash transactions occur in informal ways too, Ganti recounts an incident where a production crew member filed all transactions in a production on Excel, only to be told off by the accountant who asked him to destroy this record because he did not want fiscal authorities to overtax the project (2012: 225). This fear of overbearing taxation has been just as important throughout the history of commercial cinema in Egypt (Flibbert,

2001: 86). Yet Ganti takes this incident as evidence that the work culture in Bollywood is highly oral, to the point where even inscribing monetary trans-actions is suspicious. Today's Egyptian film industry is "oral" in the sense that *viva voce* conversation is the standard means by which contracts are negotiated and monetary information circulated, but accounting paperwork remains integral to the practice of coordinating the shooting. Throughout the production process, the imponderable budget and cash flow are medi-ated by specific crew members thanks to various written mediators. These mediators do not just retrospectively record the spent amounts, but also summon crew members to anticipate prospective costs.

Scheduling

Setting aside budgeting, the greatest imponderable problem in film prep-arations is scheduling. The shooting schedule is the assistant director's primary responsibility, yet the assistant director can never know, in the pre-sent, all the factors that will lead to the execution of any one shooting day, let alone the entire shooting schedule. The length of the shooting schedule varies according to the available budget. Well-financed productions can take six to eight weeks of shooting, while cheaper ones can take ten to fourteen days. There is a broad historical trend toward shorter schedules, which is often blamed on the film industry's so-called crisis after the 2011 Revolution. More likely, shortening schedules are a function of the fall in big-budget film numbers relative to smaller ones after 2010. What might have changed is the extent to which the shooting takes place on consecutive days. *Décor* was shot in a little over four weeks, but they extended between late December 2013 and late March 2014. According to the late casting agent Magdy Abdelrahman, six weeks would be shot within seven weeks at most in the 1980s.

Scheduling starts with a complete script breakdown indicating all times, locations, characters, props, and costumes in the film. The Arabic term for breakdown, *tafrigh*, is more evocative than the English: it means "emptying out" the screenplay, gutting it to make use of its inner parts. The screenplay itself was rarely consulted by the crew in *Décor* or *Poison-ous Roses*, except by the actors who individually rehearsed their lines or the artistic workers who discussed some specific aspect of the film's plot. In its emptied-out guise, the screenplay guides preparations as a list of loca-tions to be scouted, or a list of props to be acquired, or a list of characters to be cast and fitted. Thus, the screenplay stands as a different artifact to different crew members: to the screenwriter, it may be "the film"; to the line producer, it becomes a list of logistical demands prior to the shooting; to the cinematographer, it becomes a set of images and colors. Different crew members have different ways of breaking down the screenplay and they produce different partial breakdowns, which summon them to mediate the imponderability in their assigned activity. The assistant director remains the one worker making "official" breakdowns on set, in the sense that these breakdowns act as authoritative documents to assign blame and responsibility, as I explain below.

The assistant director Omar el-Zohairy's breakdown method illustrates what I have seen and heard other crew members do with the screenplay. In practice, he starts with the screenplay's narrative form and turns it into a functional version called a "sequential" (see Figure 3). The sequential breakdown is a serial description of all times, places, actors, and props seen on screen in every scene. After writing and reviewing the sequential breakdown, he makes a location breakdown, where he parses out each scene by location. The location breakdown allows Zohairy to start his "most important job": scheduling. With this breakdown, he can know how many shooting days are needed in each location and how he can concentrate the schedule's duration, which he cannot do with the vague estimates based on the screenplay itself. Zohairy then makes a character breakdown and a prop breakdown, while his costume script supervisor provides the costume breakdown. In *Décor*, the first round of "emptying out" the screenplay was conducted by different workers on his direction team, but it underwent numerous revisions that were ultimately approved by Zohairy. Once all the breakdowns were ready, Zohairy gave them to the production team, who followed up on gathering all the elements needed to execute the shooting.

While crafting his schedule in *Décor*, Zohairy strove to fit as many scenes as possible within the same location on the same day, while trying to reduce the number of days spent on location. Within the same shooting day, Zohairy tried to organize as few displacements *(na'lat)* as possible, to avoid getting stuck in traffic between two locations. Concerns with traffic are vital to arranging the shooting schedule as well as setting attendance times, as I detail later. The assistant director needs to consider not only the time taken by cars carrying equipment, props, and costumes to the location, but also the expected time taken by all cast and crew members from their homes to the location. The assistant director Wael Mandour told me that when he forces the crew to work hard and long hours on certain days—say,

١ – إفتتاحية الفيلم ١ – ستوديو تصوير – نهار\ داخلي :
photo montage

ـ ديكور شقة يتم بناؤه داخل ستوديو . مراحل تحويل الخشب لحوائط . وضع معدات الإضاءة و التصوير و الأرضيات . تعليق نجف بلا سقف للديكور . تحول مواد بلاستيكية و خشبية إلى مواد تبدو حقيقية . كخرسانة و طوب من الإسفنج

ـ عمال الديكور و الإكسسوار + عمال الإضاءة + فريق التصوير + عاملين البلاتوه
ـ يفضل تصوير تلك اللقطات أثناء البناء الفعلي للديكور

٢ – إفتتاحية الفيلم ٢ – مدخل ستوديو تصوير – نهار \ داخلي \ خارجي :
photo montage

ـ حارس أمن الإستوديو يجلس في زاويته متسمرا أمام بداية فيلم عربي قديم

ـ حارس أمن الإستوديو + فريق التصوير
ـ مقطع من فيلم نهر الحب + تلفاز يعمل +مراجعة كيفية عرض الفيلم على التلفاز بجودة عالية

٣- إفتتاحية الفيلم ٣ – مواقع بناء حقيقية – نهار\ خارجي :

ـ لقطات لمواقع بناء حقيقية \ لقطات لشوارع مصر

٤ – مشهد ١ – ستوديو التصوير – ديكور تصوير الفيلم – نهار \ داخلي :

ـ ستوديو ضخم . يتوسطه ديكور الشقة . معدات التصوير و الإضاءة تملأ المكان . جميع فريق التصوير حاضرين . مصورين و صحفيين في كل مكان ملتفين حول الممثلين . هناك تورتة كبيرة على ترابيزة . الجميع ملتف حولها ، المذيعات يصورن لقاءات مع المخرج و الممثلين . شريف مهندس الديكور يمزح مع مدير التصوير . ممسكا ببالونة هيليوم

ـ شريف + عمر + شهيرة + حسين + كريم + السبكي + فريق التصوير + المصورين + الصحفين + ٢ مذيعات + ٢ مصورين فيديو
ـ كاميرات فوتغرافيا محترفة حديثة تعمل جيدا و بفلاشات قوية + ٢ كاميرات فيديو تعمل جيدا
ـ مراجعة مع مدير التصوير إضاءة فلاشات الكاميرات
ـ مراجعة مع المخرج تصوير تفاصيل تصوير إنترفيوهات الممثلين داخل المشهد بكاميرات الفيديو
Exposure ـ

٥ – مشهد ٢ – ستوديو التصوير – أمام ديكور الصالة – نهار \ داخلي :

ـ مها تنشر لوح خشبي بقوة تجهز مكتبة في الديكور . يدخل شريف يساعدها و يطلب منها أن ترتاح . يظهر كريم المخرج يطلب منهم إنجاز ما تبقى من الديكور حيث تأخر وقته . يذكرهم بأن الفيلم سريع و يجب عدم الدقة في التنفيذ . مها تنظر لشريف في لوم على ذلك الوضع . مها و شريف يختصران ما تبقى من خطوات مع العمال لإنجاز الديكور

ـ مها + شريف + الساعي + عمال الديكور + كريم + فريق التصوير
ـ البالونة الهيليوم R
ـ تدريب أ \ حورية على تقطيع الخشب بالمنشار و التعامل مع مواد و أدوات الديكور

3. First page of the sequential breakdown in *Décor*, made by Omar el-Zohairy. Photograph © New Century Film Production.

because the location is only available for a limited amount of time—he gives them one or two days off to recover.

The actual adjustments involved in scheduling are best illustrated with a direct example from *Décor*. Nearly a month before shooting, I was sitting with the assistant director Zohairy and the general manager Badawy in New Century when Badawy asked Zohairy whether he had a shooting schedule in mind. Zohairy took out his location breakdown from his bag and started telling him about a shooting schedule orally, using his breakdown sheet as a guide to the locations that had been confirmed and the ones that still needed to be found. Badawy took notes, while Zohairy insisted several times that it was a *tentative* schedule. With this caveat in mind, he wanted to start with three or four shooting days in Sharif and Maha's apartment, then three or four days in Studio Misr, followed by seven or eight days in Mustafa and Maha's apartment. In between those shooting blocks, he said, the director Ahmad Abdalla would need three- to four-day breaks to edit his material. Badawy tried to convince Zohairy to get Abdalla's editing breaks after longer shooting blocks, adding that Zohairy needed to be wary because the star actress Horeya Farghaly had signed on for another movie at the beginning of December and the star actor Khaled Abol Naga had signed on for another New Century production right after *Décor*. "This isn't an independent company . . . there's a capital turnover *(dawrat ra's mal)*," he concluded.

A few days later, Zohairy made a calendar schedule in a Word document and sent it by email to all concerned crew members, including the line producer Farghalli, the director Abdalla, and the heads of each artistic team. When the art director Asem Ali next came into New Century's office, Farghalli asked him if he had any comments on the schedule. Ali took out his computer, opened his emails, and looked at it. "Why is there set building in Studio Misr in between shooting at the two apartments?" he asked. "Ahmad Abdalla wants it this way," answered Farghalli. After uttering a brief "okay," Asem added that on January 17 he would only have one day to change the set completely in Sharif's apartment. "It's the only available time," said Farghalli, because the star actor Khaled Abol Naga had booked a long trip between January 18 and 26. Ali looked unsure, but Farghalli reassured him by saying that they would pull an all-nighter and hire extra workers if necessary. The good news was that Ali would have plenty of time to build in the second apartment, because Horeya Farghaly would be away that week. Farghalli then asked Ali if he could estimate the time it would take to build the set in Studio Misr. The art director answered that it all depended on the location of Mustafa and Maha's apartment (they had not finished scouting by then). The conversation concluded with brief exchanges about minor aspects in the schedule, all conducted based on the schedule on Ali's computer.

This example shows how the imponderability of scheduling is partially broken down into a series of contingent decisions by specific crew members using certain technological devices with a situated awareness of the filmmaking process. When Zohairy is asked to recite his tentative schedule, he takes out a printed location breakdown and refers to the main locations to know which ones still need to be scouted, which operations would remain before shooting, and, crucially, how many days each step would take. Likewise, when Ali is asked by Farghalli to give his comments on the schedule, he takes out his computer and looks at the proposed calendar to know which set building responsibilities would rest on his shoulders and how much time he would have to execute each operation in turn. Without causing concerned crew members to think or act in a certain way, the paper and the computer act as reserves, summoning certain workers to their future tasks while recording what has been done already.

In this sense, the shooting schedule is a living anticipation of financial and logistical pressures, but these are just some of the variables juggled by the assistant director, because s/he also needs to consider the artistic crew members' schedule on its own. While the executive crew's daily work is bound by the project at hand, the artistic crew may work on several projects at once.[5] Well-known art directors like Mohammed Atia or Ali Hossam notoriously work on multiple projects at the same time: they may be preparing a television serial or a commercial while their movie gets shot under the auspices of the assistant decorator. This situation is inconvenient when the director insists on the art director's presence on set, as was the case with Ali Hossam on *The Cat and the Mouse* (2015). Such scheduling constraints are negotiated on a case-by-case basis, but they are never negotiated with executive crew members, who are immediately replaced when they do not fit the project's extensible schedule. A case in point was a talking extra in *Décor*, who was hired to play a doctor in one scene. When the artistic crew decided to shoot his scene on a day he was not scheduled to come, they just replaced him with the clapper Abdelsalam Radwan, who did the job just as well in their view. Scheduling therefore obeys the hierarchical logic described in Chapter 2: the artistic crew's needs take precedence over the executive workers' own.

Movie stars are the only truly irreplaceable workers on set, and they add their own constraints on the schedule. As Grimaud remarks regarding Bollywood, "the actor-who-acts is first and foremost a purveyor of dates, that is, an agent in the configuration of the time of production" (2003: 307). Egyptian stars tend to have conflicting commitments during the television drama production season preceding Ramadan. This means that the assistant director (in conjunction with the production team) needs to manage the actor's schedule between his/her own project and conflicting ones. In *Décor*, we took two long pauses in the schedule because, in the first case, there was a conflicting commitment with a serial drama in which Horeya Farghaly was starring and, in the second case, the star had planned a holiday in Thailand. Needless to say, the production would not have halted had any other crew member booked a holiday in advance.

The assistant director's balancing act thickens. In addition to assuming certain financial and logistical imperatives as well as anticipating the artistic crew's parallel schedules, s/he needs to take account of specific artistic demands. When I was assisting in the scheduling of *Poisonous Roses*, the cinematographer Maged Nader would insist on shooting in the tannery towers at very specific hours to get a specific sunlight on the yellow gelatin drying over the rooftops.[6] These hours were carefully recorded by the assistant director at the time, Hady Mahmoud. In *Décor*, Zohairy told me that Ahmad Abdalla would ask for more time to shoot some important takes or scenes, because he needed to work some more with his actors. When we were shooting the scenes in which the protagonist Maha recovers in a hospital following an accident, the set was much quieter than usual. "It's a heavy day *(yum ti'il)*," said Zohairy in an ominous tone, by which he presumably meant that the actors' performance was especially important. This day witnessed the shooting of the scenes where the male protagonists Sharif and Mustafa visit Maha to try to convince her to choose between her two lives and loves. As it happens, the start of the shooting day was delayed by about two hours, and Zohairy justified this delay with the fact that the actors needed time to prepare. When unplanned, these delays can be catastrophic to the assistant director's schedule, yet Zohairy knew that he could catch up on additional scenes because the location was rented out for the next day too. Scenes that "fall out" *(tu'a')* or canceled days are usually rescheduled at the very end of the pre-agreed schedule, no matter whether the schedule is actualized or not.

Overall, the shooting schedule is imponderable at every juncture in preparations. There are very many humans and nonhumans whose actions can affect the schedule, from adjustments to the screenplay and its break-down, to production logistics, to the artistic crew's commitments, to star holidays, to special requests. I once asked the general manager Ahmad Badawy why the initial schedules set in preparations are never followed in Egypt. "Whenever a foreign production crew comes to Egypt, I like to tell them that scheduling too much in advance is very risky in Cairo," he answers, listing traffic, shooting permits, and even demonstrations as unpredictable factors to consider when scheduling. This imponderability is partly mediated by assigning the responsibility of managing the schedule to the assistant director. Just like Farghalli mediated the imponderability of budgeting through his crew members and his Excel sheet, the assistant director relies on hierarchical assumptions and written mediators to think through the shooting's incoming future. This mediation, again, breaks down the daunting task of scheduling an entire project into smaller tasks, such as listing locations and characters, coordinating appointments, or giving more time to the director to work with actors.

Transportation

Transportation is a major logistical issue in preparations and in shooting, which is compounded by Cairo's legendary traffic. One can think of numerous mega-cities across the world with similar traffic conditions, yet the association between Cairo and traffic bears a sense of uniqueness in the minds of Egyptian filmmakers. Talking about his shooting experience in Cape Town, South Africa, Zohairy marveled at the lack of traffic there. A day's shooting in Cape Town could include six to seven location changes; in Cairo, that number would peak at three or four, because displacements that take twenty minutes in Cape Town would take hours in Cairo, according to Zohairy. Under such conditions, circumventing unpredictable yet expected traffic is integral to the everyday work of preparations and shooting. This issue is mediated based on assumptions about available means of transportation and anticipated congestion hours.

One's preferred mode of transportation indexes class belonging. This was especially striking in *Décor*: artistic workers like Ahmad Abdalla, Tarek Hefny, and Asem Ali traveled respectively by car, by motorcycle (not the working-class Vespa), and by taxi, all of which are relatively expensive means of transportation in Cairo. In contrast, executive workers like Farghalli, Setohy, and the best boy gaffer Ahmed Desha traveled by metro, by private microbus, or in the production's own microbus (which gathers several crew members on the way to work and back every shooting day). There are no inherently faster or slower means of transportation as traffic varies considerably, but there is a difference in comfort level between traveling by car or taxi and traveling in the crammed transportation system.

Assumptions about traffic extend to the usual times at which streets tend to be clogged. When production assistants came to New Century's office after a long day in the streets, they would discuss which streets they ought to have avoided or which means of transportation they should have taken, sometimes half-joking that they should have walked throughout the city.[7] For example, crew members who live next to Haram Street, one of the major arteries on the west bank of the Nile that leads to the major studios in Cairo, try to avoid this road at all costs in the middle of the day, between noon and seven o'clock in the evening. Likewise, transport is avoided in "bureaucrat" hours *(wa't al-muwazzafin)*, when government employees go to work around eight to nine in the morning and go back home around two to three in the afternoon. These streets and hours are assumed to be congested *(zahma)*, and crew members who can coordinate meeting times outside these hours prefer to circumvent the congestion. This is partly why filmmakers tend to meet at unconventional hours: late at night, in the middle of the bureaucratic day, or even on weekends (Fridays and Saturdays). It is also why the transportation of equipment or documents would take place either early in the day or late at night for *Décor*.

Assuming one can afford all means of transportation, there is often a trade-off between speed and comfort in congested hours, because the fastest ways of traveling can be less comfortable—including walking or the metro—while more comfortable motorized vehicles can get stuck in traffic for hours. Crew members who are not independently wealthy cannot choose their means of transportation, and their estimates about traffic are therefore affected by financial as well as logistical considerations. This is evident in everyday discussions about journeys via the city's transit system. When the office assistant Georges Mokhtar was talking with the assistant editor Ahmad Adil about a meeting at the Heliopolis office of Al Batrik, the production company behind *Poisonous Roses*, the director Ahmad Fawzi Saleh intervened to tell Mokhtar that he could collect him on his way at the microbus stop in Sayyida Aisha. "Why would I pay five pounds to go all the way to Sayyida Aisha when I can transit *(akhud muwaslat)* to the office for four and a half pounds?" answered Mokhtar. Fawzi conceded, because his offer of a more comfortable journey by car would have been more expensive for Mokhtar, who tried to keep within a limited budget.

Within certain financial and logistical means, executive workers coordinate their movement precisely to circumvent traffic. For instance, on a day when we had agreed to meet around noon for a scouting session in Dokki, the production manager Setohy called me around ten past noon to say that he would be late. "Just wait for me outside and I'll come soon," he said over the phone, while I waited outside New Century's building. Around one o'clock, I called Setohy again. "Are you on your way?" "Yes! I'm still finishing a few things...." "When will you be done?" "Around two." Setohy finally arrived somewhat exhausted at five o'clock, and we went out to scout around six to seven o'clock. While we were walking, he apologized to me for not being able to meet earlier in the afternoon as we had agreed. Setohy said that he was stuck scouting two apartments in the Bahr al-A'zam neighborhood in Giza, which is a twenty-minute drive from Dokki at night but can take an hour or more by day. Since the traffic was horrible, he calculated that I would not be able to make it from Dokki to where he was, so he thought that it would be better if I just stayed in Dokki until he made it back to the office—which, in the end, was barely by five o'clock.

These calculations are common to anyone who has braved Cairo's traffic, but they illustrate more significantly how filmmakers anticipate traffic in their daily work, especially for production legworkers, who do not have the luxury of avoiding Cairo's harshest congestion times. While legwork missions tend to be distributed by geographic area to alleviate cross-city journeys, these areas can be extensive enough to make traffic a significant obstacle despite all precautions taken by workers. One day in the preparations for *The Cat and the Mouse* (2015), the production manager Tamer Fathi and his assistant Khaled Ahmed came back to the office after a scouting journey. Fathi was cursing, saying they would never go on a scouting mission again. Farghalli had assigned them to look at different hotels in 6th of October City. While the roads there were normally free by day, according to Fathi, they were all somehow jammed, as were the roads between October City and Dokki. What was supposed to be a manageable scouting trip in a nice neighborhood on the outskirts of Cairo turned out to be a calamitous ride in traffic.

Planning legwork cannot do without such anticipations of traffic, whether the legwork involves traveling to successive scouting appointments or venturing into busy day-only markets to buy props and costumes. While they were sitting in Studio Misr some days before the shooting for *Décor*, the production assistant Hany Abdel Latif told his location manager Ahmad Abdallah Abdel Halim that he was supposed to go buy props in the open market in Ataba, near downtown Cairo. They were discussing how they would transport props into the studio's storage. Since it was two o'clock in the afternoon at Studio Misr, which lies near the ring road on the outskirts of Cairo, Abdel Halim declared it impossible to go downtown and back on the same day. He told Abdel Latif to plan the journey with his car driver on another day. Abdel Latif called the driver and told him that they could no longer go to Ataba that day. "It's already two," he pleaded. "Yes, tomorrow. . . . No, we can't go around the same hour . . . we have to go around nine or ten in the morning," he insisted. While Abdel Latif was talking to the driver, Abdel Halim was encouraging him to be firm, because he did not want the driver to be lazy and try to go in the afternoon given the traffic and the number of props that needed to be transported to Studio Misr before the storage closed at night. Anticipated traffic, here, had a direct consequence for the way in which a contingent task was executed.

The unpredictability of hour-to-hour traffic conditions poses a central challenge to executive workers, who need to arrange the transportation of various equipment, workers, and documents in their daily work. While anticipating traffic is not unique to the film industry, it has a direct impact on the industry's logistics and, by extension, on the mediation of imponderable traffic conditions. These conditions are not uncertain in a general sense, because workers assume that they will end up getting from point A to point B, yet the mediating steps through which the traffic will be braved remain unpredictable—hence the various assumptions used to anticipate it. This mediation is not foolproof, as is evident in Fathi's hellish journey in October City, yet it modifies an overall imponderable problem—how to move effectively around the city—into a set of contingent decisions about transportation. These contingencies reflect how logistical anticipation is never "automatic," but involves breaking down unpredictable yet expected futures into smaller tasks in the short and long term. This mediation is also evident in the more proximate decisions involved in executing a shooting day.

Avoiding Delays

In principle, preparations are meant to exhaust all eventual logistical issues to arise on set. In practice, the shooting day involves a great deal of imponderability for the workers in charge. Preparations, however exhaustive, cannot take account of all courses of action leading to the shooting's execution. The seemingly indefinite contingencies involved in executing a shooting day are perhaps better suggested with a raw example:

Today is the first shooting day in [director] Tamer Mohsen's and [screenwriter] Wahid Hamed's movie, *Qitt wa far* [*The Cat and the Mouse*]. On the previous day, [the location manager] Setohy called me over the phone to tell me that we had a *tagammu'* [meeting point] around 5 a.m. at Kouki Park near the end of Faysal St. I told him okay, and we hung up. . . .

So I arrive at the meeting point . . . around 4:55 a.m. There is a microbus on the verge of leaving with [two production assistants] Mo Fathallah and Houda (as well as a few people I don't know). I salute some people in the production team in turn: [the production assistant] Adham, Setohy, [the production manager] Tamer Fathi. When he sees me, Tamer smiles and says, "*Inta gayt al-urdar* [You came to the shooting]?" I smile back and, after kissing him, I say, "*Setohy iddani al-urdar* [Setohy gave me the shooting time]." He immediately answers with a smile, "*Ana hafshakhu dilwa'ti* [I'll kill him now]!"

I silently stand next to people in *intag* [production], along with [the casting agent] Alaa *(régie)* not too far. Tamer, Setohy, and Adham are constantly on the phone, and the question they always ask is, "*Inta fein* [Where are you]?" or "*Wasalt fein* [How far are you]?" Tamer then checks with Adham where the *malabis* people [costume team] are, and Adham ensures that they are on their way (indeed, they arrive ten to fifteen minutes later). Tamer then asks Setohy where the video-assist crew is, and Setohy says that they will go directly to the *midan* [roundabout] near the location, and [I see him calling them to] give directions over the phone.

Alaa *(régie)* is constantly on the phone with an actor, but the actor's phone is off, and Alaa expresses his frustration out loud. He says that he called at 4:15 a.m. to wake him up, and that he lives right next to Kouki Park (on Haram St.). The city's lights go dark around 5:15 a.m., when the dawn has not yet appeared. Around 5:30 a.m., Tamer Fathi brings me with Adham to the location, in his own car.

In Tamer's car, Adham receives phone calls from Amira (the assistant stylist) on his brand-new Samsung phone. She asks him to explain the road to the location every time (Adham asks where she is, and then he explains how she should go). . . . Tamer Fathi also receives a few phone calls; I guess they're about where different people are. When we arrive in the *midan* near the factory, Tamer explains to Adham how to go to the factory, then he guides a few cars and trucks behind him (including a car where [stylist] Nahed Nasrallah and her assistants are). [Indeed, a few cars and trucks seemed to have been waiting in the *midan* until a production member would guide them to the location]. (Field notes, June 7, 2014)

This excerpt from my field notes captures approximately two hours on the first shooting day of *The Cat and the Mouse*. It starts with a brief note on a phone call I received at home from Setohy. The call communicated important logistical information (where we would meet, at what time), but the fact that there was a phone call to begin with indicates that Setohy had planned on calling me. Setohy most probably did not call out of courtesy, but with the intention of contacting all the crew members who would gather at the meeting point on the next day—something I saw him doing countless times at New Century's office, with a long handwritten list of contacts on the desk.

What seems most salient is the number of phone calls made on the shooting day itself. In Chapter 3, I described how production workers always remain available by phone, thereby becoming reserves of legwork under their superior's command. Likewise, when the casting agent Alaa tried to call one of his extras without getting an answer, he was exasperated not just because the extra's absence might delay the shooting (which the production team would have blamed on him), but because the extra is expected to be on call at all times—especially on a shooting day, when his physical presence is necessary to execute certain scenes. Calling is not restricted to ensuring the presence of all cast and crew members on set: it extends to ensuring the presence of equipment, props, and costumes. When Fathi asks Setohy to call the video-assist crew, it is because he expects them to be present at the meeting point on time. He wants to make sure that they will not occasion any delays in the equipment's presence, which may in turn cause a delay on the shooting day. This delay could have been worse as the shooting took place in 6th of October City, on the outskirts of Cairo, and the video-assist crew might have gotten stuck in the commute traffic between their office and the location had they come to the meeting point a little later than dawn. Thus, phone calls act as a safety measure to ensure that everyone and everything necessary to the shooting will make it on time to the set, which is contingent on everything and everyone *actually* making it to the set.

In addition to ensuring that all cast and crew members arrive on time, the production crew oversees many unseen details that are vital to executing a "successful" shooting day—a day without delays. The production secures parking spaces for all crew members and, crucially, the equipment trucks that would have a hard time parking in Cairo (including the camera van, the gaffer's truck, the grip's truck, and the generator truck). The production ensures that all equipment, extras, props, and costumes are transported in a timely fashion to the location (prior to the shooting) and back to their storage space/companies (after shooting); they secure a perimeter around the camera to avoid unwanted interferences with the frame; they ensure that all cast/crew members receive food or allowances *(badal)* during breaks; and they ensure that the set is well kept and cleaned once all scenes are shot in a given location. Each one of these tasks was assigned to a specific crew member or a specialized subteam in *Décor*.[8] The location manager Ahmad Abdallah Abdel Halim or the production manager Setohy would negotiate parking spots with the local parking man *(sayis)* prior to a shooting day; Mahmoud Abdallah ordered the production's cars and their movement; Khaled Labanita organized lunch breaks; and the location service workers Mondy and Sayyed cleaned the location every day.

Delays *(ta'khir)* are the first and foremost problem in the execution of a shooting day. There are several reasons to avoid delays—financial ones above all. Delaying a day's schedule may cause the production to pay an additional shooting day in the very same location, with additional wages and rental costs on equipment. Most equipment is included under a rental package covering the whole schedule, no matter how long it extends, but there are always "special" items rented out by the day, such as lenses outside the standard lens set or spotlights outside the pre-agreed package. In this context, there is a financial incentive to pay "half-day" overtime wages *(nuss yum)* to avoid paying equipment, rental, *and* wages on another full day of shooting. This explains, in part, the common occurrence of shooting well beyond the conventional twelve-hour shift in Egypt. There is also a logistical reason to avoid delays, as postponed scenes can disrupt a scheduled shooting block in a single location. When actors lose concentration and repeat takes, they cause more delays. When the sun sets, daylight scenes may have to be shot on another day. These events may force the assistant director to change completely his/her ensuing plans.

The cinematographer Abdelsalam Moussa had a very cinematic anecdote to tell about setting suns and their impact on film logistics. While he was shooting in *Chaos and Disorder* (2012), there was an absolutely crucial shot he wanted to shoot at a precise hour around sunset to give the scene a certain mood. The set was gathered in a village built near the rural town of Mansuriya, some way outside of Cairo. While driving westward on the highway, he suddenly got stuck in overwhelming traffic, and he had to bear the terrible spectacle—likely made even more dramatic by the panoramic highway horizon—of a slowly setting sun while the whole set was gathered just to shoot this specific shot at this specific time. Unable to flee the traffic, Moussa witnessed his shooting day's ruin on the horizon. When he arrived on set way into the night, he managed to convince all the crew members to leave the location without pay and come back the very next day to shoot the crucial shot.

The executive crew's main concern on set is to finish without major delays the daily call sheet, which is written by the assistant director in conjunction with his direction team based on the schedule's unfolding. Zohairy made call sheets on his laptop (see Figure 2), and it had indications for all departments in the film: which scenes were to be shot on the day, who would be working, and what needed to be done by the production crew in terms of parking, equipment, important props, and costumes. Each indication was directed at a specific person or team. "Zohairy is very detailed in his job," said his script supervisor Jaylan Auf. He had such experience, in her view, that he wrote his call sheets for the worker who would get what is needed on the ground, not the line producer who would likely just print the sheet and distribute it to his/her subordinates. In practice, the call sheet is not necessarily consulted by executive workers. One day, I noticed that there was a handheld camera listed as part of the equipment in *Décor*, and I told Ahmad Abdallah Abdel Halim that I had never seen it before. He replied that Zohairy may well write everything in the order—the production only brings things when he asks for them verbally. The assistant decorator Ezzat echoed this view: in his whole career, he said, he had almost never looked at the call sheet. "I just care about attendance times and the break," he joked. In short, the call sheet is not a detailed instruction manual to executive workers as much as it is a mediator that allows them, within a certain division of labor in the filmmaking process, to recall what needs to be done or to assign blame for mistakes.

Any major delay is considered a "*drop*," a failure in execution. A failed prop delivery to the location, a lost continuity item, an actor who does not show up on time, a malfunctioning video-assist, a setting sun right before the last daylight scene—these events can be considered drops. While they all add to the unpredictability of a shooting day, they are not all the same. Farghalli made a useful distinction between a *drub qadari* and a *drub mihani*—a "fateful" and a "professional" drop. Fateful drops happen for reasons outside human control (such as when an actor becomes sick or when the camera stops working), whereas professional drops are deemed to be in the worker's control (such as when the focus puller cannot adjust the focus properly or the script supervisor tells the actress to wear the wrong costume). This distinction is not explicitly held across the Egyptian film industry, yet certain on-set events are indeed deemed to be unavoidable, while others are deemed to be professional mistakes.

On the second day of shooting in *Décor*, Zohairy was asking the art director Nihal Farouk whether the set building extras should remove wallpaper in the shot's background. "Why?" inquired Farouk. "I think it's in continuity *(rakur)*," replied Zohairy. They chatted a little when, suddenly, the power was cut in the whole studio. The cut lasted about an hour, and I later discovered that the generator had caused this drop. The generator ran out of gas, and whoever was supposed to fill it did not do it on time. Rumor had it that Farghalli experienced one of his infamous episodes of angry "transformation" *(tahawwul)* until the generator crew got the power running again. The next morning, when I entered the studio, the generator truck was a different color. I learned that Farghalli had hired a new generator. Clearly, the failure was not an act of destiny, but a predictable mistake on the part of the generator's crew, who were summarily replaced for the costly delay.

In contrast, unpredictable events interrupting the shooting are deemed unavoidable. This is vividly illustrated in an anecdote recounted by Setohy from the set of *Laylat al-bibi dul* (*The Baby Doll Night*, 2008). When they were shooting next to the Meridian Hotel on Salah Salem highway—a two-way, four-lane road crossing Cairo from southwest to northeast—the production used a large crane to take a high-angle shot. Accidentally, the crane went over the walls of a villa next to the Meridian. "Lower the gun!" cried some armed guards dashing out of the residence. They were gesturing at the crane to come down, with guns pointed straight at the crew. Amid general confusion, Setohy tried to explain to the guards that the crane was cinema equipment, but they remained very tense, ready to shoot. They told him that he needed to move the crane to the other side of Salah Salem, because it was impossible to have it hanging over the residence. Ultimately, the crew had to displace the heavy crane across the eight lanes of Salah Salem right in the middle of the day, which stopped the entire avenue and cost time on set. No one was fired or blamed for the delay, because it could not have been prevented. The villa, as it turns out, was Yasser Arafat's personal residence in Cairo.

Even if they are not blamed for unavoidable delays, like discovering that a crane is hovering over a Palestinian leader's villa, the production team still needs to reckon with them. On another set, Setohy once came on location only to find that the sewers had exploded right under the street where production cars were meant to be parked. He was alone in the morning on that day, and he had to fill the hole with sand until more production workers gradually arrived to help. "What a terrible day . . . ," he reminisced. Setohy argued that no matter one's experience in production, shooting is always extremely stressful, because any problem arising on set is expected to be solved by the production team. "On location, the word 'production' (*intag*) is like chewing gum in everyone's mouth." Through this metaphor, Setohy was referring to the common practice of calling out a team's name when their assistance is required on set, which reflects the assumption that executive workers are expected to be constantly available.

Given the looming threat of a drop, the overall logistical coordination of a shooting day remains imponderable to executive crew members, who not only have to deal with not knowing all logistical courses of action leading to the shooting in preparations, but also have to contend with logistical emergencies on the very day when they decide to shoot. These emergencies are mediated in part by the set's hierarchy of command as well as an awareness of the operations needing to be accomplished, in addition to various mediators like to-do lists, call sheets, and phone calls. Through this mediation, workers break down the imponderable shooting into a set of contingent tasks, which allow them to apprehend what comes next in a more practical manner than if they considered the shooting as a logistical behemoth. Executive crew members and technological devices act as "reserves" in this context: the crew member is summoned to apprehend future tasks while summoning his/her devices to record what has been done and what remains to be done.

Being Available and Being Faultless

Executive workers, in short, are expected to carry all the logistics of a shooting day on their shoulders, which is why the "*drop*" is such a fitting metaphor. This expectation, which is borne by the hierarchical logic described in Chapter 2, releases the artistic worker from any "technical" strains. Farghalli once imaged that "the production team is the film's line of defense *(khatt difa' al-film)*." This metaphor is highlighted in two additional and asymmetrical expectations: that executive workers should be available, and that they should be faultless. The logic of availability is partly visible in the spatial organization of the set, as shown in Figure 4. The camera stands at the center of the set. There are three main areas to consider: what the camera "sees," as shown by the V-shaped area; what is "behind the camera," which means close enough outside the V-shaped area to maintain some crew members on command between takes; and what is "behind the scenes," where cast and crew members as well as heavy equipment rest outside the immediate vicinity of the take.

While being behind the scenes is a good way to relax, several executive crew members need to remain close enough to the camera to be ready to intervene when they are called upon. Hierarchical superiors would call out loud *(yindah)* to workers or entire teams to execute their attending tasks. One hears regular cries of *ida'a* (lights) when a lighting technician is called to displace spots, or *aksiswar* (props) when a prop assistant is called to displace props, or *makeup* when an assistant needs to wipe sweat off an actor's face. Remaining available, therefore, means remaining available to be commanded by superiors to execute a task.

This expectation translates into certain bodily postures on set. On the first shooting day in *Décor*, I saw the production assistant Adham el-Sayeh and the costume script supervisor Mariam el-Bagoury standing by, idly shifting their tired legs while nothing much seemed to be happening. When I asked them why not sit down, they both adamantly refused, and they made me write two notes in my notebook: "No production team can sit" and "This kind of thing is impossible." Their adamant refusal to sit

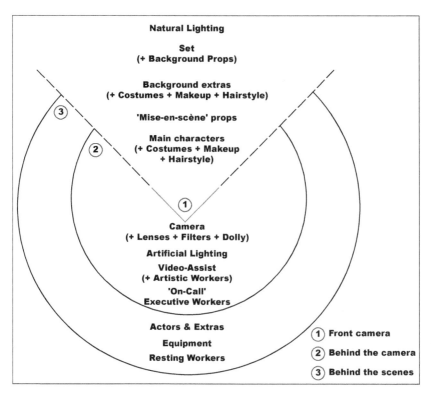

Natural Lighting

Set
(+ Background Props)

Background extras
(+ Costumes + Makeup + Hairstyle)

③

'Mise-en-scène' props

Main characters
② **(+ Costumes + Makeup**
+ Hairstyle)

①

Camera
(+ Lenses + Filters + Dolly)

Artificial Lighting

Video-Assist
(+ Artistic Workers)

'On-Call'
Executive Workers

Actors & Extras

Equipment

Resting Workers

① **Front camera**

② **Behind the camera**

③ **Behind the scenes**

4. The spatial organization of a film set.

down was expressed in good humor, yet they were committed to standing because, as subordinate workers, they could not be seen to relax on set in front of their superiors, even if they had to stand idly. On another occasion, I asked why the production assistant Hany Abdel Latif was standing by the prop car even though he looked exhausted. He went on a tirade about "stage acting" *(tamsil)* in executive work: "It doesn't actually make a difference whether I'm standing or sitting, but it looks good [in front of his superior].... If he sees me sitting, he might think that he's the one who's working hard while [I'm] just sitting down." The standing position signals a certain readiness to work, an ability to remain "on call"—an expectation that extends to equipment as well. When I asked the gaffer Mahmoud Morsi why he had so much more equipment than he used on location, he answered that he preferred having all his equipment at hand to execute whatever the cinematographer asked. "*When he ring, I bring. . . . I was born ready*," he summarized jokingly in English.

Executive workers not only remain available individually, they remain available to serve artistic workers collectively. Farghalli once stated that the production team needs to "serve all elements in the film *(yikhdim kull al-'anasir fi-l-film)*." This situation explains, in part, why the crew size in Egypt seems overinflated by Euro-American standards, because there are executive workers always at hand to carry out logistical assignments. In *Décor*, Farghalli could choose to send any of his production assistants at any time to scout a new location, to acquire a prop, or to get a permit letter signed. According to the production manager Khaled Adam, shooting locations used to be far less crowded until the 1990s. Everything that needed to be done was carried out by fifteen workers in total. It was a time where the grips were camera technicians, where all equipment would fit in one small microbus. Nowadays, according to the assistant director Karim el-Mihi, the crew can be as many as a hundred and fifty people. This is perhaps true on mega-productions, but I have never seen more than a hundred crew members on location at any one time (excluding actors and extras).

This model of production by direct command explains how Egyptian filmmakers manage the imponderability of a shooting day: by remaining available to solve any emergency on set. The expectation to remain "on call" is nominally extended to artistic crew members. However, they have greater leeway where executive workers remain rigidly on call, even though both may equally delay the shoot. To give two examples, I witnessed an actress delay an entire shooting day by thirty minutes because she did not want to come out of her lodge before the other stars did. On a separate occasion, I saw a whole set grind to a halt because the director went for a nap while the set was being prepared for a take. This asymmetry between artistic and executive workers in the expectation to be on call extends to another expectation: being faultless.

In a sense, artistic "mistakes" are considered unavoidable. The actor who repeats a take because s/he cannot learn his/her lines; the director who asks for retakes until s/he gets exactly what s/he has in mind; the cinematographer who keeps changing the lighting to get the perfect image—all are examples of artistic workers endlessly reiterating some operations without sanctions. What may be an important adjustment to the director or the cinematographer can be, to the executive crew member, a sign of inability to "know what one is doing" *(yi'raf huwwa biyi'mil eih)*. For instance, the prop assistant Mustafa Seyaha told me that the art director Nihal Farouk was too "weak" *(da'ifa)* in her job because she changed her mind too much. To evidence his claim, he referred to a room he was forced to furnish twice because Farouk saw and disliked the initial result. Seyaha did not disagree with her choices, since as an executive worker he can only execute what Farouk wants, but he still judged his superior's skill *(shatara)* harshly. He contrasted the crew in *Décor* with the crew of the well-known director Sharif Arafa, who is known to work fast, with few breaks in between takes, and to be decisive. This situation indexed Arafa's skill by contrast with Ahmad Abdalla and his crew in Seyaha's view, although Seyaha's evaluation of skill bears little consequence in practice given his hierarchically subordinate position.

In contrast with artistic "mistakes," a camera technician taking too much time to load a battery, or a grip being unable to straighten a track in a satisfactory time, or a video-assist operator being unable to get an image on the director's monitor are all unambiguous mistakes *(ghalatat)*. While these mistakes occur just as often as artistic ones, they carry weightier consequences because the mistaken party can be grounded, fired, or never rehired by the same crew. This is indeed what happened with the generator on the first shooting day in *Décor*. Mistakes are a recurrent matter of concern, even in joking conversations. One time, the whole production crew mocked the actors' manager Ashmawy because he had forgotten to call an actress on location in a previous project. "I called her, but she didn't answer!" he vehemently pleaded, looking at the mischievous worker who had started the banter with a threatening face. Farghalli kept a little red notebook with his production assistant Mahmoud Abdallah where he would calculate deductions to each crew member's wages based on his/her number of mistakes. "The deduction will be set at twenty [Egyptian] pounds per mistake in the next location," he told his crew while we were still in the middle of the shooting schedule. Everyone started joking about the notebook and teased one another about how much money they had lost (that is, how many mistakes they had made), while each crew member passionately defended him/herself from having committed any mistake. When I asked about the reason for having a deduction list, Farghalli answered laconically: "Money hurts." I was confused: how can he know whether a mistake would deserve punishment to such an extent? "Small mistakes come with a deduction, big mistakes lead to firing," he said with a hearty laugh. His laughter was certainly not meant to be reassuring: getting fired is a genuine possibility, after all.

These mistakes carried low stakes and were mentioned in good humor, but the impassioned defense on the part of guilty crew members is indicative of the primer on being faultless. The appearance of faultlessness was evidence of stage acting *(tamsil)*, according to the production assistant Hany Abdel Latif, because it smoothed out the edges of mistakes or even drops. The production team was always pretending that there were huge logistical problems in his recounting, which were constantly solved by production crew members acting as "heroes of the shadow." Abdel Latif still recognized that this performance was necessary to maintain work in executive jobs. One night at Studio Misr, when all the workers started going home slowly but surely, I asked Abdel Latif why he would not go home straight away. He looked exhausted, and since everyone was slowly leaving, I thought it would be natural for him to leave. He replied that it would be a bad mark on his résumé and that it might affect his hiring on future projects. When production heads come to taking decisions on the assistants to hire, a very small situation like leaving early could seal his fate, because he might acquire the reputation that he "doesn't finish his work." Therefore, it was important for him to remain as flawless and constant as possible. With a certain degree of perfection, he might even build the opposite reputation of being hard-working and grow in demand *(yib'a matlub)* on different projects.

When mistakes are avoided, they are often narrated in dramatic fashion to reassert one's faultless control over the situation. "What [production workers] care about is not that you make mistakes, it's that you're able to figure out [how to fix them] *(ti'raf titsarraf)*," said the assistant director Habi Seoud once. Keeping things "under control" *(taht al-saytara)* and being "in control" *(misaytar)* are highly prized traits in executive jobs, and it is a matter of professional pride to repair mistakes swiftly when they occur. A small example is when the video-assist monitor in *Décor* would go off and the director Ahmad Abdalla screamed "There's no image!" Immediately, video-assist operators would spring to the machine and ensure that the image come back as fast as possible. A more consequential example was narrated by Badawy. Once, his driver almost ruined three days of shooting in Aswan, in the south of Egypt, because he forgot to drive an actor to the Cairo airport. Badawy, who was already in Aswan, had to call to get a taxi in Cairo to pick up his actor and drive him to the airport, call the airline, get him another ticket, and stop the plane at the airport for twenty minutes to get him to Aswan. The actor arrived three hours late, but had he not arrived on that plane, he would have had to wait three days for the next flight. The production would have lost three shooting days, with a cost amounting to three hundred thousand Egyptian pounds, according to Badawy.

Whether big or small, executive mistakes are grounds for reprimand by hierarchical superiors. Assigning blame is a regular exercise in this sense. For example, in *The Cat and the Mouse*, the camera technicians did not bring a "*clip-on*" on the second shooting day.[9] When the camera technician Hamada alerted Farghalli to the missing item, the production manager Tamer Fathi quickly dispatched a production car to the camera rental office to fetch it. Soon thereafter, the focus puller came into the production room and told Farghalli that he needed to have the call sheet to know what equipment he needed on which days and what instructions to give to his technicians. Farghalli conceded the point, and when Hamada came to apologize for not having brought the clip-on, he added that he was never told by the camera assistant Yasser Zanita to bring it (since Farghalli had communicated the information to Zanita orally on the previous day). In the end, the missing piece of equipment arrived on set, but the quick exchanges between Farghalli, Hamada, and the focus puller helped establish that the production team was to blame in this case. The information, indeed, had not been communicated to the appropriate crew member, the focus puller, and, by extension, the chief camera technician. Although the production team may have reminded someone in the cinematography crew orally, and although the information could reasonably have reached its destination, the blame still went to the production team because it had not distributed the call sheet—the ultimate arbiter in this case.

Within a certain division of labor, the call sheet makes an overall imponderable outcome—who will bring what equipment on set—contingent on the crew members who are assigned to execute this task—the focus puller with the call sheet provided by the production team. The fact that Farghalli did not berate anyone on his team or on other teams and the fact that one of his production cars (as opposed to the camera van) was dispatched to the company indicates that he recognized his responsibility in this minor incident, although he may not explicitly have acknowledged it. As the focus puller did not have the call sheet, however, he could not follow up on executing his task. When I told Zohairy that not everyone read his call sheets in *Décor*, he answered that it was none of his business, because he just wants everything to be available on set. If it is not available but it is written on the call sheet, the responsibility falls back on the production team. The assistant director Karim el-Mihi reckons that this is why emails are not widely used across the industry, because it would leave a traceable record of the crew member to blame when an item is missing on set. In practice, all crew members try to discharge blame on each other. Being faultless, in this sense, is not just about trying to avoid mistakes on set, but also about trying to avoid being held responsible for mistakes by repairing them as soon as they happen, which is a concern to all executive crew members who carry out the logistics of film production.

Logistical Mediation

All in all, coordinating film production presents a set of logistical issues to executive workers, from budgeting to scheduling to transportation to executing a shooting day. In all cases, imponderability is partially mediated by the fact that only executive workers are put in charge of these issues. In addition to expectations about availability and faultlessness, the accepted division of labor between artistic and executive work allows filmmakers to mediate the complex logistics of the filmmaking process. Technological devices like paper, phones, laptops, and cameras play an equally important role in this mediation. Above, I hinted at how the budget is recorded on an Excel sheet, the flow of cash is recorded on paper, the shooting schedule relies on various breakdowns inscribed on computers, and transportation is coordinated on mobile phones. On their own, these hints are insufficient to give a sense of the importance of technological devices in coordination. They might give the impression that the relevant aspects of film logistics only occur between people—say, the accountant and the crew or the production team and the direction team—while devices serve as an inert basis on which higher-order social interactions occur. Yet these devices are important *precisely* because they summon written and oral mediators committing each crew member's attention to contingent tasks in the future, while recording past actions in the production process. In other words, they become reserves summoning filmmakers to attend to their future work. While these objects cannot allow filmmakers to take full control over the unpredictable yet expected future, they make it contingent in some respects.

For instance, accounting paperwork acts as a record of how much money can still be spent, according to the budget. These proximate evaluations are made by the line producer and the accountant. They are renewed with every week's adjustments to the budget. What counts most in these calculations is not the paperwork per se—the object inscribing transactions—but rather its role as a written mediator instantiating a relation between what has been spent and what remains to be spent. For instance, Farghalli's balance sheets *(muwazanat)* detailed what amounts had been spent on all items in *Décor* while leaving room to estimate what could be spent later. On a day-to-day timescale, the prospective outlook allowed by paperwork is well illustrated with the daily production report, which includes information on all crew members and equipment hired on a given shooting day. Farghalli told me that these reports are useful on two levels. On a technical level, they allow him to see how much equipment has been used in the week, how many days it has been used, and so on. On a financial level, he can calculate whether he will remain on budget in the coming days. For instance, if he budgeted for three hundred extras in total throughout the film, he could know how many extras he had used each day and calculate how many he had left on the budget.

These calculations illustrate how paperwork mediates the imponderable budget by breaking it down into a series of smaller costs that allow the line producer to calculate his/her adjusted budget based on past transactions and future estimates. As the production manager Setohy once put it, all coordination needs to be done "by paper and pencil" *(bi-l-wara'a wa-l-'alam)*. This is not just a metaphor of the physical inscription of logistical needs on paper (or on computer), but also a normative statement about the work's methodical nature. This expression is an instance of "boundary-work" in Ganti's sense. Like in Bollywood, the pencil-pushing worker is a better normative model than the straw-man "purely oral" colleague (Ganti, 2012: 222–25).[10] This representation of pure orality masks the proliferation of technological devices—paper, phones, and laptops—in the work of Egyptian film production. As Setohy recognizes, crew members who just communicate directives orally are likely to "run into a wall" *(mumkin yilbisu fi-l-hit)*.

While the affordances of paper and phones are obviously different, they have a similar purpose in the work of logistical coordination. They instantiate (future) logistical tasks to the (present) executive crew members, based on a (past) record of logistical planning. This record would have no use if it were simply abandoned to the paper trail, a little like bureaucrats abandon cases to the filing cabinet. This record is more like a future memory: it helps crew members in executing certain contingent operations throughout the filmmaking process, while recording what should have been done in its course, thereby allowing them to verify what remains to be done at each juncture in the process. Setohy's "paper and pencil" attitude extended into handwritten sheets that allowed him rarely to forget what needed to be done. He hung several sheets in New Century's office with the daily tasks assigned to his workers. He wrote another sheet for whatever tasks remained *(mutabaqqiyat)* over the days. He had sheets with mobile numbers in addition to the SD cards he filled with such contacts. Through this accumulation of paper and digital contacts, Setohy became a clear illustration of Clark and Chalmers' classical example of an "extended mind" (1998): a cognitive system of worker-and-paper who can remember what needs to be done, a task which would be difficult for the worker or the paper on his or its own. Of course, the worker or the paper cannot *compel* coordination in any way. It is only within an accepted division of labor between executive and artistic crew members, where everyone is aware of the operations ahead and all executive workers work with the expectation of being constantly available and faultless, that the imponderable outcome of coordination can be mediated and enacted.

Pre-light

I learn that the shooting day on December 23, 2013, will double as a *"pre-light"* day through a conversation among production assistants at Studio Misr. This day would normally include lighting and camera tests to determine how the shooting would unfold. "What they're doing right now is very unusual," they hint with a disapproving tone. As we were chatting, Ahmad Abdalla and his crew were roaming around studio number one in an effort to visualize shots in the empty set before December 23. All this work was a "waste of time" according to the production assistants, because all the decisions taken by Ahmad Abdalla would have to be re-explained later to the actors, the craftsmen, and the lighting technicians on set. "All these things will be decided by the *pre-light*," state the assistants.

I remember thinking that their tone was a bit too harsh toward what seemed like a normal desire among the artistic crew: visiting and revisiting the space of the shooting to see what the film would look like. Their conversation implied that this artistic crew was acting in an "unprofessional" manner, because professionalism would involve dead certainty in the commands given on set.

Their notion of pre-light was much more compressed in time: it was about giving directives to the actors, the craftsmen, and the lighting technicians on the spot, without visible preparation by the artistic crew.

Late in the afternoon on December 23, the cinematographer Tarek Hefny asks the artistic crew to stop shooting because he needs time to arrange his lights for the next day. The pre-light session continues until later, but I leave Studio Misr to attend a book launch. Around a month later, on January 20, I get a chance to witness another pre-light session by accident. After *firkish*, the magical word announcing the end of the shooting day, I linger with the gaffer Mahmoud Morsi and his lighting crew. They start idly playing around with spots in the living room, unlike their usual habit of keeping lights as they are or rapidly packing them before leaving the location. After a few minutes, I notice that they are creating a pre-light setup for the next day.

Morsi seems unhappy about staying longer hours. I reckon he asked Farghalli to set up these lights the next day, while the main crew was shooting the bedroom, but Farghalli would not have it. Their conflict over time and labor was no longer surprising to me. What I did not expect was Tarek Hefny coming to Morsi to give him additional instructions on the lighting before leaving. He lets his gaffer and the lighting script Hany Morsy handle the rest.

Whatever commands were communicated by Tarek are slowly relayed through the gaffer's directives to his men. He starts working on the Dedo spotlight in the dining room—a small light with a concentrated beam. Morsi has one technician over by the spot. He tells him to adjust the cardboard *(kansu)* around the light to counteract the effect of a sharper, brighter light creating a marked shadow on the wall behind the living room. The result is a circular, diffuse halo produced by the conjoined Dedo and sharp light on the wall. Morsi awaits the right moment. "A little to the right . . . a little to the left . . . fix it as it is!" Morsi asks his assistant to add translucent paper *(Forrest)* over the Dedo to diffuse the light a bit further.

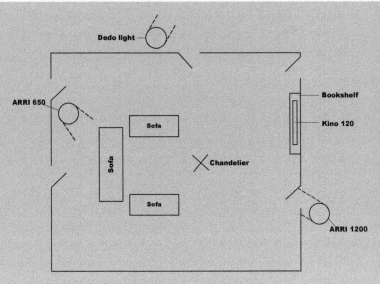

5. Lighting setup in Garden City on January 20, 2014, with a Dedo light at the top; ARRI 650 to the left; Kino 120 over the library; ARRI 1200 outside the room, and a chandelier in the middle.

This detailed technical labor produces the lighting desired by the cinematographer in a few short commands. The care taken in positioning the Dedo light is puzzling, however, as it just seems to diffuse the lighting on a peripheral wall inside the location. "Why did you put the Dedo there?" I ask Hany Morsy. "Because Tarek wants to see a little glow in the background," he answers, referring to a shot where we would get a glimpse of the wall through the dining room's slightly open door. "This will give some depth to the image."

Later, a lighting technician fixes the Kino light above the library with a "*magic arm*," a contraption that can be fixed on a flat surface to carry the weight of a spot. The gaffer Morsi sits down on the sofa lit by the Kino light and asks his technician to orient the spot's head so as to light up a specific area around the sofa. The technician moves the spot's barn doors on Morsi's command: "To the right . . . to the left . . . up . . . down. . . ." Morsi's instructions are again very brief, but he uses his own body to estimate the lit area and the way in which the light will cover the actor's body. When he is satisfied, he once again orders the technician to "fix it as it is." Morsi, it became clear to me, was visualizing the film's image much as a cinematographer would, but he would not have the last word on how the light was adjusted on set.

The last light to adjust is the ARRI 650 fixed right behind the sofa. Morsi asks Hany Morsy and me to sit on the couch so he can adjust the lights on us. He tells the technicians to move the lights according to the shadow on our faces. These lights were adjusted in anticipation of a close-up or medium shot, I thought, where shadows would be visible on the actor's face. This seemed more consequential than the diffuse Dedo light on the dining room wall, which just added another layer to the lighting without being central to the anticipated action. Once he is done with this spotlight, Morsi asks the electrician Sayyed to plug it into the master current. The setup is ready for the next day.

The pre-light comes before the lighting captured in the shooting. The lighting setup made by Mahmoud Morsi will be adjusted no doubt, but it sets certain basic moods to fulfill the cinematographer's desires. The nuances involved in coordinating these tasks explain why Tarek Hefny tells me, some months later, that it is useful to work with the same crew over several projects because everyone can then have "the same mindset" *(nafs al-dimagh)*.

Given that the lighting is always eventually adjusted, all lighting is pre-lighting in some sense, because it anticipates a moment when the light will eventually appear on screen. In the pre-light session, Morsi, Hany, and I became the actors whose bodies were lit, but the actors would differ when the shooting came, and the light would be adjusted in yet another way. A little higher, a little lower, but with an eye to how it will look in the film.

5

Visualization

On an autumn afternoon in 2013, I was working at New Century's office when the production manager Setohy came in exhausted. I asked him where he had been all day. He said that he had gone on a scouting mission at the district attorney's office *(niyaba)* in Qasr al-Nil, but that the police officers guarding the office would not allow him to photograph the building unless he received special permission from the district attorney *(al-na'ib al-'am)*. Later, the line producer Farghalli serenely walked in the office and started gathering scouting pictures on his MacBook. Each production crew member gave pictures in turn. When Setohy gave his camera's memory card to Farghalli, there were no photos of the office to show. Farghalli looked at him and asked, "Why didn't you scout the *niyaba*?" Setohy told him the whole story, to which Farghalli immediately replied, a little heatedly, "You couldn't even steal a tiny little picture? . . . I just wanted the external appearance *(khargi)* of the office!" Setohy justified himself by saying that he did not feel like he could take any photos given the guards' presence, so Farghalli sighed and asked, "What does it look like?" The answer consisted of a verbal and gestural evocation of the building's yellow color, its bulky, rectangular shape, and its architectural style, which resembles other *niyaba*s in Cairo. Farghalli seemed somewhat satisfied with the answer, but he still asked Setohy to photograph the office the next day, which he dutifully did, as he was able to steal a photo of its external appearance on his way to work.

This vignette illustrates one aspect of the work needed to estimate what a shooting location will look like on screen. Visualizing "the film" is imponderable in this sense. During preparations for *Décor*, no one knew what the final film would become, given the wide range of factors standing between the film-in-the-making and "the film" that would eventually materialize. These factors are logistical in part, as detailed in Chapter 4, but the division of labor between artistic and executive workers allows the artistic crew to offload all logistical burdens onto the executive crew. In the case of scouting, executive workers like Farghalli and Setohy oversaw the physical gathering of scouting pictures, which served as visual mediators in the crew's choice of shooting locations. Such mediators include, in addition to scouting pictures, set designs, costume pictures, casting videos, color tests, video-assist images, on-set recordings, unwanted takes in editing, the editor's notes, sound-editing *"references,"* and digital audio material—all of which serve to anticipate a specific aspect of the coming film without being part of the film per se.

Farghalli's initial question—"What does it look like?"—captures the way in which filmmakers try to foresee the film. Filmmakers are summoned to imagine the film by various reserves—cameras, phones, laptops, co-workers—to approximate its eventual look and anticipate its making. For instance, scouting pictures are summoned to anticipate what a location will look like, video-assist recordings are summoned to anticipate how shots will be composed, and sound effects are summoned to anticipate how the sound will be woven with the image on screen. The imponderable film becomes a series of contingent decisions in the hands of artistic workers through these mediators, which assist in imagining the film at each stage. This imaginative process is often said to reside in the director's head. As Ganti remarks, "all of the directors I met asserted that they had their films 'running in their heads,' discussing them in very visual terms, commonly describing onscreen action in relation to camera angles and movements" (2012: 223–24). This description ignores how technological devices anchor artistic creation, as I have argued throughout this book. Mediating images and sounds are not just inert physical supports to the artist's effort to visualize the film; they are constitutive of this very effort.

In most cases, mediators entertain an iconic relation with "the film" in C.S. Peirce's sense.[1] The film worker literally *sees* or *hears* what some aspect in the film will become on screen. When the stylist Salma Sami took fitting pictures of the star's costumes for *Décor*, she was not just trying to estimate, visually, what kinds of adornments were needed to give the actress a certain look; she was also looking at what the actress would look like in the film's image. As *Décor* was to be shot in black and white, Sami would adjust her camera settings to take black-and-white pictures. If she had simply wanted to choose costumes or accessories, she would presumably not have tried (with some difficulty) to change her camera settings to approximate the actual look in the black-and-white movie. The role of technological devices in visualizing the imponderable film is not just to "contain" an image or a sound, in this sense, but to summon individual and collective imagination to actualize some aspect of the film to come. This is encouraged not just by the iconic proximity between the mediator and the film, but also by the contingent decisions made by filmmakers within a given labor hierarchy and a given operational sequence.

One could make a similar analysis of the way in which artistic workers took time to set the camera monitor and the video-assist monitor in black and white in *Décor*, again with some technical difficulty. Everyone wanted to *see* what each take would eventually look like in editing—and, ultimately, in the film. The image on the monitor, in the studio, and on movie theater screens is technically not the same. As Abdalla once explained on set, the monitor image is just a "*look*" inserted in the camera software. The "*raw*" image—the digital content recorded by the camera and destined to be edited—is still in color to maintain its maximal quality. Most postproduction in *Décor*, likewise, was done on a black-and-white "*look*" that served as a reference to the editor, the colorist, and the mixer, although the material was still in color. In other words, what matters most is the anticipatory relation between the mediator and the film, not necessarily the material link between them.

After explaining the way in which Egyptian artistic workers approach visualization according to their specific skills and their authority on the crew, I examine three operations to illustrate how imponderable outcomes are respectively mediated in the case of scouting, image composition, and sound work. As I concentrate on the intricacies of everyday artistic decisions in *Décor* and *Poisonous Roses*, those who seek to contextualize each operation within the film's overall storyline can consult the introduction. This chapter will underplay narrative detail to stress considerations of skill, authority, and grounded technological use in the activity of filmmaking.

Skill, Authority, and Vision

Visualizing the film is partly a matter of skill *(shatara)*. While all workers are involved in the practice of visualization, their ability to visualize is never described as *shatara* except in the case of directors. The director is deemed to be the only crew member with a complete vision *(ru'ya)* of the film. His/her *shatara* consists precisely in his/her ability to imprint this vision onto the film. The term "*ru'ya*" is as ambiguous as the English term "vision":

it can imply both a concrete envisioning of images as well as an abstract intellectual project. When I asked the prominent director Daoud Abdel Sayyed what it means to "have a vision," and whether it means that the director can foresee the technical making of the film from start to finish, he replied that "vision is not about technique." What I was trying to describe, he said, was more like style *(uslub)*. When I asked whether he had specific images in mind while shooting, he answered that he would have an imagining *(takhayyul)* but no exact images. "It's not even productive," he added, because the film always looks different in the end. "It's like giving birth to a child: you know he'll look like his father and his mother, but you can't predict exactly how he will look before he's born." Having a vision is an entirely different matter in Abdel Sayyed's opinion, because it is "a general stance." For instance, in his *Kit-Kat* (1991), the main character is a blind man pretending to live a normal life despite his evident handicap, which Abdel Sayyed said was expressing his own general attitude toward Egypt. "Our society is generally backwards *(mutakhallif)*, but we still think we're the best civilization on earth."

Abdel Sayyed formulated this reflection in an interview at the Supreme Council of Culture in Cairo—an appropriate setting for such an intellectual opinion. Contrast this viewpoint with what the assistant director Wael Mandour had to say when I asked him about the importance of having a vision *(ru'ya)*. "It's a very basic question," he said with a chuckle, adding that "the director is obviously the only one who sees *(biyishuf)* the film." What he meant was that the film might begin as writing on a piece of paper, but the director can see all the locations, the actors, the movement, and so on. "No one else can see the whole project," he summarized. When I encouraged Mandour to discuss the more intellectual connotations of the term *ru'ya*, he hastened to add that this is an important aspect as well, and that the director needs to "be able to analyze human beings" before getting into technicalities. Nevertheless, Mandour's initial instinct in answering the question expresses the ambiguity inherent in the term. On the one hand, vision can be an intellectual project; on the other hand, it is the director's grasp on the whole filmmaking process—what Abdel Sayyed had earlier confined to a matter of style.

This ambiguity is again apparent in what the director Marwan Hamed told me about *ru'ya*. "It's a little like a director's imprint *(basma)*, [which is] in part formal, in part intellectual." Both aspects are inseparable in his view, because it goes back to the question of "how [s/he can] create a *film world*."

The director Ahmad Abdalla echoed this view: in addition to the basic human or philosophical concerns that he wants to express, he has an overall visual idea of his film—a *"visual concept,"* as he called it. Abdalla's visual concept and Hamed's film world are integral to what it means to "have a vision" in filmmaking. Through these terms, both filmmakers managed to break down the implicit distinction between image and intellect established by Daoud Abdel Sayyed. This distinction is central to the common representation of the director as a genius guiding the creation of the film, "someone whose very command—'Action!'—can bring the environment around him into harmony with his aims and intentions, bending each circumstance to suit a vision that had already been shaped and readied before ever setting foot in that milieu" (Pandian, 2015: 143).

Crucially, I would argue that the director's vision is not instilled in the film by an ingenious imaginative effort, but by the director's privileged position in the industry's hierarchy. When I asked Daoud Abdel Sayyed if it is necessary for the whole crew to share his vision, he answered with an emphatic "no," because only the director, or indeed the auteur *(mu'allif)*, is required to communicate a vision to the crew. This is a widely held viewpoint in the industry, and the only dissension to this otherwise consensual opinion was articulated by fellow directors. For instance, the director Ahmad Fawzi Saleh would regularly dispute the notion that the director "knows what he is doing" *('arif huwwa biyi'mil eih)*. The film is ever-evolving in his view, and it involves a constant effort to see what a location or a prop or an actor will look like on screen. Likewise, going against Abdel Sayyed's view, Ahmad Abdalla told me that everyone on his crew—including the cinematographer, the art director, and the actors—should bring some input based on his/her experience. Abdalla likes to work with a "workshop mentality" to gather everyone's ideas and let the crew own the film. "You're really democratic," I playfully retorted, to which he very seriously said that he totally objects to the prevalent notion that "the director is a god whose will must be executed." Everyone has a say in the movie, and his job as a director is to gather all these threads in a coherent manner, to make sure that "they are well interwoven *(mitwallifin)*."

Abdalla's account gives a somewhat more accurate picture of the practice of visualization. The heads of each artistic team—the cinematographer, the art director, the stylist, the sound engineer—are actively involved in visualizing their own aspects of the film. This visualization involves a similar set of skills to the director's visualization, except that it is streamlined according to each artistic worker's expertise and held to the director's final word. As Darré notes,

> In practice, indeed, the director feeds off the ideas of his collaborators as well as his actors; he chooses out of different options proposed to him; he composes the film with his collaborators. Yet, these collaborators . . . do not pretend, generally speaking, to share the work's authorship *(paternité)*. In the name of the notion of "author" . . . they most often consider that the ideas that they can bring to the director belong to him. Deriving most of their greatness from the greatness of the one they serve, they do not theoretically aspire to the public recognition reserved to him. This does not exclude internal tensions, which are sometimes publicly expressed, between their original vocation as creators, common to most technicians, and a symbolic division of labor that objectively denies their share in creation. (2006: 126–27)

Filmmakers try to see what the final film will look like *and* how the film-in-the-making will be made. In *Décor*, the art directors Asem Ali and Nihal Farouk tried to anticipate transformations to the built environment in Mustafa and Maha's apartment to create an appropriate set according to their aesthetic sensibility, their reading of the screenplay, their personal conversations, and Ahmad Abdalla's demands. When they looked at scouting pictures, their comments were not just about what would look nice in the film, but also about how they could design a set in this location, or how they could furnish it with appropriate props. There are two moments here: one where the art directors try to see how the location can be transformed while selecting it, and another where they actively eye the set's look on screen. To these ends, a variety of mediators were used to discuss artistic choices—of materials, of colors, of props—which were nested in a sociotechnical sequence where set design is contingent on previous artistic choices (the shooting location, the screenplay).

This process is presumably not exclusive to the Egyptian film industry, but its consequences have been insufficiently drawn out in existing media production ethnographies. Hoek's work on the Bangladeshi film industry stands as an illuminating exception in this sense (2014). With an interest in showing how "obscene" material is made visible/invisible in the making of an action movie, Hoek shows how filmmakers anticipate, at every juncture in the production process, the inclusion of this material at later stages. Obscenity is not just in the final film. It is made visible/invisible in screenwriting when a producer adds narrative "hooks" to allow him to insert an obscene "cut-piece" later; or in shooting, when obscene material is shot away from the main studios; or in postproduction, when different cuts of the same movie are shown to the censorship board and to theater audiences in rural Bangladesh. The necessity of considering both the final movie and its anticipated production process was as pressing to Asem Ali and Nihal Farouk, who were trying to see how a location might be designed in *Décor*, as it was to the Bangladeshi workers who tried to add obscene "cut-pieces" to their movie. In both cases, the crew member—in conjunction with various reserves—is summoned to plan *both* an upcoming, unfinished, contingent operation *and* the imponderable film.

There is no crude causality between the use of digital technologies in today's industry and the artistic worker's skill in visualizing the film. Yet given the close contact between these technologies and all artistic workers in *Décor* and *Poisonous Roses*, it is reasonable to assume that these workers underwent a lifelong apprenticeship in digital habits of visualization.[2] In analog times, artistic workers had to guess at how the image would be recorded, because the film negative was chemically affected by the environment in a way that remained invisible to the eye until treatment at the laboratory. Anticipating what the image looks like on negative is a disappearing skill today, because it is no longer necessary with video-assist monitors.[3] To quote the cinematographer Marwan Saber, "*what you see is what you get.*" Under these circumstances, it becomes important to consider how visual mediators are summoned on various reserves to anticipate some aspect of the film, and how these reserves summon artistic workers to converse, here and now, about what should be done in the film to come.

These kinds of conversations will be examined in the cases of scouting, image composition, and sound work, but I believe that the wider point about the mediation of the imponderable film holds in all operations where mediators—whether visual, written, or sonic—are used to anticipate, in the present, what some aspect of "the film" will eventually become. Whether in screenwriting, scouting, casting, set design, fitting, shooting, editing, coloring, or mixing, artistic workers try to anticipate what a given character, a given shooting location, a given actor, a given set, a given take, a given sequence of takes, a given color palette, or a given sound or musical track will "look like." What should be clear by now is that visualization is not bound by the single artistic worker's mind, but also by his/her authority over artistic choices and skill in trying to "see" the eventual film. While all crew members contribute to the labor necessary to make the film, this labor is suspended to the word of each artistic team's head and, ultimately, the director. The established hierarchy of artistic authority settles all artistic disagreements. In addition to being a matter of skill, then, visualizing the film is an exercise permeated by the micro-politics of artistic authority.

Scouting

In the opening vignette, one can sense Farghalli's irritation when Setohy tells him that he has no photo of the *niyaba* to show. Being the key inter-mediary between the production team and the artistic crew, Farghalli's interest in having a scouting picture of the *niyaba* is not about anticipat-ing what the location will look like on screen but about giving the artistic crew a good idea about the location's look. Indeed, executive crew mem-bers have a key role in helping artistic workers to visualize the film. When Setohy and I walked around the Dokki neighborhood to scout potential apartments, he was looking for buildings whose exterior appearance was in 1960s style as per the artistic crew's demands. Whenever he identified such buildings, he asked local doormen whether they had apartments willing to host a shoot and, when they were available, he photographed these apart-ments. One cannot reasonably assume that, whenever Setohy was looking at a building, or chatting away with a doorman, or taking a snapshot, he was constantly thinking about the apartment's look on screen, or even its logistical suitability as a shooting location. Rather, with a limited descrip-tion of the location in mind, Setohy's scouting contributed to narrowing down the apartment options that would be presented to the artistic crew on Farghalli's computer.

Although never acknowledged as an artistic practice, the executive work of gathering scouting pictures involves certain visual expectations. These expectations become apparent when production legworkers do not execute their scouting properly. For instance, when the production assistant Mah-moud Abdallah once got back to New Century's office after scouting trailer vans, he transferred all the scouting pictures onto Farghalli's computer. Farghalli opened the folder with the scouting pictures right away, and seeing a stream of disorganized image files he immediately asked, "Why is it not filed?" Abdallah looked dazed, and he gave some answer to the effect that the pictures were already somewhat organized in the order in which he took them, but Farghalli still asked him to separate each van in its own folder. Looking through the pictures of the first van, Farghalli again expressed deep dissatisfaction with Abdallah's work. Scrolling back and forth between two angles inside the van, he said, "There are only two pictures of the caravan's interior," which meant that he could not estimate how spacious it was. "Why didn't you take a picture like this?" at which point Farghalli aimed at the screen with two fingers stretched out in a V gesture, indicating a camera angle that would have shown an unphotographed corner in the van. Abdallah became defensive, arguing that the van was so tight that he could barely stand in it. Farghalli still kept asking why there were no more angles while browsing, to which Abdallah had no straight answer.

This interaction illustrates Farghalli's two major concerns when looking at scouting pictures. On the one hand, he tries to anticipate the logistics of shooting inside the van, which is why it is important to know its dimensions. On the other, Farghalli tries to present visuals in the best possible way to the artistic crew, who will in turn anticipate the film's look—hence the importance of filing pictures in an organized fashion and getting as many angles in the van as possible. In a way, Farghalli's criticisms of Mahmoud Abdallah's scouting were anticipating what artistic workers would tell him if they saw "missing" angles and disorganized images. When Farghalli showed scouting pictures from Alexandria to the art directors Asem Ali and Nihal Farouk, both started discussing which angles in the location would be best and how they would need to arrange the set to see these angles, using the same V gestures toward the screen that Farghalli used with Abdallah. When the art directors were missing an angle to complete their imagined picture, they would ask Farghalli whether he had a visual on it. Luckily, the scouting pictures covered their demands in this instance, but the executive crew's scouting cannot always match the artistic crew's expectations. This can have a significant impact on the artistic choice of locations, as I detail below.

When all the crew members were gathered around Farghalli's computer to look at scouting pictures for *Décor*, each artistic worker would see something different in the same image. To the art directors Ali and Farouk, it was a document of the way in which the eventual location could be transformed to give it the aspect they desired. To the cinematographer Hefny, it gave an idea of the location's natural light and atmosphere, and how he could texture the film's image. To the director Abdalla, it gave a general idea of the space in which he could stage his story. With all eyes set

6. Screen still from the contentious apartment in *Décor*, with Mustafa (Maged el-Kedwany) and Maha (Horeya Farghaly) pictured by the door. Photograph © New Century Film Production.

on Farghalli's screen while he scrolled down long lists of scouting pictures, one could easily imagine how the artistic crew's expectations concerning the eventual location (and, indeed, the eventual film) could come into conflict. While choosing Mustafa and Maha's apartment, Asem Ali adamantly refused to shoot in a Garden City apartment that both Abdalla and Hefny liked very much (see Figure 6). As he explained, the apartment's living room did not have enough "angles" *(zawaya)*, by which he meant that wherever the camera was positioned, the image's background would be a flat wall. This was aesthetically unpleasing in his estimation, by contrast with an imagined apartment that would have several layers of depth.

Ali's opposition was strong whenever he was shown pictures of the apartment, and he remained opposed to it even after he viewed it in person. Nevertheless, he eventually caved in to Abdalla's choice, because he explicitly recognized the director's ultimate authority over artistic decisions. Ahmad Abdalla, on his part, maintained that he was open to suggestions from his crew members, which is why they took time in choosing Mustafa and Maha's apartment, while putting production crew members through endless bouts of scouting. More to the point, this incident is instructive in showing how a hierarchy of authority settles artistic disputes. Even though Abdalla is a relatively open director with an interest in getting his artistic crew involved in all decisions, the hierarchical logic prevailed when Ali yielded to his judgment. Whether Ali was convinced to cede or forced to do so, the decision to shoot in one location or another would not have been settled in anyone's eyes until the director had approved it.

Moreover, this incident shows that even when the exact same image is under scrutiny, the way in which it is seen is determined by one's job on set and, specifically, one's authority over certain aspects that will materialize the film to come. This situation compounds the unpredictability involved in filmmaking, because while audiovisual possibilities can seem indefinite to the director, one can only imagine how many more possibilities are envisaged by the whole artistic crew. The crew's expectations can not only be in conflict at times, but also become mutually unintelligible, which is partly a matter of communication among artistic workers. When I asked Ahmad Abdalla whether he tries to communicate his overall vision to other crew members, he said that he tries to do it to some extent. In a more fundamental sense, he only works with people whose views he knows will not radically clash with his own—an opinion shared by all the directors I interviewed. If his cinematographer constantly wanted to have artificial lighting in settings where Abdalla saw natural lighting, and vice versa, he would not have considered working with this cinematographer in the first place. This does not mean that all crew members share an integrated vision of the film, but that some interpersonal groundwork has been done to avoid constant clashes over artistic decisions.

These clashes are unavoidable, however, because they are not strictly about linguistic (mis)communication or shared artistic background. Conflicts over visualization can represent a material difficulty in communicating images when there are divergent imaginings of the film's future look. The necessary approximations to this look are summoned by conversations among crew members with phones and laptops in hand. The scouting process for *Poisonous Roses* illustrates the central importance of these reserves in summoning mutually unintelligible ideas. In accordance with the director Ahmad Fawzi Saleh's wishes, I asked the production manager Edward Nabil to look for five missing locations: a gas station; a bourgeois bar; a hospital; Saqr's apartment in the tanneries; and a "high-class" apartment where his love interest Nahid lives. Fawzi and I gave Nabil brief verbal descriptions of what we wanted in each case and provided him with a printed copy of the screenplay to give him an idea about the film's world. A few days later, Nabil triumphantly walked into the office. "I've brought you everything, *ya basha*," he proudly boasted. When Fawzi asked to see the pictures, Nabil showed one or two photographs of what he deemed to be "high-class"

7 (above) and 8 (opposite). Exemplars from Edward Nabil's scouting portfolio, with the living room (7) and the bedroom (8) in a Mohandiseen apartment. Photograph © Al Batrik Art Production.

apartments and one long-shot photograph of a gas station, all taken on his Samsung phone. Fawzi swiftly told Nabil that the pictures were insufficient, as he (as a director) had no idea about the look of various angles within each location. Nabil proceeded verbally to describe what each location looked like, yet Fawzi would not have it: he wanted to see every angle depicted, in each location, and he methodically demonstrated to Nabil how he should go about photographing potential shooting locations (which in a way vindicates Farghalli's anxiety about scouting angles in *Décor*).

When Nabil went on further scouting missions, he brought back a more abundant portfolio of pictures, which eventually amounted to four or five "high-class" apartments, three hospitals, two gas stations, a few apartments in the tanneries, and a handful of bars. While Fawzi was impressed by the volume of images, he was not fully satisfied with the high-class apartments secured by Nabil (see Figures 7 and 8). Some were oddly painted, some had unseemly furniture, and others were partitioned in inconvenient

(continued)

ways. When Fawzi and I looked at these pictures, Fawzi would comment on various aspects of the apartment at once, including its color, its furniture, and its partitioning. When I showed the pictures to Omar Abdelwahab, the art director, and Houssam Habib, then the cinematographer, they made similar comments about the scouted apartments, although they had different opinions about which apartment they should secure. The artistic crew's indecision led Nabil on more and more scouting missions, and he grew increasingly irritated by this indecision, especially given that the low-cost yet high-class apartments he had found (most of them in the upper middle-class neighborhood of Mohandiseen) were being occupied over time. As he kept telling me, he thought that he had brought apartments with the exact specifications given by Fawzi (including a kitchen opening on a dining room, a large bathroom, high-class furniture), but the director and his artistic crew were still not convinced.

When I asked Fawzi what he had in mind for the "high-class" apartment, he would give me some evasive verbal detail. He mentioned that he wanted a "minimalist" apartment at some point. I had seen him discuss this term at length with Omar Abdelwahab and Adel el-Siwi, his artistic adviser and one of Egypt's foremost visual artists. Yet, I could not make out exactly what he wanted until he showed me generic pictures of minimalist apartments on his computer, which seemed to have been gathered on Google images (see Figures 10 and 11). We showed the folder to Nabil, who brought back pictures of new apartments in a similar style. Nabil kept referring to the new apartments as "high-class" just like the old ones, yet the thin epithet that we all used masked a vast difference between the two types of locations. The visual difference indexed a class distinction between Nabil and us. As executive workers like Nabil tend to come from more "popular" (sha'bi) backgrounds, the education of their eye—to use Bourdieu's expression (1986: 3)—is different from that of artistic workers, who tend to be middle or upper middle class. In this case, what we all took to be self-evidently "high-class" was visibly different, and the difference was made evident by the contrast between Nabil's scouting pictures and Fawzi Saleh's references.

In addition to highlighting a class difference between artistic and executive workers, this example illustrates how "executing" an artistic demand is never a mechanical matter, even when executive crew members have no say over the film's final look. Execution relies on a representation of what artistic crew members have in mind, which is admittedly difficult without

9 and 10. Exemplars from Ahmad Fawzi Saleh's list of "minimalist" apartments, with a living room (9) and a bathroom (10) in illustration. Photograph © Al Batrik Art Production.

tangible visual proxies to anchor the discussion. In the context of scouting for *Poisonous Roses*, it was vital to have enough scouting pictures to show Fawzi what the location would look like, just as it was necessary to show Nabil some pictures of minimalist apartments to give a better sense of the "high-class" apartments required. There is an obvious asymmetry, then, between the verbal descriptions given by the director to the production manager and the visual mediators exchanged between them.

Although trying to estimate the film's imponderable image is not impossible without visual mediators, it certainly seemed like the shooting locations became more tangible when they were broken down into concrete scouting pictures. This step did not exist in predigital times. According to Farghalli, the production team would select some locations to scout, then immediately get the artistic crew in a microbus to check the locations in person. The wider availability of digital cameras has allowed artistic crew members to select their preferred locations in advance. This has meant that the production's selection has become even more important and, arguably, has led to a greater specialization of scouting tasks in Egypt. In a sense, scouting pictures stand between the production team's pre-preselection of locations in daily scouting journeys and the artistic crew's preselection of locations to be seen in person. For both *Décor* and *Poisonous Roses*, final decisions were rendered after scouting in person, but the way in which locations were selected was heavily inflected by scouting legwork and the resulting pictures. "The film," in turn, became contingent on the locations eventually selected, although its overall look remained by and large unpredictable at this stage.

Image Composition

Once locations are chosen, the process whereby the image becomes gradually actualized evolves to the rhythm of each artistic department—direction, acting, cinematography, art direction, styling, and sound. Image and sound work cannot be claimed to reside within each artist's mind in this sense, because they are produced through a combination of collective labor, anticipation, and technological use. In this context, it is useful to examine the work of art directors in more depth. Watching art directors and their assistants engage in ever so slight adjustments to their designs with a click of the mouse or a stroke of the pencil, I became keenly aware of the way in which cinematic imagination was not immediately poured onto the paper or the screen, but constantly adjusted in dialogic unfolding with reserves summoning a given set or prop design to the artist's mind.

In *Décor*, the designs drawn by art directors Asem Ali and Nihal Farouk as well as their assistant Mohammed Ezzat were created using two software packages: AutoCAD, which was used to sketch floor plans, and SketchUp, which was used to draw more detailed set and prop models. Each software has a different set of affordances. AutoCAD, originally an architectural package, can produce linear designs to outline the location's skeleton. SketchUp can produce three-dimensional, to-scale, color designs that flesh out each prop on set in more detail. One software does not afford a "better" visualization than the other, as both are used along with rough pencil sketches and handwritten notes to anticipate different facets of what the design will look like on camera. What counts, in other words, is not the drawing technique per se, but the way in which this technique materializes an anticipated set or prop for the art directors who design it and the craftsmen who will execute it.

Ali, Farouk, and Ezzat discussed their designs at New Century's office. Since digital drawings came in very heavy formats, it was difficult to exchange them by email or upload them on video platforms. The software could even be troublesome in face-to-face settings. On a mid-December afternoon right before the shooting in *Décor*, Farouk and Ezzat were sitting in the office when Ali walked in. He asked Ezzat to open the apartment design they were preparing on his laptop, and the file took a long time to load. "SketchUp is tired," Ezzat joked. Later, Farouk asked the assistant decorator to bring some adjustments to the same file, but when it took too long to load, she explained the changes using a printed AutoCAD plan. The plan was covered in pencil marks, including annotated camera angles and some sketches to determine the position of furniture on set (see Figure 11). She said she wanted to enlarge the living room a little and put two additional chairs with a lamp in the corner of the next room. Ezzat made a counterproposal to insert a large futon instead of two chairs. "I don't understand, tell me more," pondered Farouk. Ezzat tried to draw his idea, but could not draw very well, at which point I intervened to explain what he meant by navigating the plan with my fingers. Ezzat agreed with the explanation. Having understood his proposal, Farouk said, "I'll think about it," before leaving the office.

This brief interaction illustrates how the software itself is not crucial to the work of designing the set, but works with other reserves to summon its imagined result. Given the unavailability of the SketchUp design, Farouk, Ezzat, the printed AutoCAD plan, and I became momentarily absorbed in imagining a small corner in Mustafa and Maha's apartment. As we saw in the case of scouting, communication about "the film" is neither transparent nor exclusive to the crew member's mind. Had Ezzat not been able to draw his proposed setup or had I not explained what Ezzat meant to Farouk, certain zones of mutual incomprehension would have remained to be clarified. This incomprehension, whether in scouting or set design, is partly what artistic workers try to overcome in the film's production process. This mediation does not solve the imponderability of imagining the set in the eyes of art directors, but it breaks it down into a series of contingent decisions, including decisions as small as setting a sofa instead of two chairs in a room's corner.

Interactions between the art directors and the craftsmen who will execute their set/prop designs further illustrate how imponderability becomes broken down into contingent decisions. I once observed Ezzat talking to a carpenter about the design of the bookshelves in Mustafa and Maha's apartment. Sitting on his computer, Ezzat showed the SketchUp design to the carpenter and detailed its measurements, its overall shape, and the decisive fact that it should be built in separate blocks. The library was indeed crucial to a shot envisioned by the director Ahmad Abdalla, where the protagonist Maha walks through an empty wall and then turns around to reveal that bookshelves had filled it. The motion was to be achieved by having the cameraman walk through the wall behind the protagonist, turn around with her, only to see craftsmen filling the wall with bookshelves (see Figures 11 and 12). In addition to discussing measurements with the carpenter, Ezzat had to explain to him *how* to build the library, because the carpenter's instinct to build one large block would have made the anticipated shot impossible. The film's image, once again, hinges on a complex division of labor between artistic and executive workers: a director's wish, an assistant decorator's design, and a carpenter's understanding.

Image composition is not just a design-to-execution affair, as this description of art direction might make it seem; it involves constant "*tests*" to ensure that the design works with the image. These tests anticipate the creation of audiovisual material on set, except that they further fragment the material into its elements: color, lighting, costumes, camera movement, actor movement. This is clear in the way in which the artistic crews on *Décor* and *Poisonous Roses* planned their shots for the upcoming shooting in the very space where the shooting was about to take place. This excerpt, noted down on December 17, 2013, at Studio Misr, illustrates this practice in *Décor*:

> AA [Ahmad Abdalla] enters on location with his backpack and explains in space what the *shot* he wants looks like. Tarek asks two

11 and 12. Final shot of the library being displaced by workers behind Maha, before the move (11) and after (12). Photograph © New Century Film Production.

kinds of questions: one is about lighting (what would the lighting look like in the shot) and the other is about the position and the angle of the camera, as well as the lens to use. . . . AA would either give him a clear answer like "I want this thing or that thing," or a less clear answer like "I guess it'll look like this" or "We'll discuss it later" or "As a cinematographer, you can decide what to do at that moment." Zohairy had his screenplay in hand and noted down all (or a great deal of) the explanations. . . .

AA uses V gestures or open-hand movements (miming the frame) to indicate where the camera is positioned and how it will move. He moves himself as though he were the camera in space (so he embodies the camera in the shot that he is explaining), and he shows through the elements around him where the actors and the objects on screen will be positioned. This visualization is a little inadequate because Tarek and Zohairy keep asking questions to know *exactly* what it will look like: exactly where the light, the camera's position, the camera's movement, the actors' movement will be. . . . Every time, AA would give some answers and impressions: one of the elements that helped him was to position himself as the camera in space, and to explain what he would "see" as the camera. . . . One question that Tarek asks very often to AA is "*ana shayif eih* [what am I seeing]?" . . .

At some point, Tarek took out his 5D camera and started taking pictures at the positions where AA imagined that he would put the camera. After taking these pictures, he would show AA on the camera's screen what the shot looks like, then AA would comment on whether it was the shot he wanted to see, or whether he wanted to modify something, or whether there would be future modifications to bring to the shot that he sees right there and then that would make it better. . . . Tarek gave different options about how the shot could be filmed, then AA would indicate whether he agreed or not. What is interesting is that the discussion is not [just] verbal, but it is about what is seen on camera.

This description summarizes the key tenets of the argument developed in this chapter: it shows how artistic imagining is not just inside the director's head, but distributed across a range of agents and mediators. It shows how reserves anticipate the future film image and its making (the 5D camera, the director's camera-body). It also shows how the imponderable image is broken down into a series of contingent decisions on movement, angle, position, frame, and so on.

It is noteworthy that the workers on *Décor* and *Poisonous Roses* all claimed that this patient testing was unusual in the Egyptian film industry. While Abdalla, Hefny, and Zohairy were visualizing their shots at Studio Misr a week prior to the shooting, the location manager Ahmad Abdallah Abdel Halim sat outside the studio, waiting late into the night so as to remain available in case they needed anything. "It's the first time I've seen a director and his crew do something like that," he said. Normally, in Abdel Halim's view, the director comes on location one day before the shooting to "study his shots well" (*yizaker al-shuttat kwayis*). He then comes the next day to shoot, adjusting the light a little, the actors' movements a little, and explaining to everyone what the shot looks like, then shoots right away. Abdel Halim thought that Ahmad Abdalla's way of proceeding was unusual and unprofessional. This can be taken as additional evidence of the boundary-work between "commercial" and "independent" filmmaking discussed in Chapter 1. According to Abdel Halim, Abdalla—who has a background in "independent" cinema—is unprofessional because he does not abide by the market's dominant working norms. Still, it is not unreasonable to believe that cheaper productions would not have the budget nor the time to allow extensive testing as in *Décor* or *Poisonous Roses*, although there is evidence to suggest that testing as a principle is not unique to these two productions.

For *Décor*, Asem Ali, Nihal Farouk, and Tarek Hefny tested lighting and color while set builders were hard at work at Studio Misr. All three stood around Hefny's Cannon 5D camera, while two to three gaffers set one lamp with a white board diffusing the light evenly over the surface of the wall (see figure 13). Prior to the test, Farouk and Ali had asked their painters to paint two different shades of yellow on either side of the wall in order to test whether they looked different on camera. After taking some pictures, Hefny showed Farouk and Ali that there was little to no difference between the two shades on his camera's screen. The discussion was especially important because all visuals had to be imagined with a black-and-white image in mind to anticipate *Décor*'s final look. On the black-and-white camera screen, both shades seemed of a dim, indistinct grey. Ali called the chief painter and asked him to get the darker of the two shades and make it three shades darker, then to paint all the walls in this same color. The imponderable image became somewhat more contingent with this decision: the wall would now have a certain yellow shade, which was decided by the art directors (given their artistic authority) with the help of a visual mediator (the Cannon 5D screen) at a specific juncture in the filmmaking process (while the set was being built).

Once again, it is important to note that the artistic work of image testing is supported by executive work. During all their tests—which also included tests on wallpaper textures, furniture textures, lighting sheen,

13. Final shot of the painted wall, seen on both sides of the door. Photograph © New Century Film Production.

glass transparency—Farouk, Ali, and Hefny would give orders to the gaffers, prop assistants, and craftsmen at their disposal to move around lights, props, or larger items on set. Even though they would be the ones speaking while all the executive workers remained in utter silence, the artistic workers were surrounded by about ten workers ready to be summoned to a given task at any moment. The parallel between executive work and technological devices acting as reserves could not be more apparent in this case. While artistic workers were summoned to imagine the film's image, they were summoning both digital devices and executive workers to produce visual mediators to help in actualizing the film to come. One must not take the silence of executive workers on artistic matters to mean that they are uninvolved in creating the film product. Rather, their intervention is conditioned by the politics of artistic authority, which gives them no say on the artistic product while being physically involved in its making.

The video-assist monitor and its attending crew have a similar role on set.[4] Not all productions can afford a video-assist, but its presence has become standard in the industry. On *Poisonous Roses*, the director Ahmad Fawzi Saleh was initially against hiring a video-assist monitor because it would cost extra money, but he recanted his position after a few days of shooting in narrow spaces, where standing next to the camera's monitor had become uncomfortable. "The best thing to happen in this film is that there's a video-assist," echoed the director Ahmad Abdalla on *Décor*. These

مدير الإنتاج

محمد سطوحي

14. High-angle shot on the chandelier while it is being raised, from the opening credits with the production manager's name on display, Mohammed Setohy. Photograph © New Century Film Production.

words were uttered jokingly while watching a high-angle shot on a small monitor sitting in his lap. The camera was positioned near the ceiling (see figure 14) and, given his fear of heights, Abdalla was glad to avoid climbing up next to the camera. Instead, he watched his little monitor while all the crew members watched a bigger monitor with a grainier image. When the video-assist operator was told by Abdalla that he did not need the big monitor because it was too grainy, he started packing it away, but Farghalli swiftly intervened to keep it because it allowed everyone to watch the image. This illustrates the way in which the practice of visualization is in effect shared by many workers on set, although it is considered the prerogative of the director (by the video-assist operator in this case).

Much like Farghalli's computer in scouting, the video-assist monitor is a central gathering point for all artistic workers on set (see Figure 15). To these workers, it mediates the imponderability of the audiovisual material by breaking it into smaller components, a little like set designs broke down sets or like image tests broke down colors, lights, and textures. I will not bore the reader with the innumerable occasions on which a director, cinematographer, art director, or stylist asked to twitch this light, move this prop, or straighten this shirt based on what they saw on the video-assist on set. What is important to bear in mind is that these adjustments are oriented toward the future film image, which is being summoned by the

15. Crew members assembled around the video-assist (foreground, left to right) Ahmad Abdalla, Omar el-Zohairy, Nihal Farouk, Mohamed Setohy; (background, left to right) Hany Morsy, a location service worker, Nadia Ahmed, three lighting technicians, and the anthropologist's forehead; Credit: Yasser Shafiey. Photograph © New Century Film Production.

video-assist monitor to the artistic workers who, in turn, are summoned to adjust it. These adjustments are possible thanks to a certain division of labor (where video-assist operators are responsible for troubleshooting all equipment issues), a certain production process (where the video-assist lies in between the scouting pictures, set designs, and image tests on the one hand and the audiovisual material on the other), and certain technological devices (such as the video-assist monitor). These elements are crucial to making an overall imponderable problem—what will the film look like?— into a series of contingent decisions on the image.

Sound Work

Sound is a neglected component of film production in Egypt. This neglect is apparent in the contrast between the video-assist monitor, which attracts all eyes on set, and the microphones, which are largely invisible and seem unimportant outside the sound engineer's hand. This sense of neglect is not just palpable in terms of equipment, it is the subject of regular complaints by sound engineers, boom operators, sound mixers, and musical composers. The issue, in part, is the lack of time, resources, and attention devoted to sound work compared with image work. On numerous occasions in *Décor*, the sound engineer Ahmad Saleh and his assistant Ahmad Abdel Nasser insisted that they were left to do a job that would be held by at least thirty crew members in Hollywood. Saleh and his assistant worked on all aspects of sound recording, design, and postproduction, while the film was mixed and the music composed by two small companies, each having hired four to five workers. Contrast this diminished manpower with the forty to fifty crew members working on different aspects of the film's image. In this context, it becomes understandable that the well-known editor Mona Rabie, who argues that the sound is "half of my editing work," could say that "a lot of producers are still not interested" in sound. "We stay three months in editing, and they want the sound in a month, or two weeks. . . . The sound is definitely coming out badly."

This neglect can be attributed to an implicit ocularcentrism in the film industry, that is, an assumed superiority of vision over all other senses. This privileging of vision over sound has been the subject of extensive criticism in the anthropology of the senses (Ingold, 2000; Howes, 2005), in sound studies (Pinch and Bijsterveld, 2004; Sterne, 2012), and even in visual anthropology (Henley, 2010). Hirschkind (2006) and Fahmy (2013) have been among the few scholars to call for an ethnographic and historical study of sound in Egypt, where there is again a marked bias toward the visual in historical and ethnographic research. Such calls have been fruitful in reinstating sound as an object of academic concern, yet they have done little to explore the relations between sound and image in situated practices of audiovisual media production. This relationship has been best explored in film studies, most notably in Michel Chion's work on the inseparability between sound and image in the experience of film perception (1994). Chion's scholarship moves away from treating sound and image as *faits accomplis*, as sensory stimuli that are interpreted differently according to different sensory hierarchies. Instead, he explores how both sounds and images integrate into an unstable and fragmented audiovisual product, which can be seen-heard in different ways. In a similar vein, some media anthropologists have described how the marriage of sound and image is anticipated by workers who, here and now, cannot hear or see what the sound/image will become in the film to come (see Grimaud, 2003: 195–222; Pandian, 2015: 181–204).

Sound work, like image work, is part of an operational sequence: on-set recording, sound editing, soundtrack composition, and sound mixing. Throughout this sequence, the digitally recorded sound is being constantly reworked by the sound engineer, the composer, the mixer, and their assistants through various technological devices (such as microphones, booms, computers). These devices act as reserves summoning the worker's mind to the eventual sound in the film, while being summoned to amplify sounds that cannot be heard except through technological intervention. The importance of these technologies is apparent on set. While we were shooting *Poisonous Roses*, the boom operator Ahmad Rashdan complained about a high-pitched noise that did not come from the refrigerator. I began distinguishing the noise when he mentioned it, but I could not identify its source. Rashdan smiled and pointed to a lamp above the kitchen counter. When I looked intently at it, the lamp's gentle flicker matched the buzzing noise that we had been hearing. Rashdan said that he started hearing the noise when he placed his boom microphone above the counter, without knowing if it was produced by an interference with the wireless signal connecting the boom to the recorder or if it was in the sound environment.

This buzzing noise would need to be removed in postproduction, but the whole issue could not have been heard until the sound equipment selected out the noise, that is, until the equipment summoned specific "unwanted" noises to the boom operator's mind. As I argue in the next chapter, such noises are unwanted because they are thought to interfere with the imagined audience's enchantment with the film. However, the very fact that they are identified as part of a process where they need to be "cleaned out" after being recorded is summoned to the operator's mind by his recording equipment, which helps him distinguish the noise from the ordinary sound environment on set. Identifying the noise takes a certain auditory skill, which is not dissimilar to the skills developed by image workers. Still, the point is not just to have a good "eye" or a good "ear," in both physical and aesthetic terms, but also to be able to anticipate what needs to be done, visually and aurally, to the recorded material.

"The most important thing is to get the dialogue clearly," said the boom operator Ahmad Abdel Nasser, who was wrapping up a long explanation of on-set recording. The operation of sound recording is designed to create sound material (with dialogue and ambiance), while ensuring that the sound edit starts with as little noise as possible. While shooting in hot weather in *Décor*, I asked Abdel Nasser whether the humming of air conditioners caused a recording problem. "It's the easiest noise to remove," he replied, explaining that it has a very different frequency from recorded dialogue. In consequence, the sound editor can isolate the sound, then either remove it or insert it outright throughout the movie, thereby making it "inaudible" by blending it into the background noise. Such anticipations are integral to the practice of sound editing. In *Décor*, the star actress' voice was a little too high-pitched and nasal on set. While cleaning the soundtrack in his initial edit, Ahmad Saleh saw a mismatch between the voice and some scenes' emotionality, so he called for its dubbing while still cleaning the sound. This kind of anticipation is reminiscent of the work done by artistic crew members in scouting, set design, and image testing. The sound worker is not just thinking about the immediate recording of sound, but the way in which this sound will be transformed at a later stage of film production and, eventually, in "the film." Perhaps more evidently than in image work, where technological devices might seem superfluous to the artist's imagination, sound equipment illustrates how anticipating the film's imponderable sound cannot be done with the ear alone but is summoned by devices making this sound concrete and contingent.

Across the Egyptian film industry, there is a common representation according to which digital equipment can integrally recreate the film's sound in postproduction. This representation illustrates the hold of ideas concerning *tiknulujya* and its multifarious powers in Cairo. While shooting in *Décor*, the set was interrupted when the sound engineer Ahmad Saleh asked production workers to shut off the water pipes, because the noise of running water overshadowed his recording. The interruption lasted around ten minutes, until the production crew was able to shut the right tap, but the line producer Farghalli could not hold back from sneaking in a caustic comment: "You know there's technology. . . . You can dub, right away, don't worry!" Saleh was deeply irritated by the remark, because it betrayed not only a neglect for his work on set, but also an unawareness of the conditions under which dubbing takes place in Egypt. Unlike recorded images, which cannot be altered as significantly, 70 to 80 percent of recorded sounds can be fixed with dubbing and sound mixing, according to Ahmad Abdel Nasser. This is not possible in Egypt, however, where the sound team is too understaffed to engage in such feats of sound design. Moreover, given the costs associated with dubbing studios and the digital sound editor's ability to mitigate many noises in sound material, dubbing on an extensive scale is not prevalent in today's industry.[5]

Whether in sound editing, dubbing, or mixing, sound postproduction involves just as much anticipation as the work of image postproduction. As the sound needs to be synchronized with the film's image, sound postproduction workers use an image "*reference*" while working. This is neither the conformed raw material nor the image treated through coloring or graphics. It is a compressed image acting as a visual mediator: close enough to the final image to allow the worker to watch it as though it were "the film," yet light enough to avoid burdening the computer's hardware and hard drives. In sound editing, the reference image serves to synchronize each sound effect with its on-screen source. In dubbing, it serves the additional purpose of indicating to the actor when and how s/he should speak, because the original performance on screen needs to be mimicked with a new voice. Yet the adjustment of sound to image is perhaps best illustrated with sound mixing.

The young mixer Abdelrahman "Mana" Mahmoud once showed me a sequence in his film *Villa 69* (2013). The scene featured a cameo by the prominent director Khairy Beshara, who was shown jogging around the protagonist's neighborhood. There was a moving medium-shot of the jogger running toward the camera, which was taken in such a way that the boom operator could not record Beshara's actual bodily exertions. Mana wanted to show me the original shot without added effects and then the same shot with added breathing and running noises. The overall impression made by the scene was transformed. As Mana and I felt, the impact of Beshara's bodily exertion was not palpable in the original material, where the character seemed to move in a ghostly manner through the frame. However, the exertion was made apparent by the mixer's additions. Mana made such adjustments whenever he felt like the image was "missing" something: a sticker noise when the protagonist removed a band-aid from his face; the reverberation of a door when a window was closed; the uneven humming of an old car in Cairo. Such contingent decisions show how the mixer's "technical" work has important aesthetic effects on the film. Moreover, it illustrates how the imponderability of the film's sound is broken into a series of smaller choices divided among sound workers working on specific equipment and inserted in an operational sequence going from on-set recording to the final mix.

"When I work, I like to try out sound effects . . . so I can feel how the shot is. . . . Sound makes a huge difference." This is how the editor Mona Rabie described the importance of anticipating the marriage of image and sound in image editing. This attention to sound is not shared by most workers on set, and it is certainly not accorded the same artistic import as the image. As Mana once deplored, there is no sound designer in Egypt to bring the score and the mix into one complete "vision" *(ru'ya)*. This aural vision is entrusted to the director in Egypt, although Egyptian directors seldom have such a vision in Mana's opinion. A case in point is the director Daoud Abdel Sayyed, who explained that he is content with giving general directives to his artistic crew, without asking for specific shots, lenses, melodies, or instruments. "I let my colleagues work," he explained. In *Kit-Kat*, he told his musical composer Rageh Daoud to put some oud music accompanied by a very nostalgic instrument. "What would be the most nostalgic instrument?" he asked him. "The organ," replied Daoud, to which Abdel Sayyed said, "Okay, oud and organ." Daoud was not convinced that the combination would work musically, but Abdel Sayyed insisted. It produced *Kit-Kat*'s unusual yet acclaimed soundtrack. A directive such as "oud and organ" is hardly what one could call a vision in sound design, yet it is with such directives that most musical soundtracks are composed in Egypt. Thus, just like scouting, set design, image testing, and all forms of sound work, musical composition relies on mediating equipment, images, and sounds, manipulated by workers within a specific operational sequence trying to anticipate what the imponderable film will look like. Scouting pictures produced by production crew members allow artistic workers to anticipate the shooting location; image tests made by the artistic crew allow them to anticipate the set's look on screen; and the image "*references*" used by sound editors and mixers allow them to anticipate the audience's reaction to an "unwanted" noise or an uncanny jogger.

Visual Mediation

A central problem in visual anthropology lies in determining the distinct value of the visual when, as Pinney argues, "the historian [or the anthropologist] reads into [images] *what he has already learned by other means*" (2005: 260). The visual, in this sense, is taken as an *illustration* of an argument whose substance is not necessarily visible. This is evident in most ethnographies of media production, where the typical attention to narrative, imagined audience and labor is very useful to situate the lifeworld of media producers, but cannot answer Pinney's challenge to examine the visual "in itself" (see Larkin, 2008; Ganti, 2012; Ortner, 2013; Wilkinson-Weber, 2014; Martin, 2016). One core reason is that these works do not engage with the role of visual (and aural) mediators in the process of media production, with some exceptions.[6] This chapter has examined how such mediators summon crew members with the appropriate skill and authority to anticipate some aspect of "the film" and its production process. I would suggest that the presence of these mediators is crucial in film production, and that their irreducible presence should attract the anthropologist as much as it attracts the filmmaker.

Anthropologists interested in the materiality of images have long argued that the sensory properties of images are vital to their social uses (Pinney, 2001, 2004; Edwards and Hart, 2004; MacDougall, 2006; Pink, 2006). While this argument is suggestive given the embodied nature of visualization in film production, it remains insufficient to explain the role of mediators and technological devices in concrete sociotechnical processes, where the sensory responses produced by mediators are not as important as their anticipatory potential. To the anthropologist, the scouting picture might look like an empty apartment; to the art director, it might look like the background of a film shot; to the director, it might look like a space where s/he can stage a story. None of these views are imagined by ingenious individual minds, as everyone relies on a concrete picture to discuss the problems at hand. Yet these pictures are virtual in Deleuze's sense, because they are "in actualization, in the process of being actualized, inseparable from the movement toward [their] actualization" (1966: 36). Crucially, the virtual scouting picture is not a property of the art director's or the producer's or even my own imagination, but a kind of visual potential inscribed within the scouting picture and manifested through the filmmaking process.

To the filmmaker, mediators are immediate iconic materializations of what a location, a set, an actor, or a sound effect will "look like" later, in the film. The conventional division of labor between artistic and executive crew members, the conventional sociotechnical sequence of film production, as well as everyday technological use are crucial in summoning this eventual film. As Grimaud has argued,

> Grasping how the film evolves through a dynamic triangulation between the screenplay, internal images, and the anticipated camera [that is, the imagined film] until shooting is trying to answer this question: how does a "production mechanism" of internal images become a form of interaction? For social actors involved in the *story session*, it is about agreeing on a "common vision," but the issue

very quickly moves away from . . . an agreement of minds (to be enacted at the level of mental images) toward the search for an organizational agreement (of means, of materials and visual effects) through interaction with the specialists (the choreographer, the costume designer, etc.) (2003: 99–100).

Whatever will be the film at any point in this interaction remains an unknowable but expected potentiality, which is made concrete through situated imaginings, conversations, and mediators. This process can seem most uncertain—I still vividly recall the director Ahmad Fawzi Saleh's angst throughout the screenwriting and preparations for *Poisonous Roses*—but "the film" is in fact imponderable, because its actualization is always already expected without being knowable in advance. The imponderable film is made contingent at every juncture in the operational sequence, such that Fawzi would say that he could "see" his protagonist better once he had chosen the actor, or that he could "see" his story better once he had looked at the material. This is not just a product of the iconic proximity between the casting pictures, the material, and the film to come. It is equally a product of cumulative decisions through which an initially hollow screenplay with paper characters gradually turns into a concrete image with on-screen incarnations. This actualization is not the preordained realization of a singular artistic "vision," as I have shown, but the result of contingent decisions made within a certain configuration of labor, anticipation, and technological use.

First Cut

"I've heard about you from Ahmad," says the editor Sara Abdalla when I first meet her. I was introduced to Sara by Jennifer Peterson, who was working on *Décor*'s marketing. "Where do you write?" she asks, thinking that I am a journalist probably. Sara is looking at two computer screens linked to a desktop tower and a hard drive in one of New Century's new editing booths. One screen shows a project in Final Cut Pro, the other shows the film's image. I recognize the scene: it is from our last day of shooting in the doctor's clinic.

When I see the image—my first glimpse into *Décor*'s post-production—I cannot help but make a nostalgic noise. "It must be the first time you see it in black-and-white," mentions Sara with a smile. "The monitors were in black-and-white on location," I answer while staring at the screen with wonder. Months after Badawy had told me about *Décor* in his office, months after scouting, set building, and shooting, I could see the fruit of all this labor in an air-conditioned office where Sara was sipping on a juice box. "How long is the cut?" I asked in a daze. "We already have a two-hour-ten-minutes-long first cut. We assembled it during the shooting." I had to leave Sara and Jennifer right away, but they both promised that I would see the cut when I came back from the United States.

Around a month later, I was beginning to feel impatient to see the cut. I had tried to contact Sara Abdalla several times to no avail. I would still come regularly to New Century's office to sit down with production crew members. One day, I arrive at the office when no one is in except the office assistant Ashraf, who brings me some tea. I call Jennifer to check whether she is in, and she invites me to her office upstairs.

We chit-chat about several things, and I ask about *Décor's* ongoing postproduction. "We've been waiting to check the color tests for a trailer, but Ahmad Abdalla is traveling tomorrow and Tarek [Hefny] is busy shooting a commercial." Jennifer mentions that Ahmad Abdalla is in the editing room with Sara Abdalla as we speak, trying to work before he travels.

A FedEx box is delivered to Jennifer's office while we chat. She opens it and finds a little red hard drive and a USB stick: they contain the expected color tests. Jennifer goes downstairs to give them to Ahmad Abdalla and I go down with her. I briefly say hi to Ahmad and Sara in the editing booth. Perhaps out of impatience and angst, I tell the director I am free to watch the film whenever he is ready to show it.

"I don't think anyone on the crew has seen the film, have they?" I ask Jennifer intently when we leave the editing room. "Well . . . I know [the well-known editor] Mona Rabie saw it, and [the well-known director] Yousry Nasrallah saw it with Ahmad Badawy in another showing," she replied. Setohy and Hany had arrived by then and were eating in the production office. I barely sit down with them when Ahmad Abdalla comes in to greet us. "Sara wants to see you," he says.

I am a little startled, but I go back to the editing room. "Come in," she says with a welcoming smile while I stand diffidently by the door. The mystery shrouding this room has made me hesitant to enter what, in this moment, seems like the temple in which the film is created. I feel a rush of excitement and curiosity. I return to the production office, take my belongings, and come back to Sara in the editing room.

"Do you have some time?" asks Sara while retrieving some files on screen. "The cut is an hour and fifty-two minutes." I nod while saying a hesitant yes. "Turn off the light." I am still in disbelief: "Did Ahmad Abdalla tell you I could watch the film?" "Yes!" she says with a hint of surprise in her voice. I sit down in front of the two computers. "The viewing conditions aren't ideal," Sara goes on, "[the film is] divided into several chapters." "Is it your way of working with Ahmad Abdalla?" I ask. "No, it's just a *technical* thing . . . we have to send each chapter to the sound-edit or the coloring or the composer so they work on each one separately." Sara is done with her setup, and the image on the small computer screen next to the Final Cut project transfers onto a larger LCD screen that I had not noticed yet, mounted right above the desk.

Sara screens the film. We watch mostly in silence. I am stunned by how easily I recognize where exactly every scene was shot, how it was shot, whether it was difficult or not, where I was standing on location while the shot was taken. I am also stunned by how much more expressive the actors look on screen as opposed to the location's experience. I cannot help but laugh in wonder, excitement, and recognition at some points in the cut: when the clapper Abdelsalam Radwan appears in his brief role as Maha's doctor, with a line that became a running joke on location ("Maha . . . Madame Maha . . ."), or when I appear as an extra in the clinic's waiting room. "Everyone who participated in the film is in it," mentions Sara. "Ahmad Saleh, Tarek, Nihal, Farghalli, Ahmad Abdalla, Zohairy, the script supervisors. . . ."

After the private screening, Sara smiles and says, "I've given you something, now you have to give me something back." I start by saying that I really liked some things in the movie: the transitions between Sharif's and Mustafa's world (especially the very first one); the final scene; the graphics. "There's a lot to be done," says Sara about the unfinished video effects. After these compliments, Sara grows impatient: "Get into the bad stuff faster!" I chuckle and mention that the *avant-titre* was a little disconcerting *(murbik)* to me, perhaps because the cuts were too fast. "I don't understand where we are, what happens, and why the rhythm is so fast compared to the rest of the movie." "I might cut less at the very beginning, but Ahmad wants the pace to be very fast," says Sara while thinking out loud. I add that I generally found the dialogue too long, in the scene where Maha asks Mustafa for a divorce, for instance.

"The scenes you've talked about were already cut down from the previous version. . . . It's a comment we've received a lot." I agree and explain to Sara that we as an audience do not need to hear the dialogue in the last scene between the three protagonists, when Maha is asked to choose between Sharif and Mustafa. "You don't think we need to hear this?" "I wouldn't want to cut it all off," I reply, "but it needs to be cut a little." Sara jots down my remarks on paper.

From mesmerized spectator, I became a test viewer, a guinea pig whose opinions might influence the shape of the film to come. This is still a first cut, one of many I am sure, but I am filled with a heady mixture of wonder and anxiety about how this impromptu screening would influence *Décor*.

6

Enchantment

Ahmad Fawzi Saleh used to recall comments he had received on his screenplay over the years while we were rewriting *Poisonous Roses*. He cherished one comment in particular: the Brazilian director Karim Aïnouz had told him that *Poisonous Roses* needed to be about the ambiguous relationship between Tahiya and her brother Saqr, all inside the world of the tanneries, without bothering about Saqr's bourgeois lover Nahid. It is no wonder that in the summer of 2015, when we rewrote the storyline to make Tahiya the protagonist, Fawzi would remember Aïnouz's comment in private and admonish himself. "I wish I had listened to him earlier," he muttered on several occasions. The fact that Aïnouz, as a Brazilian viewer, was attracted to this storyline proved to be an important reason why Fawzi was comfortable with changing his screenplay. Fawzi wanted above all to appeal to an international audience, beyond the confines of Egyptian critics and viewers, an audience contrasting with the one stereotypically imagined in the "commercial" film industry. In this sense, he would often invoke the abstract figure of the "Brazilian viewer" to describe a viewer who had nothing to do with Egypt yet would be intrigued by his story, transforming his interaction with Aïnouz into an exemplary moment of international viewership.

In a similar manner, Fawzi would often have recourse to my own judgment as an indication of what the non-Egyptian audience might understand or feel. Since I knew that this was the way in which he approached my comments, I would cheekily preface my interventions with the phrase, "As a Brazilian viewer, I would/would not. . . ." There is, of course, no sense in which Fawzi or I knew what Brazilian audiences would feel if they watched *Poisonous Roses*, and I have no illusion that I can speak in the name of these audiences. The "Brazilian viewer" was a placeholder to describe the anticipated audience of Fawzi's film, whose composition and eventual reactions remained imponderable to us. When I initially wrote these lines, *Poisonous Roses* was still in postproduction and we knew little about its prospective empirical audiences. Yet at every significant juncture in production, the imponderable audience is broken down into contingent decisions taken by filmmakers. Through these decisions, an unpredictable yet expected viewership is produced with certain assumptions in mind and mediators in hand, both inscribing the audience into the film's making.

Addressing an audience is a central component of the filmmaker's practice, yet the exact nature and scale of the imagined audience is impossible to assess in the course of film production.[1] Media anthropologists have long been interested in the way in which mass-mediated narratives allow audiences to situate their local identities within a national, regional, or global world (see Dickey, 1993; Hahn, 1994; Armbrust, 1998; Mankekar, 1999; Abu-Lughod, 2005). This interest in empirical audiences is not equivalent to the interest taken by media producers in their anticipated audiences, which has been examined in a different way by media production ethnographies. In Bollywood, Ganti describes how Bombay filmmakers anticipate their audience's reaction with "production fictions, which are truisms, axioms, and structures of belief about what is necessary for commercial success" (2012: 12). Such fictions are integral to the lay sociological analysis through which media-makers imagine their audience's composition.[2] To quote Mazzarella, "in the culture industries, it helps to maintain the fiction that media and marketing are merely 'responding' to the already-constituted desires of audiences—even as many decisions are actually made on a hunch basis by a surprisingly small group of people worldwide" (2004: 354).

Production fictions are just some of the noticeable ways in which an audience is anticipated by filmmakers, because they are often verbalized and debated. However, there are more subtle ways in which the audience's reaction is instilled *within* the practice of filmmaking, some of which are suggested in Hoek's ethnography of Bangladeshi popular cinema (2014). After explaining that the audience targeted by romantic action movies in Dhaka are young male country dwellers *(mofussil)*, Hoek demonstrates how this imagined audience is inscribed in the movie's making: how the producer asks for additional "spice" in the screenplay to sell the movie to the "lecherous" male audience; how the cameraman twists his camera in order to create surprise effects among excited viewers; how the editor inserts juicy cut-pieces to attract rural men to the theater. These practices are not production fictions, but a set of sociotechnical operations inscribing the audience into the movie's making. No matter whether the empirical audience reacts in accordance with the filmmaker's expectation, the imagined audience has practical effects on the process of film production, some spoken and others unspoken. Thus, mediating the audience's imponderable reaction involves a set of contingent actions by filmmakers, whether it is writing an extra dialogue line, twisting the camera, or inserting a new scene in the editing room.

This chapter attends to the way in which workers in *Décor* and *Poisonous Roses* have mediated the imponderability involved in anticipating their audience. Starting with the explicit production fictions involved in this mediation, the chapter moves on to the implicit inscription of an unspoken audience in sociotechnical practice. I argue that Egyptian filmmakers aim at "enchanting" their imagined viewers by trying to constrain their ability to interpret the film within the bounds of a seamless narrative *(qissa)*. Such a narrative excludes all traces of the concrete labor invested into the film. These assumptions, in addition to the reserves summoning the crew member's attention to the film ahead, contribute to breaking down the audience's reaction into smaller grounded decisions—whether an actor looks "convincing" or not, or whether a certain camera movement looks "smooth" or not. These elements are symptoms of an unspoken audience, which is thought to respond according to simple behavioral stimuli, thereby painting a different portrait of "passive" imagined audiences to the "active audience" usually discussed in media anthropology (see Hahn, 1994; Srinivas, 2016).

Imagined Audiences

Both *Décor* and *Poisonous Roses* are "artistic" movies according to industry insiders. The label serves as a tool of "boundary-work" in Ganti's sense (2012: 7), as films with an artistic mission are deemed to have more refined aesthetics, ambitions, and working practices than those with a commercial one. Such films contrast with the comedies and action movies produced in Cairo in recent years, but they are not generically exceptional insofar as they relate to a longer history of realist cinema in Egypt (see Armbrust, 1995). An artistic movie is, by default, destined to be shown at film festivals, ideally international ones, without expectations of commercial success domestically. Thus, the imagined audiences for so-called "commercial" and "artistic" projects are not the same according to industry-wide consensus. Strategies of distinction between both types of films create different expectations about the audience's composition.

Commercial value is determined by the ability to sell in local theaters and to Gulf-based satellite television channels. Since box-office returns are uncertain, however, anticipating revenues involves a certain number of "production fictions." One such fiction is the idea that a movie will not distribute well in the Gulf if it does not have a major male movie star. This fiction is so well established that when I asked the cinema journalist Walid Abul Seoud why female stars are not compensated like male stars, he matter-of-factly replied that they cannot "carry a whole film" (*yishilu film*), meaning that they do not bring the same returns as male stars. When I retorted that this gendered privilege might be a consequence of the distribution market and not anything inherent to female stars, he stated, "There have been experiments (*tagarub*) with female stars in the past, and they've all failed: *Asmaa* by Hend Sabry [2011], and *Khalti Faransa* [My Aunt France] by Mona Zaki [2004]." This anecdotal thinking has consequences for the pattern of Egyptian film production, where hiring male stars becomes an asset among producers seeking to sell their movies to distributors with narrow criteria and holding a tight oligopoly over local exhibition (see Chapter 1).

Another fiction is that commercially successful films have to appeal to a young, male, "popular" (*sha'bi*) audience in downtown Cairo. This belief is not entirely unreasonable as downtown theaters do attract large crowds of young men in the three major exhibition seasons coinciding with the Small Eid, the Great Eid, and the summer at the end of the academic year. From personal experience, however, there is still a significant contingent of young women and families in these theaters, without mentioning those audiences who watch movies outside downtown Cairo or audiences attracted to the television or the Internet. Thus, the persistence of "young urban male viewers" as a target audience cannot be attributed to empirical experience alone: it should be understood as a classist assumption among media workers. Such classism is implicit in most conversations about the "popular" crowd, which contrasts with an older, well-behaved, middle-class audience. Sometimes, it was made explicit in conversation. "You need to have movie theaters with all social classes (*kull fasa'il al-mugtama'*)," said the production assistant Mustafa Abu Zeid once. "It's not just about building in poor areas; it's about building theaters that gather as many different people as possible." Abu Zeid gave the example of the Egyptian countryside, where sometimes there is only one movie theater in an entire province. These theaters therefore gather anyone who wants to watch movies in the area. He contrasted this desirable class diversity with theaters in downtown Cairo, which "gather the nastiest segments of the population" *(awsakh fi'at al-sha'b)*, according to him. While Abu Zeid described these crowds as "nasty," he still thought they represent a vital revenue stream to the industry, which calls for making films that specifically target them.

The reasons behind each movie's success or failure are diagnosed in different ways, yet they assume that "the common man" has a taste for escapist viewing. For instance, the screenwriter Mariam Naoum attributed the commercial success of the popular cinematic genre known as "Sobky" to the heartbreak *(nakad)* in the average Egyptian's life. This heartbreak explains why the average father just wants to take his family and "see a movie with a dancer and a few gags."[3] While I sat with some production assistants prior to the Great Eid in 2014, they discussed the movies to be released in the upcoming season in a similar manner. "*Al-Gazira 2* [The Island 2] is now finished, it'll come out in the Great Eid," mentioned Abu Zeid. Everyone around the table nodded and said that the movie would make big money, but he disagreed. "It won't make money *during* Eid because the Eid clientele watches nonsensical films *(aflam hals)*." In the small Eid, he claimed, a big-budget movie like *The Blue Elephant* (2014) made little money in the initial days. This prompted New Century to remove it from the Odeon to replace it with the Sobky-style *Antar and Beesa* (2014), which made big bucks during Eid itself. Mimicking a belly dance movement, the production manager Mohammed Ibrahim said, "The Eid customer had the time of his life *(zubun al-Eid hayyas)!*"

In addition to this archetype of escapist viewing, the imagined audience of commercial cinema is understood as being authentically "Egyptian."[4] "No one makes good stories anymore," lamented the production manager Khaled Adam. He whispered into my ear that, as we were speaking, an assistant director was watching a foreign film in New Century's lobby to adapt it for an Egyptian context. This adaptation practice is widespread in Egypt, and it generates numerous accusations of theft against those who liberally borrow from foreign films. "He's watching Chinese movies now— that way no one can remember where it's coming from." Suddenly, Adam added the following comment: "That's why some plots don't make sense, because the nature of the Chinese people is not like the nature of the Egyptian people. . . . This is why people sometimes don't get [new] movies." Being Egyptian, in Adam's narrative, involves a specific way of thinking and feeling, which is not the same as—yet is modularly equivalent to—the way of thinking and feeling of other nations. This line of argument has been reproduced by the well-known cinematographer Tarek el-Telmissany, who attributed Sobky's ongoing success to his understanding of "the mindset of the Egyptian people" *(tarkibat al-sha'b al-Masri)*.

Such representations of "the people" *(al-sha'b)* are integral to guesses about commercial success. While watching an old Bollywood movie featuring superstar Amitabh Bachchan, the assistant director Abdallah al-Ghaly told me about his dream of making an Indian-style movie one day. "It reminds me of my youth," he said while recalling the days when he would wait for Eid to watch "the Indian movie" broadcast by the national Egyptian television channel. What he liked about Indian movies, and what a lot of people liked, according to him, is that the movie's low technical quality and unending entertainment "looked like them" *(kan shababhum)*. This relationship was comparable to the "C-grade" *(tirsu)* movies made by the late star Farid Shawqi with, he said, the sole purpose of emptying people's heads *(fassi dimagh al-sha'b)*. In a similar sense, the assistant director and now producer Safiy el-Din Mahmoud was adamant that the Egyptian film public is not tricked into watching low-grade cinema: they go willingly because they want to watch something entertaining, not something that will give them a headache *(ta'qid)*, as would intellectual movies *(aflam muthaqqafin)*. New Century's general manager Ahmad Badawy concurs: "If you make an artistically good film, people don't go watch it. . . . They just want to see a guy playing with a switchblade *(matwa)* and a few dancers, that's it."

These representations of "the people" do not apply to the same groups in practice, but they are useful in establishing contrasts between what "the Egyptian people" want to watch and what they do not want to watch, or what they can and cannot understand, according to filmmakers. These contrasts are not necessarily the ones made by empirical audiences, who may well disagree with filmmakers, but as production fictions, they remain central to the way in which filmmakers imagine their audiences. This is also the case with so-called "artistic" movies like *Décor* and *Poisonous Roses*, even though they are deemed to have a different prospective audience. This audience is not young, male, and popular. It is uninterested in low-brow entertainment. It is not even necessarily Egyptian or "the people." Mohammed Hosny, an accountant at New Century, once expressed the hope that *Décor* would make big money at the box office—a regular wish among workers committed to New Century's success. "It won't," answered the production manager Setohy with his usual terseness. Hosny replied that it would be unacceptable if the movie did not make money, but Setohy answered that there are other films for that, citing the soon-to-be-successful Eid movie *Antar and Beesa* (2014). "It's a film for festivals *(film mahraga-nat)*," stated Mustafa Abu Zeid on another occasion regarding *Décor*. "It'll go around the festivals, then to the SuperJet [the intercity bus lines showing movies on board]. That's it!" This potential lack of commercial success might be interpreted as a problem within a commercial company like New Century—witness Hosny's comment. However, given that New Century's management sought to bring the company's reputation to the level of the international festival circuit, the label of "artistic film" attributed to *Décor* was seen by its managers in a positive light.

The broad classist contrast between "popular" and "festival" audiences is naturalized among industry insiders. For instance, while chatting about the upcoming film *Bab al-wada'* (*The Gate of Departure*, 2014), the assistant director Jennifer Peterson argued that it was a "very art-house movie," which would most likely sell to festival audiences. Upon reflection, she chuckled and added that it was obviously not suitable for a run-of-the-mill audience consuming lowbrow entertainment in Egypt. Here, crowds of rowdy young males in downtown Cairo serve as a useful contrast to educated festivalgoers. This naturalization explains why anticipating the audience's reaction is not an entirely uncertain exercise, because there are strong conventional expectations about the audience's sociological composition and its tastes. Again, such expectations do not correspond to audience behavior systematically. If they did, producers would be much better at predicting commercial success. Still, they make the filmmaker's apprehension of the eventual audience unpredictable yet expected. What is expected is not the box-office revenue per se, but the reaction of imagined audiences, which, if aggregated, could lead to commercial success or artistic accolades. For *Décor* and *Poisonous Roses*, this reaction was mediated through a combination of labor, operational sequence, and reserves, as well as a basic behavioral assumption about the imagined audience—that is, its openness to being enchanted.

Enchantment

In her pioneering ethnography of Hollywood, Powdermaker seeks to show how "totalitarianism within the industry's social structure radiates outwards ... from the silver screen to impose empty, distracting dreams ... on passive viewers" (Askew, 2002: 4). The assumption that the industry's structure affects empirical audiences by absorbing them into an escapist narrative is not accurate according to the historical and ethnographic record, which shows, to the contrary, that viewers are more active and involved in film reception.[5] This argument cannot account for the reasons why filmmakers, in Hollywood as in Egypt, imagine films as imposing "distracting dreams on passive viewers." The question, here, is what makes filmmakers want their viewers to receive the film in a passive, "dream-like" state?

Gell's reflection on art as a "technology of enchantment" goes some way to account for the way in which spectators are imagined by Egyptian filmmakers. Gell initially defines the technology of enchantment as "all those technical strategies, especially art, music, dances, rhetoric, gifts, etc., which human beings employ in order to secure the acquiescence of other people in their intentions or projects" (1988: 7). He expands on this thought in a later essay:

> The power of art objects stems from the technical processes they objectively embody: the *technology of enchantment* is founded on the *enchantment of technology*. The enchantment of technology is the power that technical processes have of casting a spell over us so that we see the real world in an enchanted form. Art, as a separate kind of technical activity, only carries further, through a kind of involution, the enchantment which is immanent in all kinds of technical activity. (1992: 44).

Enchantment is the state in which the targeted audience is compelled to acquiesce to the intentions of their enchanters by the "enchantment of technology," which is the ability to bedazzle the audience with the barely fathomable technical skill invested in making the artwork. Likewise, filmmakers seek to produce dazzling technical displays to get their imagined audience to watch the story they have crafted, which allows them to attract box-office revenue or artistic praise, depending on the production fictions to which they adhere.

When I asked the director Marwan Hamed why people went to movie theaters less and less, he said that it was because the film industry has not yet found an answer to the question of what attracts viewers to theaters when they can watch movies on television. He expanded on this thought by providing a hypothetical scenario. A young man wants to go out with a young woman. He will have to pay for the taxi ride to the movie theater and back, the tickets, and the popcorn, which will cost him around a hundred Egyptian pounds. "This hundred pounds had better be worth it for the young man," he advised. "You have to go to the cinema to be dazzled and amazed (*tanbahir wa-tandahish*)." Earlier in the conversation, Hamed argued that the director's task is to create worlds that "overwhelm the viewer, no matter his opinions about the film," which he traces to a global trend toward increasing bedazzlement (*ibhar*) in motion pictures entertainment.

My interlocutors used various expressions to signify this enchanted engagement with a film: one can be "pulled" or "attracted" (*mashdud*), "infused" with the narrative (*mundamig*), or just happy about it (*mabsut*). All these expressions convey the way in which filmmakers anticipate their audience's reaction. The assistant director and producer Safiy el-Din Mahmoud said that he always wants his movies to provoke a reaction, whether good or bad, which is why he likes the gory action movie *Ibrahim al-Abyad* (2009). "A lot of people were disgusted by the blood and would say, 'Is this even possible' (*huwwa fi keda fi-l-dunya*)?" Mahmoud argued that movies are not required to paint a realistic picture of the world, in direct disagreement with the realist tradition favored by modernist intellectuals in Cairo. "I don't like intellectual movies," he added. "I walked out of *al-Musafir* [*The Traveler*, 2009] without any opinion about it, good or bad."

This is one reaction that filmmakers seek to avoid at all costs. It is generally described with the electrical metaphor of "unplugging" (*fasl*). When Egyptian viewers describe a film to which they are indifferent or which elicits no engagement, they say that they are "unplugged" from it. The implication is that there was a current running through them until it was switched off. I have often heard this metaphor used in editing rooms, when filmmakers watch preliminary cuts, to warn against scenes or sequences that may seem boring, unnecessary, or in need of additional work. This work is geared toward creating a product that attracts the imagined viewer. When s/he "sees through" the movie's seamless narrative, s/he cannot be genuinely enchanted. The dreaded unplugging is common among empirical viewers, however, as they are easily able to see through movies despite the best intentions of their enchanters. Once, I went out with a mixed group of American and Egyptian friends to watch *The Blue Elephant* (2014). All were deeply unimpressed by the special effects in the film, an important selling point in its marketing campaign. My friends suggested that the effects did nothing except distract *away* from the movie—a common reaction among viewers who are used to the more "convincing" effects in American cinema.

This kind of unplugging is precisely what Egyptian filmmakers try to avoid among their imagined enchanted viewers, especially with a blockbuster like *The Blue Elephant*.

In a similar sense, numerous directors told me that they seek to make something "never before seen" *('umru matshaf 'abl keda)*. Some meant it in a literal sense: they want to show images, locations, actors, props, costumes, and so on that have never been seen on screen in the history of cinema. Making something never before seen can also mean using dazzling cinematic techniques to capture the imagined audience through technical virtuosity. As the director Ahmad Fawzi Saleh put it, his primary objective is to elicit gasps from imagined viewers, pushing them to ask, "How did they do this?" *(humma 'amalu dah izzay)*. Directors presume that their audience carries a certain baggage of cinematic knowledge, and they seek to contribute something "new" to this baggage—newness being relative to the limits of the viewer's experience. An artistically minded director like Fawzi, who explicitly sought to shoot Cairo's tanneries district like "it had never been seen before," wanted to create a new film aesthetics in world cinema—and, only by extension, in Egyptian cinema. In *Décor*, Ahmad Abdalla insisted on shooting in an Alexandrian school because he did not want "viewers to see that he has filmed in yet another school in Zamalek [an upper-class neighborhood in Cairo]." Likewise, a more "commercial" director like Ismail Farouk constantly sought to introduce new locations and new characters to "the people" *(al-sha'b)*, but this newness was clearly bound by the limits of a national audience. Each in his own way, Fawzi, Abdalla, and Farouk wanted to dazzle their audience with unprecedented imagery.

While nonspecialist viewers are expected to remain dazzled by the film's making under all circumstances, viewers with some filmmaking experience can have their perception colored by their own know-how and their understanding of the time, money, and effort needed to make films. These viewers can still be enchanted given their inability to understand certain cinematic techniques—a situation anticipated by Gell's argument about the enchantment of artists who enjoy a certain degree of skill (1992: 47). While we were shooting in *Décor*, the assistant grip Ahmed Nader was chatting with the clapper Abdelsalam Radwan about an Indian movie he had recently seen. Nader was marveling at a shot in a car chase where the camera seemed to move inside the car and out, in a seamless 360° angle, without a single editing cut. His overall sense of amazement came off in the way described by Fawzi above: it was as if he were asking, "How did they do this?" Radwan replied that only a technocrane[6] could pull off the trick but Nader was not convinced: the motion moved in and out of the car without apparent obstacles. While Nader was talking, I remembered a conversation with the lighting script Hany Morsy concerning a similar one-shot scene in the American movie *Children of Men* (2006). Morsy kept marveling at the way that shot was made until he saw the making-of video online, at which point he proceeded to describe the various gripping contraptions invented to realize this shot, including a specially equipped car with a removable roof. I submitted to Nader that the Indian movie may have used such a contraption, but he remained somewhat skeptical. He was amazed by the Indians' display of technical virtuosity.

Nader's amazement is a straightforward illustration of the "enchantment of technology," especially to a skilled practitioner. Nader was particularly struck by the camera movement in this shot because he knew exactly how hard it is to rig motion equipment well enough to produce such a seamless 360° one-shot scene, especially when the camera seems to move in and out of a car. So many things can go wrong in this kind of shot, so many things can disturb the take's seamlessness, that it is incredible to think someone may have the audacity to attempt it, let alone succeed in shooting it. And even when the anthropologist gives verbal explanations to rationalize the shot, they are insufficient to reconstruct the technical know-how that allows the filmmakers to create the shot, which would have allowed Nader to execute it if he were summoned to the task. This explains why Nader was still mesmerized by the Indian movie: not because he considered "Indians" to be more skilled in general (a statement that could elicit chauvinistic disdain on the part of some Egyptian filmmakers), but because they were able to make a shot that Egyptian filmmakers cannot imagine making.

Enchanting the imagined audience is not just about the enchantment of technology. The prime objective of filmmakers is to gain the unpredictable approval of enchantable audience members. While glitzy technological tricks are certainly part of the equation, they are not the central way of producing enchantment. The independent director Hala Lotfy argued that "commercial" filmmakers surround themselves with expensive equipment to hide their incompetence in the craft of cinema. Marwan Hamed himself argued that technicalities matter little compared to the "*quality*" of the film. "There are films which were made fifty years ago with very low technical capabilities, yet they're still captivating when we watch them today," he reasoned. Likewise, even though some contemporary films spend an inordinate amount of money on technical effects, they remain "low-quality" *(radi')* in his view. "So what makes a good film?" I asked. "It's the same normal criteria that people use to evaluate a film: whether the story is good *(al-haduta hilwa)*, whether the ending is impressive, whether they identified with characters. . . ." What matters, in short, is not the means leading to enchantment but the assumption that the imagined viewer seeks enchantment through "good" seamless narratives. Goodness, in this case, varies according to the production fiction to which filmmakers adhere, whether the imagined viewer is a young urban male seeking entertainment during the Eid season or an educated festivalgoer invested in serious films.

For *Décor* and *Poisonous Roses*, the criterion of "goodness" was linked to the idea that the film ought to be realistic *(waqi'i)*, logical *(mantiqi)*, and natural *(tabi'i)* in its camera movement, set design, costumes, and even acting. Both films are heirs to the realist tradition in Egyptian cinema in this sense. It is interesting to notice how the imponderable audience is imagined to be enchanted *only* when the narrative is "realistic," "logical," or "natural." A great deal of effort was spent on highlighting these attributes during the production process in both films. During casting for *Poisonous Roses*, to give one example, we sought actors who "fit their role" *(munasib li-l-dur)*, actors that "looked the part" and could perform it. According to the venerable director Daoud Abdel Sayyed, 50 percent of the casting choice rests in the actor's looks and 50 percent in his/her performance. Actors who "look good" can still be deemed unfit for the role, because the most important criterion is that they remain convincing *(muqni')* to the enchanted audience. The audience can never become unplugged because there subsists some doubt that the actor *is* the character, either because s/he does not look the part or because s/he overacts or cannot act at all. When Ibrahim el-Nagary was cast as Saqr in *Poisonous Roses*, Fawzi cited the fact that he "looks like Saqr" to support his decision. Looking like Saqr, in this case, was both a judgment about Nagary's physical look on camera and his "natural" demeanor, that is, his way of carrying himself as one would expect a real-life tanneries worker to do.

Implicit in Fawzi's explanation is a common distinction between the technical and artistic aspects of the actor's work, between the actor's bodily appearance, position, movement, and so on, and his/her artistic "performance" *(ada')*. This performance centers on facial expressions and the ability to communicate emotion *(ihsas)* to the imagined viewer. When successful, the link between the actor's performance and the audience's reaction is immediate: it is akin to an emotional jolt to the enchantable audience's brain. Film music is deemed to act in such an immediate manner as well. The actor and composer Hani Adel argued that music is the "third party" in a scene, between the actors who express emotion in a dialogue and the spectators affected by it. Music acts as an unmediated expression of emotion under the composer's control, as though the composer were translating the film's emotionality in soundtrack form. Adel usually composes his musical themes with emotional labels—a sad theme, a happy theme, a love theme. With the director's approval, he composes each musical segment to fit the film's image frame by frame, such that each cue comes at the exact right moment to stir maximal emotion. Adel gave the example of a tear running down a character's face. If he cues the music right when the tear comes out of the eye, he will have reached his musical climax by the time the tear falls. If he cues it after a five-second silence, while the tear is halfway down the actor's face, the buildup to the climax becomes more significant. "Each composer has his own tricks to stir emotions," he concluded.

The imagined viewer, in short, can be enchanted through dazzling displays of technical skill or conventional crafts such as acting or musical composition. Ideally, the film needs to be so dazzling that the concrete labor invested in its making becomes invisible behind the screen, even to specialists. Passive enchanted viewing is a strong normative model of spectatorship among filmmakers in Egypt, and it again explains why the imagined audience's reaction is *imponderable* and not *uncertain* to them. There is a strong baseline expectation about the (passive, enchanted) conditions under which viewership will take place, such that the filmmaker's task becomes to mediate the viewers' reaction within narrow parameters. Thus, filmmakers are not stuck thinking about the myriad empirical reactions one can have to their productions. Rather, they make decisions at every juncture in the operational sequence to enhance their film's ability to enchant viewers by hiding the technical skill invested in its making. In this way, the audience's reaction is broken down into a series of contingent decisions concerning an unspoken audience.

The Unspoken Audience

The audience imagined by Egyptian filmmakers is not just visible in explicit production fictions or in intentional cinematic effects; it is also implicit in filmmaking operations. Consider the gripping craft, which in Egypt mainly consists in laying down dolly tracks and moving the dolly during shots. These operations can seem trivially "technical," because the grips just need to lay down tracks with the orientation and length desired by the cinematographer and ensure that the tracks are even, stable, and straight. The objective is to get a "smooth" camera movement *(haraka salisa)*. There seems to be little to say beyond this technical report, yet the desire for smoothness is precisely where the unspoken audience becomes manifest. Grips invest a great deal of effort in ensuring that the track and the dolly's movement remain smooth, stable, and straight when, at every moment, the equipment and the key grip's handle can puncture this smoothness. The grips in *Décor* complained that their tracks were not smooth because they were bought as second-hand equipment from Europe. This is problematic because they become chipped and uneven through use, which means that the dolly's movement is likely to be less smooth. The grip's greatest anxiety is around producing seamless movements against all odds—inadequate equipment, shivering handle, crowded on-set environment—to avoid getting the imagined viewer "unplugged" from the storyline. The assumption is that the unspoken viewer will snap out of the film if the dolly's movement becomes visible by some technical defect, which is why it is important to ensure optimal conditions for smoothness.

Grips reserve "better"—newer, smoother—tracks for quality productions like *Décor*, where the imagined audience is deeply invested in the film's aesthetics, as opposed to the more commercial projects where such details might not be as important. These different kinds of unspoken viewers were once made explicit in another context, in a conversation between the sound engineers Ahmad Saleh and Abdelrahman "Mana" Mahmoud. Saleh complained about being unable to record sound well on television sets, unlike on film sets. "You have to see the television audience as a housewife who's peeling cucumbers in front of the television," relativized Mana. This hypothetical woman might get distracted by many things, so she is not concerned with the quality of image or sound, just with ensuring a minimal standard of visibility and audibility. Moreover, the television apparatus can only transmit mid-range frequencies, which constrains the range of audible sounds between higher and lower frequencies. "You've got nothing to do with these frequencies *(ma laksh da'wa),*" Mana reasoned with Saleh. The sound engineer in *Décor* remained unconvinced. He was committed to getting as good a recording quality as possible in his work. "I'm a *perfectionist,*" he said.

The audience imagined by Saleh is an audience otherwise more discerning than the one evoked in Mana's cliché. For him, the sound ought to be as "natural" *(tabiʻi)* as possible to avoid bringing the unspoken viewer away from the story. The spectator's attention should not be caught by a sound (such as a sudden loud noise) or its absence (such as an unrecorded word in the dialogue). In practice, this means cleaning all noises emanating from the soundtrack outside the storyline, including noises produced on set or by the sound worker's own intervention. Saleh's desire for a clean sound *(sut nidif)* is intimately tied to the idea that the enchanted viewers should not feel any noise that is extraneous to the story. On another occasion, I sat down with the editor Mostafa Nour while he cleaned the soundtrack for *Poisonous Roses.* Suddenly, we both heard a glitch caused by his attempt to mend two different tannery sounds in the editing software. He heard it as I did, so he typed in a few shortcuts to insert a sound transition. When he replayed the scene, the glitch had disappeared. "Did you feel anything?" he asked as he turned toward me with a proud smile. "No," I smiled in return. "Now everything is going well *(mashya mazbut)*." This normative view about "good" and "bad" sounds is not a deeply held cultural belief: it is linked to an implicit, enchantable audience that should not feel so-called "mistakes" *(ghalatat)*.

This is nowhere as clear as in the convention of continuity *(rakur)*, which is preserved at all costs to avoid snapping the imagined audience out of the story. The principle of continuity is widely accepted in the Egyptian film industry, although lowbrow entertainment can sometimes tamper with its iron rule. The idea is to ensure that scenes shot in discontinuous moments look continuous after editing. It involves high vigilance on the part of script supervisors on set to avoid changes in costumes, actor position, and prop position, or even slight shifts in actor performance, between takes. The assistant director Omar el-Zohairy once told me that he prefers scheduling scenes in the order of performance to allow better "*dramatic flow*," so actors can keep the same costumes and the same performance *(adaʼ)*. Since schedules cannot be planned in this way in practice, the burden falls on the script supervisors to avoid any "*drops*," such as an actress wearing two different dresses in the same scene or a furniture item being visibly displaced within the same angle.

Avoiding lapses in continuity creates constant anxieties among script supervisors, who dread being blamed for any oversight.[7] "I need to be very careful about my screenplay breakdown," said the costume script supervisor Mariam el-Bagoury. She was adamant that any error in *Décor*'s costume continuity would be blamed on her. "It doesn't work if I've got perfect continuity for stars, but the extras are all dressed wrong," she continued. As a costume script supervisor, Bagoury's job was to ensure that all the actors were wearing the costume agreed upon and that the costumes were continuous across scenes that, in the film's narrative, correspond to coextensive times. To avoid missing anything, Bagoury would photograph each character with her own camera after each scene that had an eventual continuation in the screenplay. When the continuation was about to be shot, she would carefully review that each costume, accessory, and hairstyle was exactly where it was when the continuous scenes were initially captured. Jaylan Auf, the script supervisor for prop and action continuity in *Décor*, ensured a similar continuity between all remaining visible aspects in the shot. Her anxiety was no less clear: "If I make any small mistake, it's immediately visible on screen."

Visible continuity mistakes are equivalent to audible noises on the soundtrack. Their effect is to unplug the imagined viewer, and they are thereby inadmissible by industry insiders. Filmmakers tend to insist more on the normative aspect of continuity than on the unspoken viewer it assumes. Auf was concerned that any mistake would be blamed on her, because "everyone on set looks to blame everyone else for any mistake"—a typical reaction among executive workers, as I explained in Chapter 4. The logic underlying the continuity script's "mistakes" has little to do with logistical imperatives or artistic demands, but with the conventional view that the spectator should not feel any lapses in continuity. This explains the meticulous effort invested by script supervisors in creating various mediators—notes, pictures, short videos—to ensure that scenes are well connected with one another. These mediators, in turn, summon workers to restore continuity in due course. For instance, when workers were furnishing the library in Mustafa and Maha's apartment in *Décor*, they relied on a picture of the library at Studio Misr taken by Auf to return every single book and ornament to its exact location. With several weeks lapsing between the day when the library was initially shot and the shooting in Garden City, prop assistants would have had some difficulty restoring the library to its original state from memory.

Ensuring continuity, in short, is one among several practices aiming at enchanting the unspoken viewer by erasing traces of the concrete labor invested in film production. Prior to shooting *Poisonous Roses*, Fawzi would jokingly tell me that he would love to "break the illusion" (*yiksar al-iham*) produced by commercial cinema. His statement referred to the estrangement techniques developed by the Marxist playwright Bertolt Brecht to shatter the imaginary fourth wall separating actors from audiences. While we were shooting, however, the young director took great care to hide the concrete equipment and labor involved in filmmaking. Shots were systematically repeated when the artistic crew noticed workers in glass reflections or in shadows. We reshot a character's entry into an apartment a full day after the scene was completed because the editor Mostafa Nour noticed the shadow of a crew member lurking in the middle of the sequence while reviewing the previous day's material. The shadow was not evident to my eyes. I had to rewatch the sequence to see that it was well and truly there, but Mostafa's trained eyes caught this "mistake" with haste. The shadows of film workers are removed by artistic decree, because they would break the illusion if they remained in the film.

This desire to avoid breaking the illusion is again visible in another seemingly technical operation: building studio walls *(banuhat)*. The assistant decorator Mohammed Ezzat argued that such walls need to "look real" *(yikun shaklu waqi'i)*, but that they are not constructed like actual walls. As I could see while he was explaining this in studio, set builders construct large wooden frames on which they affix ready-made planks of medium-density fiber (MDF) wood. This structure creates smooth painting surfaces, giving the impression of a solid wall on camera. This impression requires some care, because any number of on-set incidents can dispel the illusion by unfixing surfaces or chipping the paint. Ezzat explained that MDF planks only recently became widely used. Historically, wall surfaces were made with thin cardboard layers *(kartun)* glued onto a canvas *(khaysh)* extended around wooden frames. Although MDF planks are more expensive, they are better, according to Ezzat, because they produce easily painted surfaces, without relying on a craftsman's willingness to carefully layer cardboard on canvas. If done without care *(min ghayr damir)*, layers of cardboard can come off and "look fake" on camera—"a disaster," in Ezzat's words. This attention to the finishing of studio walls, like the attention to seamless camera movement among grips, can seem superficially trivial, yet it is indicative of an anxiety to avoid snapping the unspoken viewer out of the film.

Whether it is the grips seeking a "smooth" camera movement or the set builders painting "smooth" walls or the sound editor removing "distracting" noises or script supervisors ensuring seamless continuity, the movie is crafted in such a way as to leave no traces of its making, thereby being at the service of the story's enchantment. The unspoken viewer is not just built into skillful handling of camera movement or studio walls, but also in the equipment that becomes intentionally invisible within the film's narrative. "The sight of immediate reality has become an orchid in the land of technology," to cite Benjamin's visionary remark in his essay on the artwork in the age of mechanical reproduction (2007: 233). This is the magic of movies, as it were, if we use Gell's notion of magic as "ideal, costless, production" (1988: 9). This perception is clearly discordant with the effort, anxiety, and imponderability involved in the film's creation. The audience's unpredictable reaction is mediated by a working process based on certain assumptions and mediators that eventually become invisible in the final film product, by the artistic crew's own design, to satisfy the expectation that the unspoken spectator is awaiting to be enchanted.

Empirical Audiences

This chapter has shown how the imponderable audience is mediated in the Egyptian film industry. Production fictions provide a lay sociological representation of the audience's composition, whether it is the rowdy young male crowd imagined in "commercial" circles or the passive educated viewer imagined by the makers of *Décor* and *Poisonous Roses*. The latter viewer is imagined to be "enchantable" in Gell's sense: s/he can be dazzled by technical displays of virtuosity or simply by the film's story. This story, in turn, is crafted in such a way as to erase all traces of labor invested in the film to leave it "smooth," "convincing," and "natural." The explicit audience articulated in production fictions becomes implicit to the sociotechnical activity of filmmaking, whether in moving a dolly, removing noises in sound editing, or ensuring continuity. In all these cases, technological devices act as reserves summoning the filmmaker's attention to the eventual enchanted audience by adjusting uneven dolly tracks or glitchy soundtracks.

Such assumptions about passive viewing are certainly not unique to Egypt, but the local division of labor, the filmmaking process, and the use of technological devices is what mediates the imagined audience's enchantment in this specific case. Needless to say, the audiences anticipated by Egyptian filmmakers do not always react like they are supposed to react in their estimation. Given the dearth of reliable research on Egyptian audiences, however, it is difficult to give a complete account of the gap between imagined and empirical viewers, let alone to measure it. Indeed, it is difficult to secure accurate data on such basic information as the number of movie theaters in Egypt. The Cinema Industry Chamber reports an implausible 544 theaters (Euromed Audiovisual, 2013), but their records are outdated and ill-maintained. The estimates of my interlocutors ranged between four hundred and six hundred screens in the whole country by 2015.[8] Several interlocutors confirmed that theaters had been slowly disappearing all over Egypt, especially in "popular" *(sha'bi)* neighborhoods and in the countryside, where old cinemas have fallen into disuse and receive little investment.

Without reliable statistics, the empirical audience's composition has been estimated according to socioeconomic considerations. Armbrust (1998) distinguishes broadly between three types of movie theaters in Cairo: lower-tier theaters tend to attract younger, male, working-class audiences; middle-tier theaters tend to attract middle-class families, teenage audiences, and young couples; and upper-tier multiplexes tend to attract upper middle-class teenagers and couples. In addition to attracting different audience segments, each kind of theater tends to screen different content. Lower-tier theaters screen re-runs and action movies, while middle-tier and upper-tier theaters only screen new releases, with a net advantage to Hollywood productions over Egyptian ones. From an exhibitor's perspective, as the producer Gaby Khoury once explained, local productions are more profitable because they are less taxed than foreign ones. These productions come in much lower numbers, however, which is partly why American movies dominate the domestic exhibition market.

This division of empirical audiences according to the kinds of theaters they attend should be apprehended with a major caveat in mind: they mirror the classist production fictions common in commercial circles. Witness the assistant director and producer Safiy el-Din Mahmoud's analysis:

> Very rich people won't pay sixty [Egyptian] pounds to go to the movies, they'll just watch stuff on OSN at home [a private satellite channel affordable to a small fraction of the Egyptian population].... Very poor people won't pay either, because they can't even live.... The industry relies on a big chunk of middle-class people who, when they have a hundred extra pounds, will spend thirty pounds to go to the movies.

Mahmoud's analysis establishes direct correspondences between audience and social class, such that socioeconomic status becomes a direct determinant of whether one goes to the movies or not. This analysis says little about the way in which this audience is instilled in unspoken ways in the filmmaking process, but it also makes little room to understand empirical audiences that behave against normative class expectations, such as educated audiences that enjoy watching lowbrow entertainment or supposedly rowdy audiences that watch American movies in silence. The slide between an audience's background and its behavior is systematic among Egyptian filmmakers, who have not only empirical expectations about what the audience receives but also normative ones about how they ought to receive it.

One might trace these expectations partly to the way in which a filmmaker acts when s/he becomes a viewer. There is a distinction to be made between lay and specialist film viewing here. Lay analyses tend to center on three core elements in the film: the storyline, the star, and the director. These elements are pervasively discussed in cinema journalism, magazines, television, and movie theaters, and among some filmmakers. Once, while I sat in a coffee shop with a cinema journalist, the director Akram Farid, and the actor Hassan Harb, the journalist asked, "Have you seen *al-Ashshash* [*The Collector*, 2013]?" Pulling on his *shisha*, Farid winked twice: first to say he had seen it, then to say he did not like it. "It's already like the story in *al-Hurub* [*The Escape*, 1988], but it's almost a copy-paste version of *Abdu Muta* [*Deadly Abdu*, 2012]." This last movie was made by the same director as *al-Ashshash*, which the journalist did not fail to mention, adding another layer of discredit to the movie and its author. "Mohamed Farag [the star actor] is very bad in the movie . . . he's imitating [the superstar] Mohammed Ramadan and all his *Abdu Muta* jokes." "But he's usually a good actor," interjected Hassan Harb. The journalist ignored the comment. "Horeya Farghaly [the star actress] isn't credible in her role," he said, because she acts in the way a rich woman thinks a "popular" dancer would act.

These comments concerned the usual suspects: the narrative and its originality, the stars and their performance, the director. This lay analysis gains additional layers, however, when filmmakers engage in more specialist commentary. What attracts the eye of filmmakers differs from lay audiences because they are skilled in the very craft that they watch and evaluate. When I went to watch *The Blue Elephant* (2014) with the photographer and director Yasser Shafiey, we sat down in a coffee shop right behind the theater before the screening. We met some of Yasser's friends from the Cairo Jesuit Cinema School by chance. Yasser asked his friends about their criticisms of the film. "Compared to Egyptian films, it's in a class of its own," said one friend. "Compared to world-class movies, it's full of problems." The set and the music were very well used, in his estimation, but there were a lot of problems with acting. "Karim Abdel Aziz [the star actor] is at 40 percent of his capacities . . . he could've been better directed . . . some scenes were very bad, there are a lot of *inserts* that don't make any sense."

With visible care to show precision in his analysis, Shafiey's friend divided the film's content into components beyond the narrative, the star, or the director, encompassing set building, music, and even such technical details as "inserts," which are short silent takes inserted between longer narrative sequences. "It should be watched, but there're a lot of problems in it," the friend concluded. Shafiey and I went to the theater to watch the film. After the viewing, he gave me his hot take. "I liked it, but there was a lot of noise in the room." He specifically singled out two young children who were sitting with their parents right in front of us and running around throughout the screening, as well as some very loud young men who kept making jokes about the film. Shafiey did not hear yet another distraction sitting next to me: an unpleasant viewer who did not cease to comment pompously on the director Marwan Hamed and his days at the High Cinema Institute. Our conversations concerning surrounding viewers evinced our own expectations regarding silent, individual spectatorship in movie theaters. These expectations can clearly contravene viewership habits in Cairo.

These varying analyses offer just a small taste of the way in which empirical audiences engage with movies in Egypt. What they show more intently is that the explicit and implicit audiences imagined by filmmakers have evident limits for predicting audience behavior. Prediction is impossible, and all filmmakers can do is to mediate the audience's imponderable reaction into a series of contingent tasks. This mediation relies on the industry's hierarchical division of labor and the filmmaking process, as well as various reserves through which the audience is instilled into the film's very fabric. In this sense, approaching the future in which the film is expected to meet its audience is not an entirely uncertain task, but an imponderable one. The encounter with the public is loaded with expectations, but the way in which it occurs in practice can shatter all prospects.

The Afterparty

Décor's premiere was scheduled for the Cairo International Film Festival on November 14, 2014. This edition had been much awaited as the turmoil following the Rabaa massacre forced the organizers to cancel the 2013 edition. The premiere was to be held at the Opera House. Ahmad Badawy left me two special invitations at the office: one to enter the film and the other to attend New Century's afterparty at the luxurious Marriott Hotel in Zamalek.

As the show is meant to start around eight o'clock, I make my way to the theater an hour in advance. The journey normally takes ten minutes without traffic, but the streets around the Opera House are completely clogged. The thorough security screening at the gate makes entry even slower, and by the time I reach the right cinema hall, a very long line has formed. Guests start filtering through the narrow doors little by little, but the slow march into the theater stops suddenly and it appears that no one else is allowed inside. As I was soon to understand, the event had been overbooked. Even guests with formal invitations did not have reserved seats. The crowd starts pushing against the gate, while some offended delegates brandish their tickets, claiming that they have special invitations.

Time passes. The screening has probably begun. The line becomes a formless crowd by the door. The commotion cedes to a long tense wait. The doors are closed, but everyone waits in silence. Suddenly, the crowd becomes agitated again: someone has come from inside the theater to try to get more people in. For a second, I see Farghalli in his elegant tuxedo right behind the door, while he tries to admit more people. "Mr. X!" he shouts when our eyes meet. I squeeze through the crowd to the door, while Farghalli grabs my arm to pull me inside without letting anyone else through. Outrage sparks again, but by this time, Farghalli has dragged me through security and into the main hall, where he tells me to find a seat upstairs.

I climb to the balcony seats. The theater is built in the style of a picture palace, with a large screen on stage, a parterre, a mezzanine, and the balcony where I sit at an awkward short angle to the screen. I arrive about fifteen minutes into the screening. The room is full. Everyone watches in utter silence. I take little notice of the audience's reaction: I want to enjoy the moment without thinking about turning this event into a core element of my study. Still, perhaps out of habit or out of embarrassment, I jot some notes on my cell phone.

The jottings are very thin as I write this thought: "decor reaction transitions." They refer to a moment during the screening where the room roared in laughter, toward the end of the film, after Maha switches between Sharif's world and Mustafa's world several times in succession. I remember the chill going down my spine when the room reacted, partly because it was striking to hear hundreds of voices screaming and shouting at the same time and partly thinking that the intended effect of the scenes was certainly not laughter. The audience seemed to laugh more in merriment than in mockery—although who knows, really.

After the screening, I have a strange déjà vu moment. The very last shot in *Décor* shows the main characters watching the premiere of the movie in which they had been acting all along, in a theater that is not dissimilar to the one where I am standing. Some of the very same filmmakers who featured in this last shot are present at the Opera House. I greet the stylist Salma Sami and the cinematographer Tarek Hefny, among others. I do not see Ahmad Abdalla or the star actors, who were on stage to collect the crowd's applause and the photographers' flashes after the screening.

I have a short conversation with a young director in the theater's lobby. He looks thoroughly unimpressed by the film. Slowly, I manage to find friends from the production crew: Setohy, Hany, Mohammed Fathallah, Yasser Shafiey. We chat and take pictures next to a large sponsor-filled banner on an abandoned bit of red carpet. The well-known celebrities are standing at a faraway door where hurried press photographers, television cameramen, and reporters flock to get a glimpse of this constellation of stars. When I remember to ask my friends about the afterparty, I am guided to a New Century microbus, which heads to the Marriott Hotel without waiting.

As hyped as the atmosphere was at the Opera House, the Marriott is at another level. A long queue of men in tuxedos and women in elaborate dresses stand by a desk near the hall, where New Century has invited the industry's cream of the crop to attend a commemoration event: sixty-five years since Dollar Film's founding in 1949, coinciding with the thirty-sixth edition of the Cairo International Film Festival. Planning these events on the night of *Décor*'s release seems like an ambitious albeit timely marketing scheme. I manage to squeeze through the crowd near the hall's entrance, where again issues have arisen regarding invitations and guest lists.

After walking through a long palatial corridor, I am surprised to find a large cabaret-style room with a stage, a small projection screen, an open bar that had run dry very early in the night, and a small photo-op station where a hired photographer asks all the major stars to stop for a picture. I glimpse such legends as Lebleba, Samir Ghanem, and Mahmoud Hemida. Away from the media machine, I manage to chat briefly with crew members whom I had not seen since *Décor*'s last shooting day. The assistant director Omar el-Zohairy briefly introduces me to the star actor Ahmad al-Fishawy; the second assistant Renad Tarek talks to me about her next film project; Farghalli is merrily running around.

The central event of the afterparty is short-lived. Badawy gives a nervous and obviously rehearsed speech about New Century's history and its future projects before everyone sits down to watch a brief trailer of Daoud Abdel Sayyed's upcoming film in New Century, *Out of the Ordinary* (2015). The singer-songwriter Hani Adel then sings "Shababeek," a jazzy remix of the famous Mohamed Mounir tune that had turned into *Décor*'s title song. Unmemorable food is served, filmmakers are left to mingle, and the party slowly dies around midnight.

"What are you doing here?"

When I go greet the star Mahmoud Hemida, he asks me this question with a hint of suspicion and surprise. I met Hemida while working with Ahmad Fawzi Saleh. His company, Al Batrik Art Production, was producing *Poisonous Roses* and he acted in a small role in the film. I explain that I was invited by Badawy to attend, and the star's nod still seems to express some confusion. What am I doing here, in a private afterparty hosted by a major player in the Egyptian film industry for a jet-setting crowd of filmmakers?

This crowd, with its world of ostentatious performance, newspaper intrigues, and television interviews, has been in some sense what I have intentionally avoided while working on "Egyptian cinema." What I have sought instead are the back channels of the industry: the everyday grind of filmmaking, the long-term sequence in which hundreds of people become engaged toward the creation of a film, the grounded use of technological devices beyond the camera and the projection screen. At each moment throughout this halting process, the makers of *Décor* were concerned that they did not know yet how it would be. In some sense, *Décor* was going to turn out as it turned out, but the everyday effort invested in mediating this future is what makes the craft of film production so captivating to me.

Retrospective

I dread, like many writers, the finality that comes with the word "conclusion," which is why I chose to write a retrospective instead. The events described in this book may have occurred, but their analysis and interpretation are not definitive. When I started writing these pages as a PhD dissertation, I intended them to contribute to the anthropology of media and mediation in three ways. First, I wanted to show what long-term ethnography can offer to the detailed description and analysis of media production in the seldom-studied Egyptian film industry. Second, I wanted to bring attention to the concrete use of technological devices in the course of media production by showing why they matter to anthropological analysis. Last, I wanted to explore how people mediate between the present and the future of a sociotechnical production process. I was not sold on the idea that the future could be described as an unknowable and unpredictable fog into which one sails inevitably, and I wanted to draft a different way in which one can conceive how media workers approach what comes next.

While turning the dissertation into a book, I wanted to make these contributions clearer. I also sought to insert more empirical descriptions to animate the narration, including the brief interludes about *Décor*'s story. I wanted to articulate the desires, anxieties, and representations of workers in the Egyptian film industry. I wanted to add a future-oriented layer to the many existing studies of media production in anthropology. With exceptions like Grimaud (2003) and Hoek (2014), the ethnography of media production is written in an *a posteriori* mode, as though media producers know what will happen all along, without considering how media workers themselves are constantly anticipating, here and now, what will come next in their activity. I have sharpened the conceptual contrasts through which the book grapples with this activity, which is why I distinguish between operational sequences and "process" in a general sense; between reserves and "objects"; between an imponderable and an uncertain future, depending on one's orientation toward it. Using these conceptual tools, I have argued that Egyptian filmmakers mediate imponderable problems in their daily work. When planning and executing a shooting day, when visualizing the film, when imagining the audience's composition and reaction, filmmakers are not at a loss—they are always already engaged in mediating an unpredictable outcome.

My contribution has been to detail all the assumptions and mediators breaking down imponderable outcomes into contingent tasks, with mitigated success, but without an immediate or a lasting resolution. Throughout the book, I have highlighted the concrete work done by Egyptian filmmakers in their everyday activity as a central area of investigation into the industry's workings *and* as an analytical resource to understand how imponderable outcomes are mediated. Without assuming a certain aesthetic theory or committing to an essentialist distinction between "technical" and "creative" work, I have shown how technical and artistic workers are equally confronted by the imponderability of filmmaking. Highlighting the labor invested in the film is not just a matter of academic interest or poetic justice, but a way of exposing how, at every juncture in the production process, with every decision made by a technical or an artistic worker, some measure of inventiveness is involved.

Moreover, the book stands as a testimony to the importance of technological objects as empirical artifacts and as analytical resources in media ethnography. Although it may have been tempting to "purify" the filmmaker-subject from technological objects (Latour, 1993), I have maintained that "reserves" summon the filmmaker's imagination and his/her social interactions in the present to work on near/far future outcomes. The distinction between objects and reserves is significant in this sense. On the one hand, it does not deny the reality of technology as a set of commodity-objects, which is how it is generally conceived in contemporary Cairo. On the other hand, it allows the analyst to examine how these objects play a broader role in media production. With this methodological resolve to examine objects/reserves, I provide a more exhaustive account of the ways in which filmmakers work through everyday issues, beyond the confines of individual cognition and social organization, into a proximate engagement with technological devices in one's immediate environment. I have argued that technological devices are invested with an anticipatory potential that, in complex processes like filmmaking, has special significance.

These devices neither determine what will happen nor serve as an invisible substratum to what would have happened anyway, but they summon an unpredictable yet expected future to the minds of social agents.

More broadly, the book makes a reflexive claim about the way in which knowing the filmmaking process, whether in anticipation or *a posteriori*, varies according to one's position in the industry. Beyond valuing working roles and hierarchies as inescapable aspects of the lived experience of filmmakers, I expose how specific types of filmmaking problems are mediated by specific roles and hierarchies—how directors, for instance, are more concerned about what actors perform on screen than how they physically get to the location. Both operations are necessary to the film's making, but by virtue of a specific division of labor, each problem is systematically assigned to a different social agent. By extension, these agents anticipate different outcomes—for example, whether the actor will look good on screen or whether s/he will arrive on location. This book connects an empirical interest in everyday labor, process, and technological use with an analytical interest in the imponderable futures mediated by social agents.

The extent to which this future has been unpredictable can be measured by contemplating the fates of *Décor* and *Poisonous Roses* after their release. Following a premiere at the 2014 Cairo International Film Festival, *Décor* went on to be shown for three weeks in domestic theaters, reaping meager box-office revenues and being quickly sold to Rotana for a standard television distribution deal. The financial losses incurred by the film matched a modest showing at international film festivals. The film never accomplished New Century's avowed ambition to reach the Cannes Film Festival. *Poisonous Roses*, on its part, debuted at the 2018 International Film Festival in Rotterdam. The film went on to be shown at over fifty festivals across the globe and reaped numerous prizes in Egypt and abroad, including three major prizes at the 2018 Cairo International Film Festival. The film was briefly showcased at the alternative film venue Zawya, and it continues to tour international venues. No one working and thinking about *Décor* and *Poisonous Roses* at the time of their making could have predicted such outcomes. Hopes and dreams about the films' success were at the edges of consciousness, unknowable and unpredictable. What was expected, however, were the lengthy mediations through which the crew, the cast, and the equipment would go to create what became *Décor* and *Poisonous Roses*. This book stands as a testimony to this journey.

Appendix 1
Division of Labor

Team	Role	Arabic title	Expected tasks // Comparative info
(1) Production	Producer	*Muntig*	The term "producer" has ambiguous meanings in Egypt. Generally, it designates the film's financer, no matter his/her experience in the film business. The more specific term *muntig munaffiz* (executive producer) is used for a subcontracted producer who finances films with another investor's money.
(Overseen by the producer)	General manager	*Musbrif'am*	The general manager is the executive head of production in a company. The producer retains the ultimate say over major production decisions—such as which scripts to fund, which stars to hire, how many movie copies to print in a theatrical run—but the general manager runs the business day to day. The manager rarely intervenes in artistic decisions, except as they concern budget constraints, logistical obstacles, or distribution imperatives (including hiring stars).
(Overseen by the general manager)	Line producer	*Muntig fanni*	The line producer is the highest member on the production team in a film project. The line producer's central task is to budget all spending made during production: wages, production fees, permit fees, transportation fees, and so on. The budget managed by the line producer covers preparations and shooting, while the postproduction budget is negotiated between the production company and the postproduction company. The line producer also signs contracts with all cast and crew members, receives money-related demands from the artistic crew, and oversees the daily activities of his/her production team. While the broad job description of a *muntig fanni* in Egypt does not greatly differ from the American line producer, the actual decisions under his/her authority cover more ground. They include following up on censorship approval, securing shooting permits, scouting apartments, or buying accessories and costumes. While his/her decisions are ultimately subordinate to the producer's authority, s/he has some autonomy in choosing his/her production team and in hiring all crew members. The line producer can also have a minor say in the artistic side of filmmaking.

(Overseen by the line producer)	Production manager	*Mudir intag*	The production manager executes in practice what the line producer oversees in principle. The production manager is the line producer's hand on the ground: s/he physically participates in all production activities that require legwork—like scouting, or getting permits, or setting meetings—while remaining hierarchically superior to the rest of the production team. The production manager directs the whole production operation on location. Unlike the line producer, who is not always indispensable on location, the production manager needs to be alert to all artistic, technical, and logistical demands from the crew.
(Overseen by the line producer and production manager)	Location manager	*Lukayshun manajir*	The location manager is a position which appeared in the 2000s. The location manager is like a super-assistant in practice: s/he overviews more tasks on set than his/her hierarchical subordinates, but is still bound to execute the work demanded by the production manager and the line producer.
(Overseen by the line producer and production manager)	Production assistants // Production executors	*Musa'id intag // Munaffiz intag*	Production assistants and executors are responsible for executing production tasks on the ground as instructed by their hierarchical superiors (for example, buying costumes and props, scouting locations, and following up on shooting permits). Once shooting begins, each production crew member takes charge of a specific department, including locations and set building, props, postproduction, costumes, transportation, and breaks.
(Overseen by the line producer and production manager)	Runner	*Ramar*	Runners are usually production trainees or workers with little experience who can be dispatched to get last-minute orders by anyone in the production team. The number of runners varies according to the size of the production.
(Overseen by the producer and general manager)	Accountant	*Muhasib*	The accountant issues payments to the crew, approving and verifying all spending in production on behalf of the film company. As all payments in the industry are in cash, the accountant is responsible for reviewing the distribution of the company's money either as prepaid production costs (*'uhad*) or as wages, given to the rest of the cast and crew.
(Overseen by the line producer)	Location services	*Khadamat*	The location services team consists of two to five people providing seats to higher-ranked crew members while being assigned to all cleaning duties.

(*continued*)

Team	Role	Arabic title	Expected tasks // Comparative info
(Overseen by the line producer)	Catering services	*Bufih*	The catering team consists of two to five independently contracted workers who serve all catering needs on set in exchange for individual fees.
(Overseen by the line producer)	Car services	*Sayyarat*	The car services team consists of a team of drivers who transport cast/crew members, equipment, or accessories. Reliable car services are prized by time-pressured production crews. Car services are different from vehicle rental services, which provide cars with specific models and colors to serve as props in shooting. Such companies are sought out on a car-by-car basis, depending on the film project's needs.
** (Overseen by the line producer)	Postproduction supervisor	*Mushrif al-bust*	The postproduction supervisor oversees the day-to-day transportation of audiovisual material between editing studios, coloring studios, and sound studios until the final film is printed. S/he is entrusted with the safety of hardware upon which audiovisual material is transported.
(2) Cast	Star	*Nigm(a)*	Stars are hired by the producer in agreement with the director and the screenwriter during preparations, usually without a casting session. Star status has different meanings in the Egyptian film industry. For some, a star is any actor who brings audiences to the box office. Stars are sought out by local and regional distributors for this reason (see Ganti 2012, 208–12). Signing a star can convince distributors to buy film rights, which guarantees revenue to the producer and encourages his/her investment. Setting aside a few indisputable (mostly male) names, some actors lay claim to star status without being perceived as commercially successful actors by distributors. These are well-known actors, who play main characters in various movies, and who receive star treatment on set (for example, having their own caravan and their own assistants, and interacting with the highest-ranked crew members).
	Secondary actor	*Mumassil(a) samawi(ya)*	Secondary actors are contracted by the production crew. Their salary is negotiated based on the length of their role in the script. The distinction between secondary actors and talking extras is not necessarily evident on screen, but it is evident in the industry's status ranking. Stars get their own caravans/hotel rooms to relax in between shots; secondary actors are made to share rooms. While stars are rarely (if ever) auditioned, secondary actors are regularly called in to audition, although they may also be directly selected by the director. Secondary actors and

Term	Arabic	Description
		extras may undergo casting, which either involves reading a short scene on camera or being selected based on a *regisseur*'s video database. Actors have no hierarchy of promotion. There is no predetermined path to becoming a star, and there is no sense in which one needs to be a secondary actor before becoming one.
Talking extra // Silent extra	*Cumbars mutakallim* // *Cumbars samit* // *magami'*	Calling someone an "actor" means that s/he engages in a central artistic role on set and, by extension, that s/he is worthy of respect. Calling someone an "extra," by contrast, means that s/he cannot act and, by extension, that s/he can be treated with less respect and, in some cases, with moral opprobrium. While all extras are at the bottom of the industry's status hierarchy, talking extras are better paid and better considered than silent extras. Silent extras serve as on-screen fillers. They come in numerous grades with a decreasing order of pay: A-class extras ("classy" Egyptian types); B-class extras ("less classy" Egyptian types); and C-class or "popular" extras (used in scenes with popular neighborhoods or parties). "Foreign" extras playing Euro-American characters have a separate hierarchy of status. While stars and secondary actors receive direct instructions from the director, extras are directed by the assistant director and his/her assistants. Silent extras are cast on looks alone, based on a headshot or a casting video, often just with the assistant director's approval.
Casting agent	*Regisseir*	The casting agent in Egypt is only responsible for casting extras, unlike in Euro-American industries, where all actors have casting agents to manage their contact with the production. As extras can come in great numbers, the *regisseir* is expected to "control" them, not just in the sense of securing their data (height, weight, headshot), but also in the physical sense of herding crowds on set. To this end, and depending on the *size* of the crowd, the *regisseir* can have several colleagues who bring their own extras and help with crowd control. Extras are paid daily by the *regisseir*, who receives a lump sum in exchange for the total number of extras on set and takes his/her share off the extras' daily wages.
Actors' manager	*Sbu'am mumassilin*	The actors' manager is hired by the casting agent to maintain phone contact with secondary actors and extras during the period of preparations and shooting, alerting them to their working schedules, their locations, the costumes they need to bring, and so on.

(*continued*)

Team	Role	Arabic title	Expected tasks // Comparative info
	Actor assistant	*Labbis*	The actor assistant manages the star's schedule and helps him/her with the wardrobe on set, usually working closely with the costume script supervisor and the stylist. Actor assistants are paid by the production, and amounts are negotiated according to the star's status.
(3) Direction	Director	*Mukhrig*	The director is the head of all artistic operations in a film. This includes, to give a brief list, contributing adjustments to the screenplay; casting actors and guiding their on-screen position, movement, and performance on set; writing down camera angles, movements, and lens sizes in a shooting script; selecting shooting locations and their design; selecting the actors' costume, hairstyle, and makeup; selecting shots to edit in/out of the film in postproduction; choosing the film's color mood; and guiding the musical soundtrack's mood. The artistic decisions overseen by the director are equally overseen by the cast/crew members holding the highest positions in their respective teams. Thus, screenwriting decisions are negotiated with the screenwriters; acting decisions are negotiated with the stars or (occasionally) the secondary actors; camera decisions are negotiated with the cinematographer; set design decisions are negotiated with the art directors; and so on. However, all artistic decisions are ultimately under the director's authority, and all disagreements are settled by his/her word. On set, the director's interactions are generally limited to the actors, the artistic crew, and the direction team led by the assistant director. In postproduction, directors always sit with editors, mixers, and musical composers, unlike in Hollywood, where directors traditionally submit the material to the studio to follow up on postproduction.
(Overseen by the director)	First assistant director	*Musa'id mukhrig*	The assistant director ensures that the director's word is carefully carried through by the production team. The assistant director is directly hired by the director, but s/he hires his/her own script supervisors and second assistants. The number of assistants varies according to the size of the production and the assistant director's preferences, but typically ranges from one to five assistants. In preparations, his/her main tasks are to make a complete script breakdown and a shooting schedule with his/her assistants and in coordination with the production team. The assistant director also casts secondary characters and extras, while following up on the director's

Role	Term	Oversight	Description
			decisions in scouting. On set, the assistant director communicates all artistic demands to the production team (for example, when a new location needs to be scouted, when a new character needs to be cast, when a new prop needs to be bought), while guiding the timely execution of the daily call sheet with his/her assistants. S/he is also responsible for the roll call and the extras' movement during shots. Assistant directors cannot argue artistic decisions, but they can discuss financial or logistical limitations to the director's vision.
Movement script supervisor	*Script baraka*	(Overseen by the assistant director)	Continuity script supervisors act as the assistant director's assistants, unlike in Euro–American industries, where they are strictly responsible for ensuring continuity. Script supervisors assist with various breakdowns, casting sessions, or meetings with artistic crew members. In shooting, movement script supervisors follow movement continuity, as well as assisting in giving directions to secondary actors and extras.
Costume script supervisor	*Script malabis*	(Overseen by the assistant director)	In addition to assisting the assistant director with managerial tasks, the costume script supervisor follows costume continuity on set. S/he will write a daily call sheet to list each actor's costumes. Costume script supervisors interact with actors, their assistants, and the styling team to make sure that the actors are wearing the right costume with the right makeup and hairstyle in each shot.
Props script supervisor	*Script aksiswar*	— (Overseen by the assistant director)	A script supervisor is sometimes appointed to follow prop continuity specifically in bigger productions, but this position is usually filled by the movement script supervisor.
Second assistant director // Trainee	*Musa'id tani //* Trayning	(Overseen by the assistant director and script supervisors)	Second assistants are employed to direct extras and to help script supervisors with daily direction tasks. Like the production runner, s/he is expected to absorb the rudiments of the job gradually, on his/her own, until the assistant director deems him/her worthy to upgrade within the team's hierarchy, from continuity script supervisor, to assistant director, to director. Numerous exceptions exist to this promotion model, but it is the widely expected pattern in Egypt. This career makes little sense in a Euro–American context, where continuity script supervisors, assistant directors, and directors have separate professions with separate career paths.

(continued)

Team	Role	Arabic title	Expected tasks // Comparative info
(Overseen by the director)	Clapper	*Clak*	The clapper helps with the synchronization of sound and image with regular claps before each shot, while writing up shooting reports that are a vital resource in indexing disconnected takes prior to postproduction. Unlike in Euro-American industries, the clapper works under the director, not the cinematographer. The profession is accorded little respect in the industry, whether in terms of salary or hierarchical status, and promotion follows no clear path.
Video-assist subteam (overseen by the director)	Video-assist operator	*al-Assist*	The video-assist operator plugs in cables and monitors to give a live image of ongoing shots on set, while troubleshooting all issues related to video-assist equipment. Operators cannot advance within their own profession unless they open a separate equipment office. Most operators get promoted into production or cinematography. The video-assist operator is usually chosen by the director.
(Overseen by the video-assist operator)	Video-assist assistant	*Musa'id assist // Kablagi*	The assistant is usually tasked with rolling up cables before and after shooting, while ensuring that the video-assist monitor runs without glitches.
Gripping subteam (overseen by the director)	Key grip	*Mashinist // Usta bansar*	The key grip owns and rigs all camera motions (dolly tracks, dollies, cranes), while commanding a team of gripping workers on set. The key grip is usually hired by the director, since he has the final say over camera movement. While grips outside Egypt are responsible for rigging all equipment on set, Egyptian grips only deal with camera motions. Equipment is rented out at a separate rate from the grip's daily wage, but the key grip usually negotiates a lump sum deal with the production. Until the 1990s, the key grip was also the chief camera technician, as rental companies owned both analog cameras and their motions.
(Overseen by the key grip)	Best boy grip	*Musa'id (mashinist) awwal*	The best boy grip is second in line after the key grip when it comes to rigging camera motions and dolly tracks. When the key grip is away, as happens when equipment is divided between two or more locations, the best boy takes over all the key grips' commanding tasks on set.

(Overseen by the key grip and best boy grip)	First/second assistant	*Musaʿid (mashinist) tani/talit*	First and second assistants are responsible for laying down dolly tracks according to the key grip's or the best boy's directives, and for carrying around heavy equipment on set.
(Overseen by the key grip and best boy grip)	Trainee	*Trayning*	Grip trainees usually stay by the equipment car or the equipment deposit on set. They may be called upon to lend tools to the grips (door stubs, wrenches).
— (Overseen by the director)	Steadicam operator	*Stidikam*	The Steadicam operator becomes the cameraman in shots needing a Steadicam rig. The operator is usually chosen by the director, but the decision can revert to the cinematographer or the line producer in cases where the director has no preferences.
(Screenwriting)	Screenwriter	*Sinarist //* *Maʾalif*	Egyptian screenwriters enjoy a relatively high status insofar as they are treated as the film's authors—unlike in Bollywood, where they are little valued because they inscribe ideas discussed in preproduction "sittings" and "narrations" (Ganti 2012, 222–23), and unlike in Hollywood, where they are submitted to several checks by studios until they receive the "green light" to shoot (Wasko 2003, 15–36). Screenwriters sometimes write scripts on their own, or by receiving a commission from a producer or a movie star. Usually, directors will bring adjustments to the script in conjunction with the screenwriter during preparations. Screenwriters are contracted by the producer, sometimes in conjunction with a specific director or a specific star, other times separately. After getting a screenplay accepted by a production company, the screenwriter's main working interactions are with the director—except, of course, in cases where the screenwriter *is* the director. The screenwriter exerts no influence on preparations, shooting, or postproduction beyond the writing of a script. Thus, the script everywhere guides the film's execution, yet the screenwriter is absent throughout the production process—hence his/her ghostly presence.

(*continued*)

Team	Role	Arabic title	Expected tasks // Comparative info
**	Editor	*Muntir*	The (image) editor assembles different image cuts of the film based on the screenplay, the shooting script, the available material, and the director's instructions. The editor usually has his/her own insight into the film as an artistic product and discusses how best to execute it with the director. This insight into the takes to select, scenes to include in the cut, and rhythm to adopt in cuts is under the director's purview, but the editor argues in the editing room to improve the overall product. The editor, much like the composer and the screenwriter, is a relatively solitary worker: s/he works with equipment to craft the final film with the director's occasional intervention. The Egyptian editor is additionally endowed with the role normally reserved for the "technical director" in Euro-American industries: s/he supervises the technical quality of the film product, from the audiovisual material to the film's printing. Before the advent of digital shooting, there was a specialized editor who transferred the work done by the main editor using positive footage onto the raw negative material. These negative editors (*muntir nigatif*) were far and few, as their jobs had the greatest consequence for the producer's capital, distilled into edited negatives.
** (Overseen by the editor)	Assistant editor	*Musa'id muntir*	The assistant editor's main job is to synchronize image and sound material and convert the raw material into a workable format for the editor. The assistant editor can sometimes help in "building" scenes (*tarkib*), but the editor remains responsible for building and rearranging each cut in conversation with the director. When film material was still analog before the 2010s, the assistant editor would also create a list of edge numbers to synchronize cuts with the negative editor.

(4) Cinematography	Cinematographer	*Mudir taswir*	The cinematographer is the artistic reference in most matters concerning the film's image: lighting, camera equipment, camera settings (exposure, frame-rate), lens types, and lens filters. While it is common to say that "the image belongs to the cinematographer," two decisive image-related decisions are in the director's hands in Egypt: lens size, which determines the frame's size on screen, and camera movement. In addition to his/her artistic duties, the cinematographer manages a very large team on set, which can have between twenty and thirty crew members. This team includes his/her core crew, the camera crew, and the gaffing crew. The cinematographer hires his/her own cameraman (when not the one manipulating the camera), focus puller, lighting script supervisor, and gaffer.
(Overseen by the cinematographer)	Cameraman	*Kamiraman*	The cameraman adjusts camera settings and manipulates the camera while shooting according to the cinematographer's and the director's orders.
(Overseen by the cameraman)	Focus puller	*Fukas pular*	The focus puller replaces lenses and filters while adjusting the depth-of-field in given shots.
— (Overseen by the cinematographer)	Lighting script supervisor // Trainee	*Skript ida'a // Treyning*	The lighting script supervisor notes down all visible sources of light to ensure lighting continuity between discontinuous takes. Trainees who are brought along to learn on a cinematography crew are usually given the lighting script supervisor's position.
Camera subteam (overseen by the cinematographer)	Chief camera technician	*Usta camera*	The chief camera technician carries around the camera on set. S/he is selected by the equipment rental company, but his/her pay comes out of the production's budget directly. The chief camera technician chooses his/her own crew and ensures the safety of the company's equipment. Given such responsibilities, the chief camera technician enjoys a relatively higher status by comparison with runners, extras, or their hierarchical subordinates.
(Overseen by the chief camera technician)	First/second camera assistant	*Musa'id kamira tani/ talet*	The first and second camera assistants can carry around the camera and its attending equipment, but usually defer to the chief camera technician in this matter. Their number varies according to the size of the production and the amount of equipment on set.

(*continued*)

Team	Role	Arabic title	Expected tasks // Comparative info
(Overseen by the chief camera technician)	Trainee	*Trayning*	Camera trainees carry the boxes containing filters and lenses on set. They are expected to observe how their superiors handle the camera and the location before being allowed to handle it themselves.
	Operator	*Idir-kamira*	The operator works with the camera crew to transfer all digital material filmed on set onto several hard drives containing the film material that is sent to the editing office. The operator is a job that appeared with the digital era: s/he has replaced the "loader" from the analog era, who used to be responsible for changing and storing film negatives until they were sent to the editing office. The difference now is that the operator can look at the material live on location and check on lighting and color, communicating with the artistic crew about the quality of the material. The operator knows which memory cards are in use, which ones are coming from the camera, and which ones go back to the camera after being backed up.
Gaffing subteam (overseen by the cinematographer)	Gaffer	*Usta ida'a*	The gaffer rigs all artificial lights and attending equipment as ordered by the cinematographer. Unlike in Euro-American industries, where gaffers create a lighting plan to be rigged by the grips, the Egyptian gaffer and his/her team rig all lighting equipment under the cinematographer's direct command. Gaffers usually own their equipment, and there are dense networks of borrowing and lending spotlights among gaffing crews.
	Best boy light	*Musa'id (ida'a) awwal*	The best boy light is second in command behind the gaffer when it comes to rigging lights and instructing the gaffing crew. In the gaffer's absence, the best boy can adjust lighting on his/her own and work directly with the cinematographer.
(Overseen by the gaffer and best boy light)	First/second assistant	*Musa'id (ida'a) awwal/tani*	First and second assistants are responsible for rigging spotlights under the gaffer's or the best boy's guidance, and for carrying heavy lighting equipment around the set. First assistants are usually more experienced than second assistants, and have more knowledge about lighting setups, but all assistants execute a similar job.

(Overseen by the gaffer and best boy light)	Trainee	*Trayning*	Gaffing trainees keep by the equipment car or the equipment deposit on set. They may be called upon to lend tools, gels, or spotlights to the gaffers.
**	Colorist	*Kulurist*	The colorist executes the color grading of the film's image in agreement with the cinematographer. Whereas the editor can argue with a director over specific takes or scenes, the colorist is under much stricter time pressure from the production company. While film companies now tend to be equipped with their own editing stations (that is, Mac computers with Final Cut Pro software), coloring is still done in specialized postproduction venues with a permanent workforce. Coloring sessions are costly and production factors in little time to work through coloring in postproduction.
**	Graphics supervisor and assistants	*Grafiks*	The graphics supervisor works with his/her team on adding video effects to the scenes in need of adjustments. Like the colorist, the graphics supervisor and assistants work in specialized postproduction companies and have no say over the film's overall artistic direction. Graphics sessions are costly and production companies factor in little time to work through graphics in postproduction.
(5) Art direction	Art director	*Muhandis dikur*	The art director makes all artistic decisions concerning set design, prop design, and prop hiring. The art director manages a large team of workers, between ten and thirty crew members depending on the workforce needed to build the set. S/he hires his/her own first assistant, the chief builder (who hires all set building workers), and the prop master (who hires all prop assistants). Unlike production designers in Hollywood, who supervise the film's style overall, Egyptian art directors are directly tasked with designing and executing all sets, as well as being directly involved in designing or choosing all props (a job normally reserved to the "prop master" in Hollywood). Much like the French *chef décorateur*, the Egyptian art director concentrates all authority over the background of the film image.

(continued)

Team	Role	Arabic title	Expected tasks // Comparative info
(Overseen by the art director)	First assistant decorator	*Musa'id muhandis dikur*	The first assistant decorator assists the art director with set and prop design, while overseeing building to ensure that it is executed to the art director's specifications. While art directors are largely absent on location except to check on the set's and props' finishing, the assistant decorator supervises set building workers daily.
(Overseen by the first assistant decorator)	Second/third assistant // Trainee	*Musa'id tani/talet //* Trayning	Second and third assistants tend to follow up on specific aspects of set building and prop design, usually to train in the specific skills needed to supervise these works. Second and third assistants often act as trainees to the art director.
Props subteam (overseen by the art director and first assistant decorator)	Prop master	*Usta aksiswar*	The prop master hires or buys all props needed by the art director at the lowest possible cost and using the exact image *"reference."* Prop masters also supervise furnishing before each shot. While prop masters in Euro-American industries are well-versed in the screenplay and the props' continuity, Egyptian prop masters just execute furnishing according to the direction team's guidance.
(Overseen by the prop master)	Prop assistant	*Musa'id aksiswar*	Prop assistants move around props on set and, in cases where props are hired, bring them back to their storage when the shooting is done.
Building subteam (overseen by the art director and first assistant decorator)	Chief builder	*Munaffiz dikur*	The chief builder hires and supervises all craftsmen involved in building sets or decorating apartments, from the first to the last nail. While the chief builder supervises the whole building operation, each craft is headed by a "lead" worker (commonly called *usta*). All chief builders train as cinema carpenters before becoming builders. Some chief builders are attached to the studio where they work, but most have their own workshops. While most set-building workers are paid by the day, the chief builder receives a weekly wage.
Carpentry subteam (overseen by the chief builder)	Chief carpenter	*Usta naggar*	The chief carpenter oversees the building and finishing of all wood-based products on set, including walls and furniture. He is the most important set-building craftsman, because he is involved in nearly all set-building and prop-making operations.

(Overseen by the chief carpenter)	Carpenters	*Naggarin*	Carpenters build the basic structure of the set and all wooden props. Cinema carpenters are specialized craftsmen: they work under tight schedules, with any type of material, with an eye to making sets and props that have a convincing "finish" on camera, not a durable existence as normal carpenters would build.
Painting and varnishing subteams (overseen by the chief builder)	Chief painter // Chief varnisher	*Usta na"ash // Usta ustur*	The lead painter supervises the painting of all surfaces in sets and props. The lead varnisher lays the finishing touch on anything varnished (parquet, furniture). The lead painter and lead varnisher hire their own respective crews to assist with their tasks.
(Overseen by the chief painter/ varnisher)	Painters // Varnishers	*Na"ashin*	Painters and varnishers work under their chief to paint and varnish all items needing their intervention.
—(Overseen by the chief builder)	Electrician(s)	*Kahraba'i silisyun*	An electrician is called in whenever work is needed on an apartment's electricity or non-cinematic lights. The electrician's knowledge differs from that of the gaffers, who specialize in cinema equipment.
Subteam(s) under the chief builder	Glass worker(s) // Metal worker(s) // Plumber(s) // Upholsterer(s)	*'Amil izaz// Haddad // Sabhak // Minaggid*	The glass worker, the metal worker, the plumber, and the upholsterer are contracted on specific tasks when needed on set. These workers are hired by the chief builder, but have no permanent presence on set.
(Overseen by the chief craftsmen)	Trainees	*Trayning // Sabi*	Craftsmen trainees pass on tools and assist their superiors with menial tasks on set. Much like in the gaffing and gripping team, trainees are brought to observe work, and with time can be promoted to working in set-building operations.

(*continued*)

Team	Role	Arabic title	Expected tasks // Comparative info
(6) Styling	Stylist	*Staylist*	The stylist oversees all decisions concerning the actor's look—hair, makeup, and costume—much like the "HMC" department in the United States and in France (Rot 2014, 22). The look's style/color is made to match the movie's aesthetics in collaboration with the artistic crew. The stylist also works with the costume script supervisor to ensure that all actors are fitted with the right costumes prescribed by the screenplay. The role of stylist emerged in the 2000s. Before then, star actors would choose their own costumes, and secondary actors' and extras' costumes were included under art direction.
(Overseen by the stylist)	Assistant stylist	*Musa'id staylist*	The assistant stylist helps with designing, acquiring, maintaining, and keeping track of costumes, while making sure to dress each actor appropriately on set in collaboration with the costume script supervisor. The assistant ensures, in particular, that all extras are donning the right look.
Subteam (1) under the stylist	Chief costumer	*Munaffiz malabis*	The chief costumer would supervise the execution of the stylist's designs prior to the 2000s. Since costume design has declined as an industrial practice, the chief costumer now simply oversees the daily maintenance of costumes with his/her assistants.
(Overseen by the chief costumer)	Costume assistants	*Musa'id malabis*	Costume assistants maintain, repair, wash, and iron all costumes on set. While the chief costumer may work on several projects at once, the assistants must remain available on location.
Subteam (2) under the stylist	Hairstylist/ Makeup artist	*Kwafir/ Mikab artist*	The hairstylist and the make-up artist execute or supervise the execution of hairstyles and makeup as determined by the stylist. The head makeup artist or coiffeur checks the actor's look at the beginning of each scene, and whatever changes happen to the look throughout the day are followed through by assistants, who can do touch-ups on the actors whenever they sweat a little or become disheveled. Stars often bring their own hairstyling and makeup crew, which means that the production's hairstylist or makeup artist works more with secondary actors and extras.

(Overseen by the hairstylist/makeup artist)	Hairstyling assistant(s)/ Makeup assistant(s)	*Musa'id kwafīr/ Musa'id mikab*	The hairstylist or make-up artist's assistants execute basic hairstyles and looks on set and, whenever needed, make additional touch-ups between takes. The number of assistants is determined by production needs: at least one assistant must remain on set at all times, but extra assistants are hired depending on the overall number of extras.
—Subteam (3) under the stylist	Costume designer	*Musammim azyaʾ*	The costume designer creates costume concepts and executes them from scratch. Few productions now use costume designers, except in historical dramas.
(7) Sound	Sound engineer	*Muhandis sut*	The sound engineer is responsible for recording all sounds on set, while ensuring the general quality of recorded sound (avoiding background noise, ensuring dialogue is loud enough). The sound engineer can interrupt takes or ask for re-takes when there is a technical issue with sound, but this authority is generally subordinated to the director's and the cinematographer's authority.
(Overseen by sound engineer)	Boom operator // Sound assistant	*Giraf // Musa'id sut*	The boom operator installs individual microphones on actors and holds the boom microphone while recording on set. In larger productions, additional sound assistants are hired to install ambient microphones and heavy recording equipment.
**	Sound editor	*Muntir sut*	The sound editor cleans the recorded soundtrack with dialogue and ambient sound of all noises. In Egypt, the sound editor tends to be the sound engineer on set.
** —(Overseen by sound editor)	Assistant editor	*Musa'id muntir*	Assistants can be hired to help with repetitive tasks such as cleaning tracks or exporting material. The number of assistant (if any) varies according to the sound editor's personal needs and preferences.
**	Sound mixer	*Mixir*	The sound mixer harmonizes the film's image with the dialogue soundtrack, various effect tracks, and the composer's music.

(*continued*)

Team	Role	Arabic title	Expected tasks // Comparative info
** —(Overseen by the sound mixer)	Assistant mixer	*Musa'id mixir*	Assistants can be hired to help with tasks such as creating sound effects and exporting material. The number of assistants (if any) varies according to the sound editor's personal needs and preferences.
**	Composer	*Mu'allif*	The composer crafts the film's soundtrack according to the director's minimal directives, while trying to infuse his/her own feeling and insight into it. More than any operation in sound postproduction, the soundtrack is perceived as the main "artistic" operation, in contrast with "technical" concerns like sound editing or sound mixing. Most composers work on their own, but small companies have emerged to divide the load of composition, recording, and mixing.

Key

** Postproduction workers who are not involved in preparations or shooting.

— A position that is not necessary on all film sets according to industry conventions.

Appendix 2
Operational Sequence

Egyptian film production can be divided into four overarching stages: 1) screenwriting; 2) preparations; 3) shooting; and 4) postproduction. These stages can roughly be mapped onto the "preproduction–principal photography–postproduction" triptych in Euro-American industries, yet the operations constituting each stage are somewhat distinct in Egypt. Each stage comprises operations with mediators leading to the next stage: screenwriting produces a scenario that guides preparations; preparations produce actors, costumes, sets, props, camera equipment, and so on necessary to shooting; shooting produces all the audiovisual material manipulated in postproduction; and postproduction produces "the film." These operations are not always linearly antecedent to one another, but some operations are technically antecedent to others. In relevant areas, then, I highlight which operations are logically dependent on previous operations.

Stage	Operation	Arabic name	Expected tasks // Comparative info
(1) Screenwriting	Screenwriting	*Kitābit sinaryu*	Screenwriting is technically an act of graphic inscription like permit making or script breakdowns, yet it is deemed an artistic practice and enjoys a more flexible timeline. Unlike in Hollywood, there is no "development" stage prior to the writing: preproduction is thought to begin with the screenplay's first draft. Screenplays are either adapted from a film or novel, or based on an idea by the screenwriter, the director, the star actor, or the producer. The screenwriter writes the action on screen, the characters' internal states, and the dialogue, sometimes in two separate columns (following the French style), but more often in succession (following the American style). Conventionally, the screenplay includes little detail on image composition and sound, which are left to the director and his/her artistic crew. Although the screenplay can always be adjusted during preparations, the core work starts with a version containing at least all the main characters and locations.
(2) Preparations		*Taḥḍīr*	"The film" begins and ends at different points for different crew members, if it ever goes beyond screenwriting or preparations. Different crew members are contracted at different points in the project's unfolding. For *Décor*, for instance, the art directors Asem Ali and Nihal Farouk started working about two weeks prior to the stylist Salma Sami, while some assistants were hired several weeks into preparations. Likewise, gaffer and grip teams finish the project once shooting is over, even though "the film" is not released until several months later.

Script breakdown(s) *(Tafrighat)*

The screenplay undertakes a complete breakdown by the assistant director and his/her assistants. Each assistant director has a different way of breaking down the script, but all breakdowns are now made in digital format (as a table in a Microsoft Word or Excel file, or using specialized software such as MovieMagic). This operation sometimes takes an intermediary calligraphic stage, with a printed script copy colored with highlighters and annotated by pen and pencil. The assistant director produces a general breakdown of all locations, characters, props, and costumes in the scenario, as well as a sequential breakdown divided by scene. While the sequential breakdown is used to make the shooting schedule, the general breakdowns are distributed to the production team and each concerned team head (for example, the character breakdown to the stylist, the prop breakdown to the art director). The breakdowns are the most exhaustive list of logistical elements needed in shooting.

Scouting	*Mu'aynat*	Scouting is a complex operation involving several discrete steps, all aimed at securing shooting locations. First, a location breakdown is written by the direction team and given to the production team, which starts scouting main locations before the complete breakdown is ready. Then, scouting pictures are gathered by legwork production workers, who take to the streets every day in preparations to take pictures. In some cases, production teams have recourse to fixers to secure locations in some neighborhoods in Cairo or in other Egyptian cities. Unlike professional scouts in Euro-American industries, these fixers broker between the production team and a specific location, distributing payments to the local owners and taking a commission on their work. Once all pictures are gathered by the line producer, they are shown to the artistic crew, who narrow down a selection of locations to be scouted in person. After scouting in person, final locations are selected by the artistic crew and secured by the production team.
Set/Prop design	*Tasmim dikur/ aksiswar*	The art director and his/her assistants design and create sets and props. His/her focus is to transform the script into a believable background to the film's image. When s/he receives a script, the art director begins by imagining what the characters' everyday environment would look like: where they live, where they go to school, and so on. Then, s/he starts producing images, whether using pencil sketches or computer designs, of these places as described in the script.
Set building	*Bana dikur*	Once the set/prop design is complete, it is printed and given to the chief builder and the craftsmen who build given set/prop items. These designs are annotated by hand, both by the art director and the craftsman, to include unspecified measurements or special demands. Once materials necessary to build the set/props are acquired by the production team, the craftsmen start building the set. Set building starts after scouting decisions are finalized, except in studio shooting, where the set design can begin while scouting is ongoing.

(*continued*)

Stage	Operation	Arabic name	Expected tasks // Comparative info
	Prop acquisition // manufacture // rental	*Shira // tasni' // igar aksiswar*	The art director chooses all props either in person or using picture references. His/her assistants ensure that the prop master and the production team bring the right props on location. Unlike larger Euro-American productions where the acquisition of props is handled by specialized companies (see Vonderau 2015), props are acquired by different teams on an Egyptian film crew. Furniture (*farsh*) can be rented out from a prop storage by the prop master, manufactured by the set building team, or bought from commercial stores by the production team. *Mise-en-scène* props can be either rented from a storage by the prop master or bought by the production team. Some props are kept in the production company's own storage, but most props on a given film set are either rented, made, or bought.
	Casting	*Kasting*	Casting is usually directed by the assistant director, who both runs casting sessions with secondary actors and selects extras based on picture and video data with the casting agent. Casting sessions can range between filming an actor facing the camera without asking him/her to chat much and acting out several scenes (sometimes in groups) in front of the camera. While the director makes final decisions on main and secondary roles (using the assistant director's recommendations), the assistant director usually makes final decisions on talking and silent extras. The line producer gets no say over which extras are chosen, but s/he can negotiate the number of extras brought on set (which can burden overall production costs).
	Fitting	*Pruvit malabis*	Once an actor is cast and contracted, s/he goes through fitting. Based on a costume breakdown verified with the costume script supervisor, the stylist takes the actor's measurements to buy clothes, get them from storage, or ask the actor to bring clothes from his/her own wardrobe (as was the most common practice until the 2000s). Costumes are now seldom designed for specific films, except period dramas. Once enough clothes are gathered, each fitting session consists of trying on costumes in several combinations and, crucially, in taking pictures of each costume combination on the actor's body. The pictures are sent to the line producer and the director, who approves the final look in person usually. In some cases, the stylist will coordinate the look with the art direction team, to ensure that it matches the film's overall color palette. The cycle of gathering clothes, taking pictures, and discussing looks goes on until all costumes in the breakdown are filled—and, in the star's case, until all hair and makeup are settled.

Camera tests	*Tist kamira*	Cinematographers run tests on the film camera using several filters and lenses under different lighting, whether filming short clips or taking pictures. When the production company owns its own equipment, the cinematographer has no choice but to use its camera. In cases where there is no company camera, however, tests are used to determine which camera will be hired by the production team. These tests are discussed by the cinematographer and the director to settle which camera, camera settings, lenses, and filters will be used in shooting.
Rehearsals	*Pruva*	Rehearsals with actors during film preparations are not the norm across the industry, but when they do happen they take the form of a table reading between the director and the stars.
Pre-light	*Prilayt*	Once all locations are scouted and built, the cinematographer traces a general lighting plan with the gaffer, who ensures that the plan is physically feasible (that is, that there is enough space to rig certain spots on set, that the cables are long enough to reach all spotlights). This general plan is amended in "*pre-light*" sessions, where the cinematographer indicates to the gaffer, on location, where s/he wants to rig lights and how s/he wants to orient natural lighting sources using flags, reflectors, or similar equipment. The pre-light arrangement is liable to be adjusted immediately prior to the shot.

Call sheet (*Urdar*)

The call sheet is produced daily by the assistant director in conjunction with his/her assistants to list the order of shots on a given shooting day as well as all logistical demands to be secured by the production team. Communication on set is primarily oral, but the call sheet serves as a primary memory aid and reference point in case of a "drop."

(3) Shooting	*Taswir*	Shooting days are organized to create the audiovisual material that will be used in postproduction, but the logistics surrounding the shooting day go beyond the moment at which the material is recorded.

(*continued*)

Stage	Operation	Arabic name	Expected tasks // Comparative info
Shooting script (*Dikupaj*)			

The scenario's closest extension is the shooting script (*dikupaj*), which is written by the director to divide each scene into a list of shots. Shooting scripts vary greatly in their form according to each director's preference. Some complete a shooting script on paper before the shooting begins, others decide on their shots at the beginning of each shooting day, and yet others rely on scouting images and videos to leave a margin for improvisation on set. Storyboarding or sound planning are unusual practices in the Egyptian film industry.

Stage	Operation	Arabic name	Expected tasks // Comparative info
	Furnishing	*Farsh*	The first day-to-day operation on set is furnishing. On every shooting day in a new location, the art direction team guides the prop master and his/her crew in positioning the *mise-en-scène* props in the upcoming scene, either by executing the arrangements prepared in floor plans or by adjusting them on location. Such adjustments can come on the director's initiative. Furnishing is repeated with every scene change.
	Lighting	*Ida'a*	After the set is furnished, the cinematographer takes the space to set his/her lights according to his/her aesthetic preferences, the position of the sun, or the director's indications on camera movement. The cinematographer gives indications to the gaffing crew on where to rig the spots and which gelatin filters to add. The gaffer gives quick verbal cues to the lighting technicians, who physically manipulate the lights, while looking at the light's direction, angle, surface, hardness, and so on. The gaffer can tell the technician to adjust the tripod's position, the orientation of the spot's head (which is determined by the tripod's position, partly but also by the rotation on the head's axis), the tilt of the spot, the light's aperture, and, when needed, the gelatin, the flags, the frames, and the foam boards.

Dressing and makeup	*Libs wa makiyaj*	While the set is being furnished and lit, actors and extras are readied behind the scenes. They are dressed and styled according to the prepared look by the stylist's assistants, the hairstyling team, and the makeup team. In exceptional circumstances, stars may refuse to put on the agreed-upon look, which leads to extensive negotiations between the actor, the stylist, and the costume script supervisor to avoid shooting delays. The director can take this time to review the actor's performance in the upcoming scene. In complex scenes, the main script supervisor will try to catch actors to review the dialogue.
Camera setup	*Tabdir kamira*	The chief camera technician carries the camera to the location designated by the cinematographer. His/her assistants clean the camera and, when needed, help him/her set it on a tripod or a dolly. The cameraman or the focus puller changes lenses, filters, and camera settings with the camera assistants' help, following the cinematographer's commands.
Sound setup	*Tabdir sut*	The sound assistant helps actors in setting their microphone receivers discreetly, while the sound engineer tests the microphone connection from his/her control board. Conventionally, the sound engineer will set the microphone on his/her first encounter with a star, to introduce him/herself, but this task is normally undertaken by the assistant. When needed, sound assistants add recorders around the set to record ambient sounds and set the boom microphone to be operational before each take.
Rehearsals	*Pruva // Tist*	Once actors are ready and brought on set, there are rehearsals to test the mechanics of the actor's action (including dialogue lines and main movement) and/or the camera movement (that is, composition, speed, duration). Directors explain in space, before the shot, how they want to set the camera and move it in dialogue with the cinematographer. Rehearsals are usually recorded on the video-assist by the video-assist operator to be reviewed by the artistic crew. The assistant director starts a short roll call for these video rehearsals, starting with a usual "silence on set" (*budu'*), then "video" (to which the video-assist operator replies "rolling"), and "action." The rehearsals are instrumental in adjusting the image's composition by displacing props, or changing spotlight positions, or altering the camera frame, lens, filter, and movement, or the actor's performance (*ada'*).

(continued)

Stage	Operation	Arabic name	Expected tasks // Comparative info
	Image/sound recording	*Taswir/Tasgil sut*	The main operation in shooting is the "take," which is a specific image-cum-sound capture with a given camera movement and angle. All takes within a given angle constitute a shot, and all shots in the same location with a similar action constitute a "scene" (*mashhad*, plural *mashahid*). When a take is set to be taken, the assistant director and the location manager will shout out "*Hudu*" (Silence on set!) or "*Nibda*" (Let's calm down!) to quiet the hustling and bustling set before sound recording. The assistant director (in some cases the director) starts a roll call including "sound" and "[camera] speed," followed by a vocal confirmation by the sound engineer and the cameraman that the machine is running (*rolling* or *dayir*). The clapper then reads the scene and shot number, and claps to synchronize the recording of sound and image. The movement within the take starts when the director yells "action" and ends when s/he yells "stop" or "cut"—the sound and image recording ceases just as on-camera action. The roll call can be amended to include specific commands, including a call for "mark" when the clap needs to be taken again or a call for "movement" (*haraka*) when extras need to be moving in the background prior to the main movement. Actors perform, extras move, props are manipulated, and equipment records the whole assemblage to take a snippet of audiovisual material, thereby materializing a particular shot (in the director's shooting script) in a particular scene (in the scenario). Barring any error or artistic change, the serially recorded takes follow the assistant director's call sheet, which sets the order of scenes and (when the shooting script is known in advance) the order of shots within each scene. After each take, adjustments are made to image composition, camera movement, and actor performance after sometimes extensive conversations among artistic crew members. The shot is repeated with its camera angles, lenses, movements, lighting, and action (although it may involve slight adjustments in one or another element) until the director (and, secondarily, the cinematographer and the sound engineer) is entirely satisfied with the audiovisual material distilled in the shot. The camera is thereafter displaced for the next shot, with a new angle/ movement. The entire cycle of furnishing, rigging lights, setting tracks or tripods, changing lenses, changing costume/hairstyle/makeup starts all over again, in line with what is set for the next scene or shot in the call sheet.

	On-set photography	*Futughrafya*	After each shot, the photographer asks the actors to maintain the pose in order to take a studio shot, which is used in promotional material by the production company. This practice was inherited from the analog era, but it is no longer systematically executed after each shot, given time constraints and the ability to extract promotional material from the digital film itself. The on-set photographer can be, although s/he is not always, the "making-of" photographer.
	Break	*al-Brayk*	Break meals are ordered by a production assistant or executor. This worker will come early, with a pen and paper, to take individual orders on location. The choice of restaurants is limited for all workers except the stars, but each worker gets to order his/her own meal. Some workers, especially in gaffing, gripping, and art direction, prefer to take a per diem (*badal*) instead of a meal. Mealtimes are called roughly in the middle of the shooting day, after six hours of work, but are often skipped if the shooting is running late.

Shooting report (*Rahur*)

The clapper notes down in a shooting report all the information inserted on the clap before each take, including the shooting date, scene number, shot number, take number, the camera card's serial number, the lens number, and the name of the film, director, cinematographer, and production company. The scene and shot numbering is usually decided by the direction team and communicated to the clapper.

	(4) Postproduction	*al-Bust*	Much like in Hollywood (Wasko 2003, 50–51), Egyptian postproduction starts with image editing while shooting is ongoing. Although the term "*bust*" (an Arabized abbreviation of "post"- production) is common in today's industry, the postproduction process is still metonymically known as "*muntaj*" (editing).

Audiovisual material (*al-Matiryal*)

The audiovisual material constitutes the very matter of postproduction work. It is akin to a distilled extract produced, drop by drop, through the alembic of shooting. The daily yield of audiovisual material is backed up on hard drives, converted into a workable format, and synchronized by the assistant editor.

(*continued*)

Stage	Operation	Arabic name	Expected tasks // Comparative info
	Image editing	*Muntaj*	Using the treated image material, the editor starts "building" scenes (*tarkib*), which involves selecting takes and sequencing them, more or less, in the order prescribed by the screenplay or the shooting script. Once shooting is over and the material built, the editor works with the director on moving around shots and selecting different takes until they reach a final cut. Unlike in Hollywood, where the executive producer traditionally gets the last word on the final cut, the Egyptian director traditionally settles his/her own final cut (with some exceptions where the producer or the star interfere with the cut).
	Sound editing	*Muntaj sut*	Sound editing also relies on the synchronization made by the assistant editor after each shooting day. The edit starts with cleaning (*tandif*), which involves cutting away all "noise" in the dialogue and sound effect tracks. Once cleaning is over, the sound editor can start dubbing (*dublaj*) with the talking actors and the director. Once all operations are done, the sound-edit is traditionally sent back to the image editor to double-check on technical details (for example, whether the synchronization still works, whether all dialogues are clearly audible). Until the advent of digital technologies, the sound edit was performed by the image editor or his/her assistant in Egypt, adding three magnetic strips onto the reel: one for music, another for dialogue, and a last one for effects (*bruy*).
	Graphics	*Grafiks*	When a "final cut" is ready, the scenes needing video effects are sent to the graphics supervisor and, later, the entire cut is sent to the colorist. The technical sequence going from a final cut to video graphics to color applied to the updated cut can be thwarted in practice and reiterated if, for instance, a fault in the graphics is discovered while coloring.

Final cut

The cut is sent out to the mixer, the colorist, and the composer in twenty-minute chapters.

Color grading	*Kulur*	When the graphics are ready, the cut is conformed (that is, the editing decisions made on the lower-quality working image are transferred onto the higher-quality raw material). The conformed cut is sent to the colorist in twenty-minute chapters. S/he works with the cinematographer to enhance the film's colors. Given time pressures, color grading in commercial cinema usually involves matching color values across the whole movie without discriminating between intensities in specific scenes. The colorist's work is thus reduced to applying settings and exporting the material with the cinematographer's approval.
Composition	*Musiqa taswiriya*	After watching the first cut, the composer composes a track and records it in a studio with live musicians or, in some cases, using software. The recorded tracks are mixed into a single musical soundtrack, which is approved by the director and sent to the mixer.
Mixing	*Miksaj*	Mixing involves the final assemblage of the "final cut" (after graphics and coloring) with all recorded soundtracks, including the dialogue, the sound effects, the music, and the *foley* (that is, the sounds made by the movement of bodies and objects on screen). Time permitting, the mixer engages in a similar iterative process to the image and sound editor, whereby s/he matches certain rises and falls in dialogue, diegetic sound, and extradiegetic music according to his/her idea of image/sound balance, in collaboration with the director.
Printing	*Tiba'a*	Most domestic theaters were still equipped with thirty-five millimeter projection equipment by 2015, which means that the digital mix needs to be converted into a printable format and sent to Studio Misr, the Egyptian Media Production City, or Aroma, the only facilities with direct-to-print technology (through which digital material can be printed in thirty-five millimeter format). While printing is conceived as a fairly automatic operation, it is a very costly one, which is why producers ration printed copies.

Notes

Introduction

1 Continuity is a principle of filmmaking in which space-times recorded in a disjointed way on set are reassembled in a continuous sequence in editing. The continuity script supervisors ensure that when all recorded material is viewed in postproduction, no continuity lapses will occur (for instance, no objects will seem to appear or disappear in between two consecutive shots, no actors will change clothes in the same scene, and so on).

2 Under this broad umbrella, one can include well-known studies of "popular" *(sha'bi)* quarters in Cairo (Hoodfar, 1997; Ghannam, 2002; Ismail, 2006), middle-class consumption practices (de Koning, 2009; Peterson, 2011), or Islamic ethical movements (Starrett, 1998; Mahmood, 2005; Hirschkind, 2006).

3 The heightened sense of uncertainty wrought by country-wide unrest has encouraged some anthropologists to attend to the futures imagined in response to the postrevolutionary context (see Rommel, 2015; Schielke, 2015; Winegar, 2016; Armbrust, 2019). In Middle Eastern media studies, a similar concern has yielded analyses of social media use with various emphases, including cyber-activism (Herrera, 2014), political mobilization (see Markham, 2014; Wolover, 2016), and the body as a medium of protest (Kraidy, 2016).

4 This is corroborated by the fact that the industry's most recent fall in production numbers occurred in 2009–2010, nearly a year prior to the Revolution (Euromed Audiovisual III, 2013).

5 These disruptions also affect the theater audience's ability to attend films in person, with significant effects on box-office success. The production assistant Hany Abdel Latif mentioned the dire fate of *365 Yum Sa'ada* (*365 Days of Happiness*), which was released on January 25, 2011, and consequently incurred a sizeable loss.

6 The relative absence of the Revolution in the film industry's work might be related to the fact that I started fieldwork at a time that looks, in hindsight, like the beginnings of an ongoing counter-revolution and return of military might at the helm of the country.

7   Badawy made this demand given the company's concerns over leaks of visual materials to the press prior to the film's release. Therefore, I never took any personal pictures in New Century. The reader expecting behind-the-scenes illustrations of Egyptian film production will not find them in these pages, because this was a central condition of my access to New Century.

8   In addition to participant observation, I conducted around forty formal interviews with directors, cinematographers, screenwriters, producers, and editors. I also collected several newspaper articles, promotional materials, and internal writings and images related to commercial film production.

9   This commitment is visible in the anthropology of television (Ginsburg, 1991; 1993; Dornfeld, 1998; Born, 2004; Abu-Lughod, 2005; Salamandra, 2005; 2008; Moll, 2010; Pype, 2012; Barkin, 2013; 2014; Matzner, 2014), advertising (Moeran, 1996; Dávila, 2001; Mazzarella, 2003; Shankar, 2015), and newsmaking (Peterson, 2005; Bird, 2010; Boyer, 2005; 2013; Bishara, 2013; Gürsel, 2016).

10 For literature on the value of ethnography in media research, see Ginsburg et al. (2002) and Ganti (2014).

11 This perspective on technical action was perfected by the French school in the anthropology of technology (see Lemonnier, 1976; 1992; 2004; Coupaye, 2009; Cresswell, 2010 [1976]).

12 With a noted exception: the mobile phone has accrued its own anthropological literature over the years, but little attention has been given to the use of mobile phones in production processes (see Horst and Miller, 2006; Madianou and Miller, 2012; Postill, 2011: 69–85; Archambault, 2017).

13 Against a strictly Heideggerian reading, I do not take "reserves" as a technological imperative imposed by *Gestell*, a mysterious rationalizing force in Heidegger's description (1977)—a totalizing way in which reality is ordered. Most critiques targeting Heidegger's conception of modern technology aim at his "abstract," "monolithic," and "nostalgic" understanding of *Gestell* as an omnipresent, omnipotent, technological mode of revealing reality (see Verbeek, 2005: 61–75).

14 "Summoning" is a somewhat inadequate translation for the original Heideggerian term, *Herausfordern*. The German implies a sense of provoking, of forcibly bringing-forth into the world, of extracting something out of the world—what most translators have rendered as "challenging-forth." I have preferred the term "summoning" for the sake of readability.

15 In media anthropology, a similar attention to process can be found in the works of Dornfeld on the PBS series *Childhood* (1998), Boyer on the digital newsmaking process in Germany (2013), and Gürsel on wire-service photography in the Associated Press (2016).

16 Examples include Luhmann's concern with the way in which Western technocratic experts have sought to predict the future, with mitigated success historically (1998); Guyer's lament about the disappearance of the "near-future" in policy talk (2007); Adam and Groves' historical sociology of futures (2008); Rabinow's anthropology of the "contemporary" as a window onto a

posthuman future (2008; with Dan-Cohen, 2006); Augé's musings about the disappearance of the future *tout court* in a neoliberal world order (2011); and Pels' interest in how anticipated futures act on expert prediction in the present (2015).

17 An uncertain existential future is at stake in ethnographies of austerity in Europe (Knight and Stewart, 2016; Knight, 2017a; 2017b); economic uncertainty in Africa (Johnson-Hanks, 2005; Cooper and Pratten, 2014; Goldstone and Obarrio, 2016); global migration (Pine, 2014; El-Shaarawi, 2015; Sandoval-Cervantes, 2017); global security governance (Holbraad and Pedersen, 2013); and environmental degradation (Tsing, 2015).

Chapter 1. Industry

1 There are no other public cinema schools in Egypt, but several private schools have emerged in recent years: the International Advanced Media School (IAMS, which grants a degree in conjunction with Cairo University), the Cairo Jesuit Cinema School, Raafat el-Mihi's school, and the American University in Cairo's film studies program. There are also a variety of acting workshops, most notably Khaled Galal's workshop at the Opera House, Ahmad Kamal's workshop, Marwa Gibril's workshop, and the AUC's theatre program. The School of Fine Arts and the School of Applied Arts in Helwan University have trained some workers in the art direction field, including in costume design.

2 Since 1973, state-controlled institutions have been peripheral, by and large, to the financing of commercial films. The two notable exceptions were the Cinema Organization (*gihaz al-sinima*) at the Egyptian Media Production City (EMPC) as well as the Production Section (*qita' al-intag*) in the Egyptian Radio and Television Union (ERTU), which were both headed by Mamdouh al-Leithi until 2011. Both stopped funding movies by 2010. The Ministry of Culture administered a fund of twenty million Egyptian pounds for filmmakers in 2008 and 2012.

3 The Chamber is the organ representing the interests of the film industry to the government via the Federation of Egyptian Industries since 1972. It is officially supposed to propose new legislation to support the industry's activity and collect data on its economy. In practice, the Chamber's influence on state policy is almost null, and the gathered data is largely inaccurate, per the public testimony of an ex-member (the producer Mohammed el-Adl) in an episode of *Live Stream (Bathth mubashir)* that aired on CBC+2 on October 28, 2013.

4 Shafik reports that there were eighteen films made in 1994, twenty-five in 1995, and twenty-six in 1996, by contrast with the average of over sixty films per year in the 1980s (1998: 43).

5 These loans have taken two main forms according to the head of Film Clinic, Mohammed Hefzi: "lump-sum" deals, where the distributor buys exclusive rights to the film in exchange for a negotiated sum, and "minimum guarantee" deals, where the distributor gives partial loans to sustain production

while guaranteeing the producer a certain percentage of exhibition profits. According to Hefzi, minimum guarantee deals are not very frequent in Egypt, and the evidence presented by the amount of post-2000s films whose negatives (or original copies) are owned by ART and Rotana suggests that Hefzi's assertion is correct.

6   There are historical precedents to this model. In the 1980s, "contract movies" (*aflam al-mu'awlat*) were made with small capital on a short schedule and almost immediately released on VHS to be sold in the Gulf. The term "*mu'awlat*" refers to the financing pattern used by construction workers to secure one-off jobs in Cairo. The term is still used in the press to attack what is considered to be "low-quality" cinema, even though the *mu'awlat* production model has, properly speaking, disappeared.

7   By several estimates, stars making between five hundred thousand and one million Egyptian pounds were suddenly offered two to seven million pounds; and writers who made in the hundreds of thousands made millions. The producer Hussein al-Qalla, for instance, was asked by Good News to estimate a budget for *The Yacoubian Building* (2005). He initially proposed a twelve-million-pound budget with one superstar in mind. After this budget, al-Qalla was dismissed from the project. Good News thought it better to hire an unprecedented range of stars, which raised the movie's costs to a staggering forty-three million Egyptian pounds in al-Qalla's estimation, setting it among the most expensive Egyptian movies of all time.

8   These suspicions are difficult to verify, but it should be noted that such accusations have been part of the industry's lore since the 1940s (Armbrust, 2004: 81). They are also integral to the discourse of film industries across the world (in Bombay, see Ganti, 2004: 56-62; or in Hong Kong, see Martin, 2016).

9   International co-production has never been an established mode of financing in the Egyptian film industry, and it was agreed to on an ad hoc basis. For example, in the 1980s, the well-known director Youssef Chahine had strong links with French producers and made several French-Egyptian co-productions. This pattern subsided once Chahine's company, Misr International Films, stopped investing in film production in 2008.

10   For instance, *al-Fil al-azraq* (*The Blue Elephant*, 2014) was co-produced by Albatros (headed by producer Kamel Abu Ali), El-Shorouk (headed by media mogul Ibrahim el-Meallem), and Lighthouse (headed by the film's director, Marwan Hamed).

11   These facilities are no longer used today except to print thirty-five millimeter film copies destined to local exhibition venues, many of which are still not equipped with digital projection equipment (in DCP format). They are also among the few locations licensed to print in Dolby 5.1 sound.

12   Improvements to the digitized workflow are still expected. The cinematographer Marwan Saber explained, for instance, that some cameras produce file formats that are too large to be edited as such, so they need to be converted, then edited, then reconverted into the final format. Equipment

companies are working on unifying formats to allow postproduction operations needing different machines to proceed without format conversion, which should smooth out the workflow.

13   This description applies to "commercial" as well as "independent" production. However, "independents" tend to seek funding in various national, regional, and international organizations, including the Egyptian Ministry of Culture, grants from regional film festivals (such as the now-defunct Dubai, Abu Dhabi and Doha Film Festivals), regional cultural initiatives like the Beirut-based Arab Fund for Art and Culture (AFAC) and the Culture Resource (al-Mawrid al-Thaqafi), and international film funds (such as the World Cinema Fund at the Berlin International Film Festival; the Hubert Bals Fund at the Rotterdam International Film Festival; the Centre National du Cinéma Fund in France).

14   Egyptian TV drama production has been heavily promoted by the state since the 1960s, but under the auspices of a public-sector company. There were institutional boundaries between television production and commercial cinema until the early 1990s.

15   The website elcinema.com, managed by the marketing agent Alaa el-Karkouty, publishes box-office figures. Yet these figures are likely to be inflated to attract more audience members, since they are estimates based on reports by the production company while the movie is still in theatres.

16   External sales follow different conventions: the external distributor tends to buy exclusive rights to the film on all platforms (cinemas, television, Internet), with a different payscale depending on whether the film will sell to smaller or bigger audiences in the distributor's estimation. For instance, a film to be sold to the on-demand channel OSN is cheaper than a film to be sold to the giant Rotana, and starpower is an important facet of these calculations.

17   This is true in local *and* regional distribution. I have systematically heard that it is impossible to distribute in the Arab world without having a pan-Arab movie star (such as Adel Emam, Ahmad Helmy, Karim Abdel Aziz). This is especially true in the Gulf, which accounts for "the overwhelming majority of sales" internationally since the 1980s (Flibbert, 2001: 87).

18   Since salaries are paid out in cash, the accuracy of rumoured numbers can never be fully ascertained unless one is party to the transaction. My estimates rely on second-hand reports by directors and production crew members—especially line producers, who work daily with the budget. However, even a line producer's or a company's records may not faithfully reflect the actual salary paid to a star, given the incentive to deflate salaries on paper to avoid taxation. One should also remain aware of the propensity to inflate a star's monetary worth, which can be cultivated by the star him/herself to increase his/her market value.

19   In contrast, the greatest stars would be paid five thousand Egyptian pounds in the 1980s according to the late casting agent Magdy Abdelrahman, with a total movie budget around two hundred or two hundred and fifty thousand pounds. Male stars in today's industry are far more valuable than female ones,

but this pattern of privilege has only developed after the 1960s, when star female actresses like Faten Hamama and Shadia made higher salaries than their male counterparts (al-'Ashari, 1968: 75).

20 I have no accurate estimates on salaries in television or in advertising, but I was told that the salaries in advertising tend to be double (per shooting day). Salaries in television are comparable with film production for most crew members, except that the length of TV drama shooting (twelve to sixteen weeks, as opposed to three to four weeks in films) makes income streams more regular when the production company pays on time.

21 For instance, Al Nasr was inherited by Sharif Ramzy from the late Mohammed Hassan Ramzy, who in turn inherited it from his father, Hassan; Hany Gerges Fawzi inherited his company from his father, Gerges Fawzi; Misr International Films was inherited by Gaby Khoury from his uncle, the illustrious Youssef Chahine; the Sobky companies were initially inherited as a single company by Ahmad and Mohamed El Sobky from their father, Hassan.

22 Younes was supposed to be the costume script supervisor in *Décor*, yet she was unable to commit to the movie given her own scheduling issues, which is why el-Bagoury was hired.

23 Conventionally, artistic crew members and production crew members get a lump-sum contract, while technical workers receive weekly payments. In the latter case, payment is delivered by the production team to the head of the unit (such as the gaffer, the key grip, the prop master), who redistributes the money to his crew in turn. Unit heads are responsible to assess how many workers they need on any given day and how much they pay each worker.

24 Some cross-industry standards prevail in exceptional cases. Set building craftsmen, for instance, are paid by the day: in 2014, a carpenter received one hundred and twenty-five Egyptian pounds per day, while a lead carpenter received one hundred and seventy-five pounds.

25 There are precedents for such raises, however, particularly in tightly-knit professional networks such as the one created by cinematographers trained at the High Cinema Institute.

26 In principle, workers are only paid once the camera rolls, which means that all work invested in preparing the shooting, whether before the beginning of the shooting schedule or on a given shooting day, is unpaid. If workers show up to work on location, but the camera does not roll because the star is absent or tired, as happened on some occasions in *Décor*, the day is called off and no one gets paid.

27 The distinction between zero-budget and independent cinema is not uncontested: Hala Galal argues that independent director Ibrahim Battout's experience with very low budget cinema (as well as her own experience) shows how it is possible to make movies without having to go through censorship, or to get shooting permits, or to do any of the standard work of commercial film production.

28 Zohairy was alluding to the common stereotype according to which just about anyone can pretend to be a filmmaker in downtown Cairo, which

has its own closed scene of short film festivals outside the market circuit. According to Zohairy, these festivals show "some of the worst movies I've ever seen," and he was referring both to the product's technical finishing as well as its content.

Chapter 2. Process

1   This connection is most visible in the oral histories of skill transmission between *khawagat* (Egyptians of foreign origin, mostly European) and Egyptian craftsmen. Elyachar reports, for instance, that one of the great master craftsmen in the Hirafiyeen neighborhood in Cairo learned his skill at repairing automatic car transmissions from the *khawaga* Antoin, and that this mode of transmission was frequent in the Heliopolis neighborhood (2005: 111–15). Similarly, the clapper Abdelsalam Radwan told me that the generation of cinema workers that had learned from *khawagat* was the most skilled, because they had original knowledge of the cinema craft, which is now somewhat corrupted by its transmission via Egyptian workers. Abdelsalam's folk history of the industry rejoins the accepted historical narrative concerning this pattern of transmission, most notably through the education of Studio Misr technicians in Germany and France in the 1930s (El-Hadari, 1995: 89–90).

2   There is no typical time to promotion in this sense, because it depends on the availability of contracts and the superior's willingness to promote a worker, in addition to the worker's own sense of when to "flip." However, it seems that the expansion of the Egyptian film industry into television and advertising has led novices to quicker promotion since the 1990s. This is partly because they can do the same job for lower salaries in a market in constant need of additional labor, but also because the amount of work has increased if one counts all three industries combined.

3   A light-box is a large, assembled cubic metal frame hung from the ceiling with a diaphane cloth underneath it and spotlights that give an even lighting over a square surface.

Chapter 3. Reserves

1   For a fuller treatment of the conflicting on-stage and off-stage discourses about "culture" at this kind of conference, see Winegar (2006, 2009) and Mehrez (2010).

2   This point was well made in Spitulnik's (1998; 2002) and Larkin's (2008) work on radio technology in Zambia and Nigeria, respectively.

3   All equipment items have an established daily rental price. According to the gaffer Mahmoud Morsi, they are negotiable just within a ten percent margin, but as a rule, larger productions try to negotiate a lump sum deal with equipment companies or owners to cover equipment needs throughout the production.

4   The cinematographer Marwan Saber says that the Cannon 5D and 7D cameras, which are digital photography cameras with video capability, have

been used in the industry since the mid-2000s. However, these cameras are not engineered for cinema, contrary to the Red or the Alexa.

5   Prior to the spread of Final Cut Pro, the editor Heba Othman said that the most common editing software was Avid. It was used by two companies: Elixir (which later bought Studio Misr) and Lightworks (where the now-prominent editors Mona Rabie, Dalia Nasser and Rabab Abdel Latif used to work).

6   The assistant director Wael Mandour told me that industry insiders thought that the industry would digitize within ten to fifteen years, but they would never have thought that it would occur as fast as it did. For instance, the cinematographer Wael Darwish was still buying thirty-five millimeter cameras until 2010–2011, but these cameras had been made obsolete by 2013.

7   As Saber explained, Focus only buys equipment by "*trial-and-error*," that is, by testing whether the equipment can survive or not in local working conditions. These conditions include excessive heat, dust, and working hours, which explains why it is important to buy equipment that can "carry the load" (*yishil*).

8   Repairs are handled by European equipment companies except in limited areas (including batteries, lighting equipment). Any repair attempted outside these companies is liable to void the equipment's guarantee. Reda Zanita complained that the monopoly held by foreign companies over repairs allows them to comfortably set their own prices, thereby adding a great financial burden onto Egyptian equipment owners.

9   This potential can be thwarted in practice when production crew members avoid answering the phone. On set, for instance, all crew members silence their mobile phones to avoid disturbing the ongoing recording, and they must leave the immediate vicinity of the shoot to talk freely.

10   The video-assist can be impracticable in a financial sense, but it can also be impracticable in a logistical sense. In *Décor*, in an extreme long shot where the protagonists Sharif and Maha appeared in the distance on a rocky beach in Alexandria, Ahmad Abdalla had to come next to the camera's monitor to check his takes, because the wireless video-assist had a maximal range of thirty-five meters in clear conditions and just about twenty-five meters in the troubled morning weather.

11   The well-known editor Mona Rabie insists that digital technologies have not made editing work "faster," because editors who were optimally trained on analog technologies could produce films within a similar timeframe. However, digital technologies made it possible (time-wise and cost-wise) to try more combinations of takes and scenes than the analog process.

12   See, in the Egyptian case, Barak's history of the development of modern time in tune with the rise of new modes of transportation and communication in the colonial era (2013).

Chapter 4. Coordination

1   These logistical problems have presumably existed since the industry's beginnings, yet I have not gathered enough material to historicize the way in which logistics were handled before the early 2000s, when computers and mobile phones became widespread. Prior to these technological devices, production studios or downtown cafés like *Ba'ra* acted as central logistical nodes where cast and crew members could meet, call sheets could be distributed, etc. Such geographical constraints have now largely disappeared, although a great deal of logistical work is still carried out in production offices.

2   In practice, this meant that trusted crew members in *Poisonous Roses* had their payments delayed to cover for more pressing costs (for instance, paying for a prop or a costume bought in a commercial boutique, or paying workers who cannot accept payment by installments, which is still a common practice in the industry).

3   This sum includes the postproduction budget, which was not taken into account by Farghalli in his calculations, since it was negotiated on a separate basis between New Century and the different postproduction companies where the project was finished. However, the difference of 3.6 million Egyptian pounds between Farghalli's initial budget and the final cost cannot be nearly accounted for by postproduction or marketing.

4   In smaller productions or in emergency cases (for instance, when an unexpected sum of money is needed to keep the shooting day alive), cash can be handled by trustworthy emissaries until it reaches the location. In *Décor*, these emissaries have been legwork production workers or trusted drivers. This is not preferred by production teams, however, given suspicions of theft and the necessity to record transactions.

5   Some executive chiefs like the gaffer, the key grip, and the chief builder can also work on several locations at once, yet they will always "send someone" *(yib'at hadd)* equally qualified to stand in their place. In *Décor*, the chief builder Wezza would leave his chief carpenter Hosny on location, while the gaffer Mahmoud Morsi would leave his best boy Desha. This is in part why gaffing, gripping, or building crews are so large, because everyone can be asked to step up when a superior leaves the location.

6   Tanning workshops produce several animal-based products, including yellow gelatin. The process begins with boiling the excess grated off the skins destined to become leather, then the boiled extract is cooled in water basins, cut into wiggly slices, and arranged on very tall towers on the rooftop of tanning workshops to dry in the Cairo sun.

7   Workers can indeed walk great distances without using the metro, the microbus or the taxi, even though Cairo is an unfriendly urban environment for pedestrians (Sims, 2010: 236–37). This is partly because they can then assess journey times more accurately than in more comfortable motorized transportation, but it is also because it is sometimes necessary to "get somewhere" as fast as possible, which may well be by foot.

8   Of course, this division of labor depends on the overall size of the crew. In principle, all these tasks can be executed by a single legwork crew member: Edward Nabil, the production manager in *Poisonous Roses*, worked on his own in Hala Lotfy's *Coming Forth by Day* (2012).

9   A clip-on is a piece of equipment necessary to assemble the steadicam, which is a rig allowing the cameraman to latch the camera onto his body and move around the set while keeping the frame relatively stable.

10   One way in which Egyptian filmmakers regularly articulate the distinction between their own industry and Euro-American ones is precisely by saying that Europeans only work "by paper and pencil," while Egypt remains an "oral" industry.

Chapter 5. Visualization

1   In Peirce's words, "an *Icon* is a sign which refers to the Object that it denotes merely by virtue of characters of its own, and which it possesses, just the same, whether any such Object actually exists or not." (1932: 2.247).

2   I could not elaborate on these habits beyond the specific projects that I have witnessed between 2013 and 2015. Only a longer-term study could demonstrate the link, if any, between digital technologies and the filmmaker's ability, here and now, to accurately anticipate how some aspect of "the film" will look later. In such a study, the weight of artistic decisions in past projects could more clearly be linked to the way in which artistic workers make decisions based on similar mediators. It would be interesting then to examine to what extent filmmakers reproduce certain sociotechnical conditions to yield similar results in different projects.

3   Crew members in analog times had some access to "rushes," which were printed out of the negative during the shoot, but these stills were comparatively more expensive and time-consuming than the moving images available on the video-assist today.

4   Video-assist technology was introduced into the film industry via the advertising sector in the early 2000s. At the time, some equipment companies started specializing in video-assist equipment. The video-assist came to constitute an autonomous "subteam" on set. Each rental office sends its own men to operate its own equipment, partly to ensure that the operator has the appropriate skills to make the equipment work, and partly as an insurance policy with expensive equipment.

5   Unlike in Bollywood and Dhallywood, where dubbing is the norm given the noise made by analog cameras (Ganti, 2012: 227–29; Hoek, 2014: 65), contemporary Egyptian films only resort to dubbing when it comes to correcting "mistakes" in an actor's performance or in sound recording (for instance, when a dialogue line has been unclearly recorded).

6   In Chennai, Pandian briefly described how production workers survey "the city with a digital camera" to flow with the director's "wishes, however obscure" (2015: 60). Describing a scouting session filmed by two assistants, Grimaud indicates that "scouting is above all trying to see 'what [the place]

gives to the image' (. . .) whether it is mentally or with the help of a photo or video camera (. . .)" (2003: 230–31).

Chapter 6. Enchantment

1 In Hollywood, there is an important "technical" discourse based on quantitative metrics to anticipate audience behavior (see Zafirau, 2009). This discourse is reflected in—and supplemented by—an important film economics literature (see Litman, 1998; Eliashberg et al., 2006). Reliable quantitative metrics are inexistent in Egypt, and as such, evaluating film success relies on "intuitive" categories to use Zafirau's expression.

2 This phenomenon has been ascertained in commercial cinema (Hughes, 2006; Ganti, 2012), television (see Matzner's work on "maids" as an archetype of working-class female consumption in Bombay, 2014), and advertising (see Mazzarella's work on the archetypal "middle-class Indian consumer" as a marketing target, 2003).

3 "Sobky" is a form of cinematic entertainment named after two well-known producers, Ahmad and Mohamed El Sobky. The genre is based on popular songs, belly dancing, cheap gags *(iffihat)*, and fantasies of male violence. It is worth noting that these formal characteristics are not unique to the Sobky genre, whether in the contemporary industry or in historical terms. Yet the recent dominance of Sobky films over the Egyptian cinema landscape has made this specific genre a target for much public criticism and scrutiny (see El Khachab, 2019).

4 This nationalist phenomenon has been extensively documented in various areas of Egyptian popular culture (see Armbrust, 1996; Abu-Lughod, 2005), as well as in other media industries (see Mazzarella, 2003, and Ganti, 2012, on the "Indian audience").

5 See Hahn (1994) on how spectators borrow conventions of spectatorship from interactive song-and-dance performances known as *faiva* in Tonga; or Armbrust (1998) on interactive viewing in popular *(sha'bi)* movie theatres in Cairo; or Ethis on similar audience behavior in early twentieth-century France (2009); or Srinivas on contemporary Bangalore (2016).

6 A technocrane is a kind of gripping equipment allowing the camera to move on a 360° axis, at a distance and at different heights.

7 This anxiety is not strictly an Egyptian phenomenon: Rot (2014) has written extensively about the script supervisor's worries in France.

8 With an estimated population of 82 million Egyptians, this would put Egypt at a rate of one screen per 330,000 to 410,000 people. As Shafik notes, West Germany counted 3,664 cinema halls in 1983 with a comparable population to Egypt, which only had 267 halls in 1986 (1998: 40). Since then, the number of Egyptian movie theatres has decreased while the overall population has only been increasing.

Bibliography

Abu-Lughod, Lila. 2005. *Dramas of Nationhood: The Politics of Television in Egypt.* Chicago, IL: University of Chicago Press.

Adam, Barbara, and Chris Groves. 2008. *Future Matters: Action, Knowledge, Ethics.* Leiden: Brill.

Akrich, Madeleine. 1993. "Les formes de la médiation technique." *Réseaux* 60: 87–98.

———. 1987. "Comment décrire les objets techniques?" *Technique et Culture* 9: 49–64.

al-'Ashari, Mohammed. 1968. *Iqtisadiyat sina'at al-sinima fi Misr: Dirasa muqarana.* PhD diss., Cairo University.

Amin, Hussein. 1996. "Egypt and the Arab World in the Satellite Age." In *New Patterns in Global Television: Peripheral Vision*, edited by John Sinclair, Elizabeth Jacka, and Stuart Cunningham, pp. 101–125. Oxford: Oxford University Press.

Aouragh, Miriyam. 2012. "Social Media, Mediation and the Arab Revolutions." *tripleC: Communication, Capitalism and Critique* 10, no. 2: 518–536.

Appadurai, Arjun. 2013. *The Future as Cultural Fact: Essays on the Global Condition.* London: Verso.

———. 1986. "Introduction: Commodities and the Politics of Value." In *The Social Life of Things: Commodities in Cultural Perspective*, edited by Arjun Appadurai, pp. 3–63. Cambridge: Cambridge University Press.

Archambault, Julie. 2017. *Mobile Secrets: Youth, Intimacy and the Politics of Pretense in Mozambique.* Chicago, IL: University of Chicago Press.

Armbrust, Walter. 2019. *Martyrs and Tricksters: An Ethnography of the Egyptian Revolution.* Princeton, NJ: Princeton University Press.

———. 2004. "Egyptian Cinema On Stage and Off." In *Off Stage/On Display: Intimacy and Ethnography in the Age of Public Culture*, edited by Andrew Shryock, pp. 69–98. Stanford, CA: Stanford University Press.

———. 1998. "When the Lights Go Down in Cairo: Cinema as Secular Ritual." *Visual Anthropology* 10, no. 2–4: 413–442.

———. 1996. *Mass Culture and Modernism in Egypt.* Cambridge: Cambridge University Press.

———. 1995. "New Cinema, Commercial Cinema, and the Modernist Tradition in Egypt." *Alif: Journal of Comparative Poetics* 15: 81–129.

Askew, Kelly. 2002. "Introduction." In *The Anthropology of Media: A Reader*, edited by Kelly M. Askew and Richard R. Wilk, pp. 1–13. Malden: Blackwell Publishers.

Augé, Marc. 2011 [2008]. *Où est passé l'avenir?* Paris: Éditions du Seuil.

Balfet, Hélène. 1991. "Des chaînes opératoires, pourquoi faire?" In *Observer l'action technique: Des chaînes opératoires, pourquoi faire?*, edited by Hélène Balfet, pp. 11–19. Paris: CNRS Éditions.

Banks, Miranda J., Bridget Conor, and Vicki Mayer, eds. 2015. *Production Studies, the Sequel! Cultural Studies of Global Media Industries*. London: Routledge.

Barak, On. 2013. *On Time: Technology and Temporality in Modern Egypt*. Berkeley, CA: University of California Press.

Barkin, Gareth. 2014. "Commercial Islam in Indonesia: How Television Producers Mediate Religiosity among National Audiences." *International Journal of Asian Studies* 11, no. 1: 1–24.

———. 2013. "Reterritorialization in the Micromediascape: Indonesian Regional Television amid the Rise of Normative Media-Islam." *Visual Anthropology Review* 29, no. 1: 42–56.

Baudrillard, Jean. 1972. *Pour une critique de l'économie politique du signe*. Paris: Gallimard.

Bechky, Beth A. 2006. "Gaffers, Gofers, and Grips: Role-Based Coordination in Temporary Organizations." *Organization Science* 17, no. 1: 3–21.

Beck, Ulrich. 1992. *Risk Society: Toward a New Modernity*. London: SAGE.

Becker, Howard. 2008 [1982]. *Art Worlds*. Berkeley, CA: University of California Press.

Benjamin, Walter. 2007 [1935]. "The Work of Art in the Age of Mechanical Reproduction." In *Illuminations*, edited by Hannah Arendt, pp. 217–252. Translated by Harry Zohn. New York: Schocken Books.

Bird, S. Elizabeth, ed. 2010. *The Anthropology of News and Journalism: Global Perspectives*. Bloomington, IN: Indiana University Press.

Bishara, Amahl. 2013. *Back Stories: U.S. News Production and Palestinian Politics*. Stanford, CA: Stanford University Press.

Blair, Helen. 2001. "'You're Only as Good as Your Last Job': The Labour Process and Labour Market in the British Film Industry." *Work, Employment and Society* 15, no. 1: 149–169.

Boelstorff, Tom. 2008. *Coming of Age in Second Life*. Princeton, NJ: Princeton University Press.

Bolter, Jay David, and Richard Grusin. 2000. *Remediation: Understanding New Media*. Cambridge, MA: The MIT Press.

Born, Georgina. 2004. *Uncertain Vision: Birt, Dyke, and the Reinvention of the BBC*. London: Secker and Warburg.

———. 1997. "Computer Software as a Medium: Textuality, Orality and Sociality in an Artificial Intelligence Research Culture." In *Rethinking Visual Anthropology*, edited by Marcus Banks and Howard Morphy, pp. 139–169. New Haven, CT: Yale University Press.

Bourdieu, Pierre. 1986. *Distinction: A Social Critique of the Judgment of Taste*. London: Routledge.

————. 1977. *Outline of a Theory of Practice*. Cambridge: Cambridge University Press.

Boyer, Dominic. 2013. *The Life Informatic: Newsmaking in the Digital Era*. Ithaca, NY: Cornell University Press.

————. 2012. "From Media Anthropology to the Anthropology of Mediation." In *The SAGE Handbook of Social Anthropology*, edited by Richard Fardon, pp. 383–392. London: SAGE.

————. 2007. *Understanding Media: A Popular Philosophy*. Chicago, IL: Prickly Paradigm Press.

————. 2005. *Spirit and System: Media, Intellectuals, and the Dialectic in Modern German Culture*. Chicago, IL: University of Chicago Press.

Bryant, Rebecca, and Daniel M. Knight. 2019. *The Anthropology of the Future*. Cambridge: Cambridge University Press.

Caldwell, John T. 2008. *Production Culture: Industrial Reflexivity and Critical Practice in Film and Television*. Durham, NC: Duke University Press.

Callon, Michel. 1986. "Some Elements of a Sociology of Translation: Domestication of the Scallops and the Fishermen of St. Brieuc Bay." In *Power, Action and Belief: A New Sociology of Knowledge?*, edited by John Law, pp. 196–223. London: Routledge.

Chakravarti, Leila Zaki. 2016. *Made in Egypt: Gendered Identity and Aspiration on the Globalised Shop Floor*. New York: Berghahn.

Chamoux, Marie-Noëlle. 2010 [1978]. "La transmission des savoir-faire: Un objet pour l'ethnologie des techniques?" *Technique et Culture* 54–55, no. 1: 139–161.

Chion, Michel. 1994. *Audio-vision: Sound on Screen*. New York: Columbia University Press.

Christopherson, Susan. 2008. "Beyond the Self-Expressive Creative Worker: An Industry Perspective on Entertainment Media." *Theory, Culture and Society* 25, no. 7–8: 73–95.

Clark, Andy, and David Chalmers. 1998. "The Extended Mind." *Analysis* 58, no. 1: 7–19.

Cooper, Elizabeth, and David Pratten, eds. 2015. *Ethnographies of Uncertainty in Africa*. New York: Palgrave Macmillan.

Couldry, Nick. 2008. "Mediatization or Mediation? Alternative Understandings of the Emergent Space of Digital Storytelling." *New Media and Society* 10, no. 3: 373–391.

Coupaye, Ludovic. 2009. "Ways of Enchanting: *Chaînes Opératoires* and Yam Cultivation in Nyamikum Village, Maprik, Papua New Guinea." *Journal of Material Culture* 14: 433–459.

Cresswell, Robert. 2010 [1976]. "Technique et Culture: Les bases d'un programme de travail." *Technique et Culture* 54–55, no. 1: 23–45.

Curtin, Michael, and Kevin Sanson, eds. 2017. *Voices of Labor: Creativity, Craft, and Conflict in Global Hollywood*. Berkeley, CA: University of California Press.

————. 2016. *Precarious Creativity: Global Media, Local Labor*. Berkeley, CA: University of California Press.

Dajani, Karen F. 1980. "Cairo: The Hollywood of the Arab World." *International Communication Gazette* 26: 89–98.

Darré, Yann. 2006. "Esquisse d'une sociologie du cinéma." *Actes de la recherche en sciences sociales* 161–162: 122–136.

Darwish, Mustafa. 1998. *Dream Makers on the Nile: A Portrait of Egyptian Cinema.* Cairo: American University in Cairo Press.

Dávila, Arlene. 2001. *Latinos, Inc.: The Marketing and Making of a People.* Berkeley, CA: University of California Press.

De Koning, Anouk. 2009. *Global Dreams: Class, Gender, and Public Space in Cosmopolitan Cairo.* Cairo: American University in Cairo Press.

De l'Estoile, Benoît. 2014. "'Money is Good, but a Friend is Better': Uncertainty, Orientation to the Future, and 'the Economy.'" *Current Anthropology* 55, no. S9: S62–S73.

Deleuze, Gilles. 1966. *Le Bergsonisme.* Paris: Presses Universitaires de France.

Dickey, Sara. 1993. *Cinema and the Urban Poor in South India.* Cambridge: Cambridge University Press.

Dickinson, Kay. 2012. "Introduction: In Focus—Middle Eastern Media." *Cinema Journal* 52, no. 1: 132–136.

Dornfeld, Barry. 1998. *Producing Public Television, Producing Public Culture.* Princeton, NJ: Princeton University Press.

Edwards, Elizabeth, and Janice Hart. 2004. *Photographs, Objects, Histories: On the Materiality of Images.* London: Routledge.

Eisenlohr, Patrick. 2010. "Materialities of Entextualization: The Domestication of Sound Reproduction in Mauritian Muslim Devotional Practices." *Journal of Linguistic Anthropology* 20, no. 2: 314–333.

———. 2009. "Technologies of the Spirit: Devotional Islam, Sound Reproduction, and the Dialectics of Mediation and Immediacy in Mauritius." *Anthropological Theory* 9, no. 3: 273–296.

———. 2006. "As Makkah is Sweet and Beloved, so is Madina: Islam, Devotional Genres and Electronic Mediation in Mauritius." *American Ethnologist* 33, no. 2: 230–245.

El-Hadari, Ahmed. 1995. "Les Studios Misr." In *Égypte: 100 ans de cinéma*, edited by Magda Wassef, pp. 86–97. Paris: Institut du Monde Arabe/Éditions Plume.

El Khachab, Chihab. 2019. "The Sobky Recipe and the Struggle over 'the Popular' in Egypt." *Arab Studies Journal* 27, no. 1: 34-61.

———. 2017. "State Control over Film Production in Egypt." *Arab Media and Society*, 23 (Winter/Spring).

El-Shaarawi, Nadia. 2015. "Living an Uncertain Future: Temporality, Uncertainty, and Well-Being among Iraqi Refugees in Egypt." *Social Analysis* 59, no. 1: 38-56.

Eliashberg, J., A. Elberse, and M. Leenders. 2006. "The Motion Picture Industry: Critical Issues in Practice, Current Research, and New Research Directions." *Marketing Science* 25, no. 6: 638-661.

Elyachar, Julia. 2005. *Markets of Dispossession: NGOs, Economic Development, and the State in Cairo.* Durham: Duke University Press.

Engelke, Matthew. 2010. "Religion and the media turn: A review essay." *American Ethnologist* 37, no. 2: 371-379.

Ethis, Emmanuel. 2009. *Sociologie du cinéma et de ses publics.* Paris: Armand Colin.

Euromed Audiovisual II. 2008. *The Mediterranean Audiovisual Landscape* (Report).

Euromed Audiovisual III. 2013. *Statistical data collection project on film and audiovisual markets in 9 Mediterranean countries. Country Profile 1. Egypt*

Fahmy, Ziad. 2013. "Coming to Our Senses: Historicizing Sound and Noise in the Middle East." *History Compass* 11, no. 4: 305-315.

Flibbert, Andrew. 2001. *Commerce in Culture: Institutions, Markets, and Competition in the World Film Trade*. PhD diss., Columbia University.

Ganti, Tejaswini. 2014. "The Value of Ethnography." *Media Industries Journal* 1, no. 1: 16-20.

———. 2012. *Producing Bollywood: Inside the Contemporary Hindi Film Industry*. Durham and London: Duke University Press.

———. 2004. "The Production and Distribution of Popular Hindi Cinema." In *Bollywood: A Guidebook to Popular Hindi Cinema*. New York and London: Routledge.

Ganz, Adam and Lina Khatib. 2006. "Digital Cinema: The Transformation of Film Practice and Aesthetics." *New Cinemas: Journal of Contemporary Film* 4, no. 1: 21-36.

Gell, Alfred. 1992. "The Technology of Enchantment and the Enchantment of Technology." In *Anthropology, Art and Aesthetics*, edited by Jeremy Coote and Anthony Shelton, pp. 40–63. Oxford: Clarendon Press.

———. 1988. "Technology and Magic." *Anthropology Today* 4, no. 2: 6-9.

Ghannam, Farha. 2002. *Remaking the Modern: Space, Relocation, and the Politics of Identity in a Global Cairo*. Berkeley: University of California Press.

Ginsburg, Faye D. 1993. "Aboriginal Media and the Australian Imaginary." *Public Culture* 5, no. 3: 557–578.

———. 1991. "Indigenous Media: Faustian Contract or Global Village?" *Cultural Anthropology* 6, no. 1: 92–112.

Ginsburg, Faye, Abu-Lughod, Lila and Brian Larkin, eds. 2002. *Media Worlds: Anthropology on New Terrain*. Berkeley: University of California Press.

Goldsmith, Ben, Susan Ward, and Tom O'Regan. 2010. *Local Hollywood: Global Film Production and the Gold Coast*. St Lucia: University of Queensland Press.

Goldstone, Brian and Juan Obarrio, eds. 2016. *African Futures: Essays on Crisis, Emergence, and Possibility*. Chicago, IL: University of Chicago Press.

Graeber, David. 2012. "The Sword, the Sponge, and the Paradox of Performativity: Some Observations on Fate, Luck, Financial Chicanery, and the Limits of Human Knowledge." *Social Analysis* 56, no. 1: 25-42.

Grimaud, Emmanuel. 2003. *Bollywood Film Studio, ou Comment les films se font à Bombay*. Paris: CNRS Éditions.

Guillory, John. 2010. "Genesis of the Media Concept." *Critical Inquiry* 26: 321-362.

Gürsel, Zeynep D. 2016. *Image Brokers: Visualizing World News in the Age of Digital Circulation*. Berkeley: University of California Press.

Guyer, Jane 2007. "Prophecy and the Near-Future: Thoughts on Macro-Economic, Evangelical, and Punctuated Time." *American Ethnologist* 34, no. 3: 409-421.

Hahn, Elizabeth. 1994. "The Tongan Tradition of Going to the Movies." *Visual Anthropology Review* 10, no. 1: 103-111.

Hannerz, Ulf. 2016. *Writing Future Worlds: An Anthropologist Explores Global Scenarios*. London: Palgrave MacMillan.

Heidegger, Martin. 1994. "La Chose" In *Essais et conférences*. Translated by Jean Beaufret. Paris: Gallimard.

———. 1977. "The Question Concerning Technology." In *The Question Concerning Technology and Other Essays*. Translated by William Lovitt. New York: Harper Colophon Books.

Henley, Paul. 2010. "Seeing, Hearing, Feeling: Sound and the Despotism of the Eye in 'Visual' Anthropology." In *Beyond the Visual: Sound and Image in Ethnographic and Documentary Film*, edited by Gunnar Iversen and Jan Ketil Simonsen. Højbjerg: Intervention Press.

Hepp, Andreas and Friedrich Krotz, eds. 2014. *Mediatized Worlds: Culture and Society in a Media Age*. London: Palgrave MacMillan.

Herrera, Linda. 2014. *Revolution in the Age of Social Media: The Egyptian Popular Insurrection and the Internet*. London: Verso.

Hesmondhalgh, David and Sarah Baker. 2013. *Creative Labour: Media Work in Three Cultural Industries*. London: Routledge.

Hetherington, Kregg. 2016. "Surveying the Future Perfect: Anthropology, Development and the Promise of Infrastructure." In *Infrastructures and Social Complexity: A Companion*, edited by P. Harvey, C. B. Jensen and A. Morita, pp. 40-50. London: Routledge.

———. 2014. "Waiting for the Surveyor: Development Promises and the Temporality of Infrastructure." *The Journal of Latin American and Caribbean Anthropology* 19, no. 2: 195-211.

Hirschkind, Charles. 2006. *The Ethical Soundscape: Cassette Sermons and Islamic Counterpublics*. New York: Columbia University Press.

Hjarvard, Stig. 2013. *The Mediatization of Culture and Society*. Abingdon and New York: Routledge.

Hoek, Lotte. 2016. "Revelations in the Anthropology of Cinema." *Anthropology of this Century* 16.

———. 2014. *Cut-Pieces: Celluloid Obscenity and Popular Cinema in Bangladesh*. New York: Columbia University Press.

Holbraad, Martin and Morten Axel Pedersen, eds. 2013. *Times of Security: Ethnographies of Fear, Protest and the Future*. London: Routledge.

Hoodfar, Homa. 1997. *Between Marriage and the Market: Intimate Politics and Survival in Cairo*. Berkeley: University of California Press.

Horst, Heather A. and Daniel Miller. 2006. *The Cell Phone: An Anthropology of Communication*. New York and Oxford: Berg Publishers.

Howes, David, ed. 2005. *Empire of the Senses: The Sensual Culture Reader*. Oxford: Berg Publishers.

Hughes, Stephen P. 2006. "House full: Silent Film Genre, Exhibition and Audiences in South India." *The Indian Economic and Social History Review* 43, no. 1: 31-62.

Hutchins, Edwin. 1995. *Cognition in the Wild*. Cambridge: The MIT Press.

Ingold, Tim. 2000. "'Stop, look and listen!' Vision, Hearing and Human Movement." In *The Perception of the Environment: Essays on Livelihood, Dwelling and Skill*. London: Routledge.

———. 1997. "Eight Themes in the Anthropology of Technology." *Social Analysis* 41, no. 1: 106-138.

Ismail, Salwa. 2006. *Political Life in Cairo's New Quarters: Encountering the Everyday State*. Minneapolis: University of Minnesota Press.

Johnson-Hanks, Jennifer. 2005. "When the Future Decides: Uncertainty and Intentional Action in Contemporary Cameroon." *Current Anthropology* 46, no. 3: 363-385.

Khouri, Malek. 2010. *The Arab National Project in Youssef Chahine's Cinema*. Cairo: American University in Cairo Press.

Kinsley, Sam. 2012. "Futures in the Making: Practices for Anticipating Ubiquitous Computing." *Environment and Planning A* 44, no. 7: 1554-1569.

———. 2010. "Representing 'Things to Come': Feeling the Visions of Future Technologies." *Environment and Planning A* 42, no. 11: 2771-2790.

Kittler, Friedrich. 1999. *Gramophone, Film, Typewriter*. Stanford: Stanford University Press.

Kiwitt, Peter. 2012. "What is Cinema in a Digital Age? Divergent Definitions from a Production Perspective." *Journal of Film and Video* 64, no. 4: 3-22.

Knight, Daniel M. 2017a. "Anxiety and Cosmopolitan Futures: Brexit and Scotland." *American Ethnologist* 44, no. 2: 237-242.

———. 2017b. "Fossilized Futures: Topologies and Topographies of Crisis Experience in Central Greece." *Social Analysis* 61, no. 1: 26-40.

Knight, Daniel M. and Charles Stewart. 2016. "Ethnographies of Austerity: Temporality, Crisis and Affect in Southern Europe." *History and Anthropology* 27, no. 1: 1-18.

Kraidy, Marwan. 2016. *The Naked Blogger of Cairo: Creative Insurgency in the Arab World*. Cambridge: Harvard University Press.

Ladner, Sam. 2008. "Laptops in the Living Room: Mobile Technologies and the Divide between Work and Private Time among Interactive Agency Workers." *Canadian Journal of Communication* 33, no. 3: 465-489.

Larkin, Brian. 2008. *Signal and Noise: Media, Infrastructure and Urban Culture in Nigeria*. Durham: Duke University Press.

Latour, Bruno. 2005. *Reassembling the Social: An Introduction to Actor-Network-Theory*. Oxford: Oxford University Press.

———. 2000. "The Berlin Key or How To Do Words With Things." In *Matter, Materiality and Modern Culture*, edited by Paul Graves-Brown, pp. 10–21. London: Routledge.

———. 1996. "On Actor-Network Theory." *Soziale Welt* 47: 369-381.

———. 1993. *We Have Never Been Modern*. Cambridge: Harvard University Press.

———. 1988. "Mixing Humans and Non-Humans: The Sociology of a Door-Closer." *Social Problems* 35, no. 3: 298-310.

———. 1987. *Science in Action: How to Follow Scientists and Engineers through Society*. Cambridge: Harvard University Press.

Latour, Bruno and Steve Woolgar. 1979. *Laboratory Life: The Social Construction of Scientific Facts*. Beverly Hills: SAGE.

Law, John. 1992. "Notes on the Theory of the Actor Network: Ordering, Strategy and Heterogeneity." *Systems Practice* 5: 379-393.

Lebow, Alisa. 2018. *Filming Revolution*. Stanford: Stanford University Press.

———. 2016. "Seeing Revolution Non-Linearly: www.filmingrevolution.org" *Visual Anthropology* 29, no. 3: 278-295.

Lemonnier, Pierre. 2004. "Mythiques chaînes opératoires." *Technique et Culture* 43/44: 25-43.

———. 1992. *Elements for an Anthropology of Technology*. Ann Arbor: University of Michigan.

———. 1976. "La description des chaînes opératoires: Contribution à l'analyse des systèmes techniques." *Technique et Culture* 1: 101-150.

Litman, Barry, ed. 1998. *The Motion Picture Mega-Industry*. Boston: Allyn and Bacon.

Livingstone, Sonia. 2014. "Mediatization: An Emerging Paradigm for Media and Communication Studies." In *Mediatization of Communication*, edited by Knut Lundby, pp. 703-724. Berlin: Mouton de Gruyter.

———. 2009. "On the Mediation of Everything: ICA Presidential Address 2008." *Journal of Communication* 59, no. 1: 1-18.

Luhmann, Niklas. 1998 [1992]. "Describing the Future" In *Observations on Modernity*. Stanford: Stanford University Press.

MacDougall, David. 2006. *The Corporeal Image: Film, Ethnography, and the Senses*. Princeton and Oxford: Princeton University Press.

Madianou, Mirca and Daniel Miller. 2012. *Migration and New Media: Transnational Families and Polymedia*. London: Routledge.

Mahmood, Saba. 2005. *Politics of Piety: The Islamic Revival and the Feminist Subject*. Princeton and Oxford: Princeton University Press.

Malafouris, Lambros. 2013. *How Things Shape the Mind: A Theory of Material Engagement*. Cambridge: The MIT Press.

Mankekar, Purnima. 1999. *Screening Culture, Viewing Politics*. Durham: Duke University Press.

Markham, Tim. 2014. "Social Media, Protest Cultures, and Political Subjectivities of the Arab Spring." *Media, Culture and Society* 36, no. 1: 89-104.

Martin, Sylvia J. 2016. *Haunted: An Ethnography of the Hollywood and Hong Kong Media Industries*. Oxford: Oxford University Press.

Martín-Barberio, Jesus. 1993. *Communication, Culture and Hegemony: From the Media to Mediations*. London: SAGE.

Martinelli, Bruno. 1997. "Sous le regard de l'apprenti: Paliers de savoir et d'insertion chez les forgerons Moose du Yatenga (Burkina Faso)." *Technique et Culture* 28: 9-47.

Mateer, John. 2014. "Digital Cinematography: Evolution of Craft or Revolution in Production?" *Journal of Film and Video* 66, no. 2: 3-14.

Matzner, Deborah. 2014. "'My Maid Watches It': Key Symbols and Ambivalent Sentiments in the Production of Television Programming in India." *Anthropological Quarterly* 87, no. 4: 1229-1256.

Mayer, Vicki. 2011. *Below the Line: Producers and Production Studies in the New Television Economy*. Durham: Duke University Press.

Mayer, Vicki, Miranda J. Banks, and John T. Caldwell, eds. 2009. *Production Studies: Cultural Studies of Media Industries*. New York and London: Routledge.

Mazzarella, William. 2006. "Internet X-Ray: E-Governance, Transparency, and the Politics of Immediation in India." *Public Culture* 18, no. 3: 473–505.

———. 2004. "Culture, Globalization, Mediation." *Annual Review of Anthropology* 33: 345-367.

———. 2003. *Shoveling Smoke: Advertising and Globalization in Contemporary India.* Durham: Duke University Press.

McLuhan, Marshall. 1964. *Understanding Media: The Extensions of Man.* New York: New American Library.

Mehrez, Samia. 2010. *Egypt's Culture Wars: Politics and Practice.* Cairo and New York: American University in Cairo Press.

Messuti, Pablo. 2014. "El impacto de la digitalización en la industria del cine argentino: Políticas de fomento, dinámicas productivas y nuevas ventanas de exhibición." *Hipertextos* 2, no. 3: 23-42.

Meyer, Birgit. 2015. *Sensational Movies: Video, Vision, and Christianity in Ghana.* Berkeley: University of California Press.

———. 2011. "Mediation and Immediacy: Sensational forms, Semiotic Ideologies and the Question of the Medium." *Social Anthropology/Anthropologie Sociale* 19, no. 1: 23-39.

Miller, Daniel. 1987. *Material Culture and Mass Consumption.* Oxford: Blackwell.

Miller, Daniel and Don Slater. 2000. *The Internet: An Ethnographic Approach.* Oxford: Berg.

Miller, Toby, ed. 2001. *Global Hollywood.* London: British Film Institute.

Miyazaki, Hirokazu. 2004. *The Method of Hope: Anthropology, Philosophy, and Fijian Knowledge.* Stanford: Stanford University Press.

Moeran, Brian. 1996. *A Japanese Advertising Agency: An Anthropology of Media and Markets.* Honolulu: University of Hawaii Press.

Moll, Yasmin. 2018. "Television is Not Radio: Theologies of Mediation in the Egyptian Islamic Revival." *Cultural Anthropology* 33, no. 2: 233-265.

———. 2010. "Islamic Televangelism: Religion, Media, and Visuality in Contemporary Egypt." *Arab Media and Society* 10: 1-27.

Nippert-Eng, Christena. 2010 [1996]. *Home and Work: Negotiating Boundaries Through Everyday Life.* Chicago: University of Chicago Press.

Ortner, Sherry B. 2013. *Not Hollywood: Independent Film at the Twilight of the American Dream.* Durham: Duke University Press.

———. 2010. "Access: Reflections on Studying Up in Hollywood." *Ethnography* 11, no. 2: 211-233.

Pandian, Anand. 2015. *Reel World: An Anthropology of Creation.* Durham: Duke University Press.

———. 2010. "The Time of Anthropology: Notes from a Field of Contemporary Experience." *Cultural Anthropology* 27, no. 4: 547-571.

Parks, Lisa and Nicole Starosielski, eds. 2015. *Signal Traffic: Critical Studies of Media Infrastructures.* Urbana, Chicago and Springfield: University of Illinois Press.

Peacock, Vita. 2015. "The Negation of Hierarchy and its Consequences." *Anthropological Theory* 15, no. 1: 3-21.

Peirce, Charles Sanders. 1932. *Collected Papers of Charles Sanders Peirce. Volume 2: Elements of Logic*. Edited by Charles Hartshorne and Paul Weiss. Cambridge: Harvard University Press.

Pels, Peter. 2015. "Modern Times: Seven Steps toward an Anthropology of the Future." *Current Anthropology* 56, no. 6: 779-796.

Peterson, Mark Allen. 2011. *Connected in Cairo: Growing Up Cosmopolitan in the Modern Middle East*. Bloomington: Indiana University Press.

———. 2005 [2003]. *Anthropology and Mass Communication: Media and Myth in the New Millennium*. New York: Berghahn Books.

Pfaffenberger, Bryan. 1992. "Social Anthropology of Technology." *Annual Review of Anthropology* 21: 491-516.

Pinch, Trevor and Karin Bijsterveld. 2004. "Sound Studies: New Technologies and Music." *Social Studies of Science* 34, no. 5: 635-648.

Pine, Frances. 2014. "Migration as Hope: Space, Time, and Imagining the Future." *Current Anthropology* 55, no. S9: S95-S104.

Pink, Sarah. 2006. *The Future of Visual Anthropology: Engaging the Senses*. London: Routledge.

Pinney, Christopher. 2005. "Things Happen: Or, From Which Moment Does That Object Come?" In *Materiality*, edited by Daniel Miller, pp. 256-272. Durham: Duke University Press.

———. 2004. *Photos of the Gods: The Printed Image and Political Struggle in India*. London: Reaktion Books.

———. 2001. "Piercing the Skin of the Idol." In *Beyond Aesthetics: Art and the Technologies of Enchantment*, edited by Christopher Pinney and Nicholas Thomas, pp. 157–179. Oxford and New York: Berg Publishers.

Plantin, Jean-Christophe and Aswin Punathambekar. 2019. "Digital Media Infrastructures: Pipes, Platforms, and Politics." *Media, Culture and Society* 41, no. 2: 163-174.

Postill, John. 2011. *Localizing the Internet: An Anthropological Account*. New York: Berghahn Books.

Powdermaker, Hortense. 1950. *Hollywood, the Dream Factory: An Anthropologist Looks at the Movie-Makers*. Boston: Little, Brown.

Pype, Kathrien. 2012. *The Making of the Pentecostal Melodrama: Religion, Media and Gender in Kinshasa*. Oxford: Berghahn Books.

Rabinow, Paul. 2008. *Marking Time: On the Anthropology of the Contemporary*. Princeton: Princeton University Press.

Rabinow, Paul and Talia Dan-Cohen. 2006. *A Machine to Make a Future: Biotech Chronicles*. Princeton: Princeton University Press.

Rajewsky, Irina O. 2005. "Intermediality, Intertextuality, and Remediation: A Literary Perspective on Intermediality." *Intermédialités* 6: 43-64.

Rommel, Carl. 2015. *Revolution, Play and Feeling: Assembling Emotionality, National Subjectivity and Football in Cairo, 1990-2013*. PhD diss., SOAS University of London.

Rot, Gwenaele. 2014. "Noter pour ajuster: Le travail de la scripte sur un plateau de tournage." *Sociologie du travail* 56, no. 1: 16-39.

Rot, Gwenaele and Laure de Verdalle, eds. 2013. *Le Cinéma: Travail et organisation*. Paris: La Dispute.

Salamandra, Christa. 2008. "Creative Compromise: Syrian Television Makers between Secularism and Islamism." *Contemporary Islam* 2, no. 3: 177-189.

———. 2005. "Television and the Ethnographic Endeavor: The Case of Syrian Drama." *Transnational Broadcasting Studies* 14 (Spring/Summer).

Samimian-Darash, Limor. 2013. "Governing Future Potential Biothreats: Toward an Anthropology of Uncertainty." *Current Anthropology* 54, no. 1: 1-22.

Sandoval-Cervantes, Iván. 2017. "Uncertain Futures: The Unfinished Houses of Undocumented Migrants in Oaxaca, Mexico." *American Anthropologist* 119, no. 2: 209-222.

Sanson, Kevin. 2018. "Stitching It All Together: Service Producers and the Special Dynamics of Screen Media Labor." *International Journal of Cultural Studies* 21, no. 4: 359-374.

Schielke, Samuli. 2015. *Egypt in the Future Tense: Hope, Frustration, and Ambivalence Before and After 2011*. Bloomington: Indiana University Press.

Schielke, Samuli and Mukhtar Saad Shehata. 2016. "The Writing of Lives: An Ethnography of Writers and Their Milieus in Alexandria." *ZMO Working Papers* 17: 1-25.

Scott, Allan J. 2002. "A New Map of Hollywood: The Production and Distribution of American Motion Pictures." *Regional Studies* 36, no. 9: 957-975.

Szczepanik, Petr and Patrick Vonderau, eds. 2013. *Behind the Screen: Inside European Production Cultures*. London: Palgrave MacMillan.

Shafik, Viola. 2007. *Popular Egyptian Cinema: Gender, Class and Nation*. Cairo and New York: American University in Cairo Press.

———. 2001. "Egyptian Cinema." In *Companion Encyclopaedia of Middle Eastern and North African Film*, edited by Oliver Leaman, pp. 23-129. London and New York: Routledge.

———. 1998. *Arab Cinema: History and Cultural Identity*. Cairo: American University in Cairo Press.

Shankar, Shalini. 2015. *Advertising Diversity: Ad Agencies and the Creation of Asian American Consumers*. Durham: Duke University Press.

Shehata, Samer S. 2009. *Shop Floor Culture and Politics in Egypt*. Albany: State University of New York Press.

Sigaut, François. 2009. "Techniques, technologie, apprentissage et plaisir au travail . . ." *Technique et Culture* 52-53: 40-49.

———. 2003. "La Formule de Mauss." *Technique et Culture* 40: 153-168.

Silverstone, Roger. 2002. "Complicity and Collusion in the Mediation of Everyday Life." *New Literary History* 33, no. 4: 761-780.

———, ed. 1994. *Television and Everyday Life*. London and New York: Routledge.

Sims, David. 2010. *Understanding Cairo: The Logic of a City out of Control*. Oxford: Oxford University Press.

Singerman, Diane and Homa Hoodfar, eds. 1996. *Development, Change, and Gender in Cairo*. Bloomington: Indiana University Press.

Snowdon, Peter. 2014. "The Revolution *Will* be Uploaded: Vernacular Video and the Arab Spring." *Culture Unbound* 6: 401-429.

Spitulnik, Deborah. 2002. "Mobile Machines and Fluid Audiences: Rethinking Reception through Zambian Radio Culture" In *Media Worlds: Anthropology on New Terrain*, edited by Faye D. Ginsburg, Lila Abu-Lughod and Brian Larkin, pp. 337–354. Berkeley, Los Angeles and London: University of California Press.

———. 1998. "Mediated Modernities: Encounters with the Electronic in Zambia." *Visual Anthropology Review* 14, no. 2: 63-84.

Srinivas, Lakshmi. 2016. *House Full: Indian Cinema and the Active Audience*. Chicago: University of Chicago Press.

Stankiewicz, Damien. 2016. "Against Imagination: On the Ambiguities of a Composite Concept." *American Anthropologist* 118, no. 4: 796-810.

Starrett, Gregory 1998. *Putting Islam to Work: Education, Politics, and Religious Transformation in Egypt*. Berkeley: University of California Press.

Steinhart, Daniel. 2019. *Runaway Hollywood: Internationalizing Postwar Production and Location Shooting*. Berkeley: University of California Press.

Stephanie, Lena, Ravi S. Sharma, and Narayan Ramasubbu. 2012. "The Digitisation of Bollywood: Adapting to Disruptive Innovation." *Media Asia* 39, no. 1: 3-16.

Sterne, Jonathan. 2012. "Introduction." In *The Sound Studies Reader*, edited by Jonathan Sterne. London: Routledge.

Storper, Michael and Susan Christopherson. 1987. "Flexible Specialization and Regional Industrial Agglomeration: The Case of the U.S. Motion Picture Industry." *Annals of the Association of American Geographers* 77, no. 1: 104-117.

Strandvad, Sara Malou. 2011. "Materializing Ideas: A Socio-Material Perspective on the Organizing of Cultural Production." *European Journal of Cultural Studies* 14, no. 3: 283-297.

Telmissany, May. 1995. "Sinima al-dawla sinima badila: Qira'a fi tajribat al-qita' al-'am al-sinima'i fi Misr". *Alif: Journal of Comparative Poetics* 15: 70-84.

Thompson, Edward P. 2009 [1964]. "Time, Work-Discipline, and Industrial Capitalism." In *Industrial Work and Life: An Anthropological Reader*, edited by Massimiliano Mollona, Geert de Neve and Jonathan Parry, pp. 9–39. Oxford and New York: Berg (London School of Economics Monographs in Social Anthropology).

Thompson, John B. 1995. *The Media and Modernity: A Social Theory of the Media*. Cambridge: Polity Press.

Tsing, Anna. 2015. *The Mushroom at the End of the World: On the Possibility of Life in Capitalist Ruins*. Princeton: Princeton University Press.

Veblen, Thorstein. 1899. *The Theory of the Leisure Class*. London: MacMillan.

Verbeek, Peter-Paul. 2005. *What Things Do: Philosophical Reflections on Technology, Agency, and Design*. University Park: The Pennsylvania State University Press.

Villi, Mikko and Matteo Stochetti. 2011. "Visual Mobile Communication, Mediated Presence and the Politics of Space." *Visual Studies* 26, no. 2: 102-112.

Wasko, Janet. 2003. *How Hollywood Works*. London: SAGE.

Wassef, Magda, ed. 1995. *Égypte: 100 ans de cinéma*. Paris: Éditions Plume and Institut du Monde Arabe.

Westmoreland, Mark R. 2016. "Street Scenes: The Politics of Revolutionary Video in Egypt." *Visual Anthropology* 29, no. 3: 243-262.

Westmoreland, Mark R. and Diana K. Allan. 2016. "Visual Revolutions in the Middle East." *Visual Anthropology* 29, no. 3: 205-210.

Wilkinson-Weber, Clare M. 2014. *Fashioning Bollywood: The Making and Meaning of Hindi Film Costume*. London: Bloomsbury Academic.

Williams, Raymond. 2005 [1975]. *Television: Technology and Cultural Form*. London: Routledge.

Winegar, Jessica. 2016. "A Civilized Revolution: Aesthetics and Political Action in Egypt." *American Ethnologist* 43, no. 4: 609-622.

———. 2009. "Culture is the Solution: The Civilizing Mission of Egypt's Culture Palaces." *Review of Middle East Studies* 43, no. 2: 189-197.

———. 2006. *Creative Reckonings: The Politics of Art and Culture in Contemporary Egypt*. Stanford: Stanford University Press.

Wolover, D. J. 2016. "An Issue of Attribution: The Tunisian Revolution, Media Interaction, and Agency." *New Media and Society* 18, no. 2: 185-200.

Zafirau, Stephen. 2009. *Imagined Audiences: Intuitive and Technical Knowledge in Hollywood*. PhD diss., University of Southern California.

Zaloom, Caitlin. 2009. "How to Read the Future: The Yield Curve, Affect, and Financial Prediction." *Public Culture* 21, no. 2: 245-268.

———. 2004. "The Productive Life of Risk." *Cultural Anthropology* 19, no. 3: 365-391.

Zeitlyn, David. 2012. "Divinatory Logics: Diagnoses and Predictions Mediating Outcomes." *Current Anthropology* 53, no. 5: 525-546.

Index

Page numbers in *italic* indicate images.

Chalmers, David 144
Chaos and Disorder (2012) 133
Chion, Michel 173
cinema equipment: cameras 90–93,
    249n4; cameras and negatives,
    predigital 252n3; and electrical
    infrastructure 94; lights 145–47;
    rentals 90, 132–33, 249n3; repair
    of 95, 250n8; selection of 250n7;
    sound equipment 93; sound
    equipment, microphones 104–105;
    transition to digital 90–93; video-
    assist monitors 104, 151, 170–72,
    171, 172, 250n10, 252n4. *See also*
    technological devices; technological
    devices, digital; technology, digital
    filmmaking; *tiknulujya*
Cinema Industry Chamber *(ghurfat
    sina'at al-sinima)* 31–32, 200–201,
    245n3
Cinema Organization *(gihaz al-sinima)*
    245n2
cinematographers 235, 236
cinematography team and labor
    division 223–25
clappers 220, 239
Clark, Andy 144
classism *(taba'iya)*: class differences in
    visualization 159–60, 162; digital
    devices as class markers 95–96;
    in film industry 56–58; in target
    audiences 186–87, 189, 201–202;
    transportation mode as class
    marker 126–27. *See also* labor
    division; labor hierarchies
colorists and labor division 225
Coming Forth by Day (2012) 252n8
commercial cinema *(al-sinima
    al-tugariya)* 45, 47–50
continuity 197–99, 219, 243n1
contract movies *(aflam al-mu'awlat)*
    246n6

coordination: artistic demands on
    scheduling 125; avoiding delays
    130–36, 138; being available
    136–38; being available and
    faultless 131, 136–42; being
    faultless 138–42; budgeting
    and accounting 116–20; cash
    circulation 118–19, 251n4;
    logistical mediation 142–44;
    logistics pre-early 2000s 251n1;
    scheduling 113–15, 120–26;
    transportation 126–29, 251n7;
    transportation, car services 216;
    vignette 113–15. *See also* budgets;
    enchantment of audience;
    mediation of imponderable
    outcomes; operational sequence;
    reserves; visualization
co-production 32–33, 246n9, 246n10
costumes: and continuity 197–98, 219;
    fitting 234; and labor division
    228–29
costume script supervisors and labor
    division 219

Daoud, Rageh 177
Darré, Yann 68, 154
Darwish, Wael 250n6
Décor (2014): cost of 118, 251n3;
    exhibition and distribution of 211;
    interpersonal links in production
    and distribution 41–43; plot
    summary 8; premiere 203–207;
    prospective audience 188–89; and
    realism 194; screenplay adjustments
    70–71; shooting, day one 73–76;
    star budget 37; video effects 76.
    See also Badawy, Ahmad
Décor art directors. *See* Ali, Asem;
    Farouk, Nihal
Décor assistant art director. *See* Ezzat,
    Mohammed

Mahmoud, Safiy el-Din 77, 188, 191, 201–202
Makram, Michel 64
Mandour, Sherif 32
Mandour, Wael: on digital technologies 91, 92, 250n6; on having a vision 152; personal links 42; on scheduling 121, 123
Al-Masa (production company) 32, 35
Mazzarella, William 184
el-Meallem, Ibrahim 246n10
media anthropology: and audiences 184–85; media ethnography 209–10; methodology 10–12
mediation of imponderable outcomes: in budgeting 118, 120; in coordinating 101, 115–16, 142–44; in daily work of filmmakers 210; foremediation 19–20; futures, types of 16–21; mediation, meanings of 18–20; mediatization 19; and objects/reserves distinction 85; in scheduling 126, 129; in scouting 164; in set design 166–69; in shooting 115; in sound work 175–76, 177; streetlight road photo 22–24; and technological devices 13–14, 19, 104–106; in transportation 129; in visualizing film 149–51, 155, 171–72; visual mediation 177–79, 252n6. *See also* apprenticeship; budgets; coordination; enchantment of audience; labor division; labor hierarchies; mediators; operational sequence; reserves; visualization
mediators: anticipation of subsequent operations through 80, 83; audiovisual material and report 76; of budget and cash flow 120; in coordination 115, 126, 134, 135, 142; in daily work of filmmakers 210; as icons 150–51, 252n1; versus intermediaries 12; in operational sequence 70, 73–74, 231; script supervisors' use of 198; visual 102, 177–79; in visualizing film 154, 155–56, 168–70; visual mediators in postproduction 176; visual mediators in scouting 85, 150, 163–64; and worktime 108; written mediators in screenwriting 98. *See also* mediation of imponderable outcomes; reserves
el-Mihi, Karim: on independent cinema 48; on production crew sizes 138; on use of emails 141–42
Miller, Daniel 18, 84
Misr International Films 35
mixing 241
Mizrahi, Togo 37
mobile phones: and being available 99–101, 131, 250n9; as class markers and status symbols 95–96; and coordination 131–32; enchantment with technology 87–88; as reserves 14, 84–85, 99–102, 142
Mohammed, Hossam 42
Mohsen, Tamer 130–31
Mokhtar, Georges 127–28
money laundering 32, 246n8
Morsi, Mahmoud: on being available 137–38; personal links 42; pre-light setup 145–47; promotion of trainees 66–67; on rental costs 249n3; sending someone in his place 251n5; training of assistants 62
Morsy, Hany 145, 146, 147, 193
Moussa, Abdelsalam 91, 133
movement script supervisors and labor division 219
movie stars. *See* stars
Moviola editing suites 90–91, 92

Poisonous Roses production manager (Edward Nabil) 159–60, 162–63, 252n8
pop culture references 8–9
Port Said stadium massacre documentary 87
postproduction: audiovisual material 239; color grading 33, 241; graphics 240; image editing 240; infrastructure 38; mixing 33, 241; music composition 177, 195, 241; printing 241; printing films 241; and reserves 104; sound editing 240; state control of 33, 246n11; transition to digital 90–91, 250n5. *See also* enchantment of audience; operational sequence; reserves; visualization
postproduction team and labor division 216
Powdermaker, Hortense 189
preparations: call sheets 102, *103*, 141–42, 235; camera tests 235; dressing and makeup 237; fitting 234; for imponderable outcomes 115–16, 130–31; lighting 144–47, *146*, 169–70, *170*, 235, 236; location breakdown 113, 121; as operational sequence 74, 232–35; props 2, 121, 129, 216, *233*, 234; rehearsals 235, 237; script breakdowns 101, 120–21, *122*, 197–98, 232; sets 108–112, 136–38, *137*, 199, 233; transportation 126–29, 216, 251n7; vignette 108–112. *See also* coordination; operational sequence; scouting; shooting
production costs. *See* budgets; salaries and wages
production fictions 184–89, *186*
production models 34–36, 247n13

production teams: detailed tasks of 132, 252n8; labor division in 214–16
promotion in career 66–69, 249n2
props: acquisition/rental of 2, 129, 234; design 233; script breakdown 121; vehicle rentals 216. *See also* preparations; sets
props scripts and labor division 219
props team and labor division 226

al-Qalla, Hussein 246n7
Qitt wa far (The Cat and the Mouse, 2015) 9, 43–44, 124, 128, 130–31, 141–42
Qudrat ghayr 'adiya (Out of the Ordinary, 2015) 9, 37, 117, 206

Rabaa massacre 7, 203–204
Rabie, Mona 33, 173, 176–77, 180, 250n5, 250n11
Radwan, Abdelsalam 75, 79, 124–25, 181, 192–93, 249n1
Rags and Tatters (Farsh wa ghata, 2013) 5
Ramsis, Georges, Jr. 41, 113, 119
Rashad, Mohammed 47
Rashdan, Ahmad 174
rehearsals 235, 237
remediation 19
Renaissance Cinemas 34–35
Renaissance theater-owning group 42
reserves: overview 13–16, 84–85, 209–10, 244n13; across stages of production 100–105; and anticipating audience 185, 189, 200, 203; in coordination 136, 142–44; in image composition 164–66, 168; and mediation of imponderable outcomes 105; versus objects 15, 85, 210; in scheduling 124; in scouting 14, 159–60, 162; in screenwriting 97–99; in sound work 174;

tiknulujya as 96–97; in visualizing film 150, 155, 157–60, 162; and worktime 105–108. *See also* mediation of imponderable outcomes; technological devices as reserves

Revolution, January 2011 4–6, 120, 243nn4=6

Rotana satellite television channel 31–32, 211, 245n5, 247n16

Rotterdam International Film Festival 211

runners and labor division 215

Saber, Marwan: on brokerage *(samsara)* production model 32; on digital cinema technologies 88–89, 94–95, 155, 249n4; on equipment in Egypt and elsewhere 93, 250n7; on improvements expected 246n12

Sabry, Farouk and Walid 35

Sabry, Hend 186

Sadat, Anwar 30–31

el-Said, Tamer 45–46

salaries and wages: cash payment of 118–19; contract basis 44–45, 248n23, 248n24, 248n26; deductions for mistakes 139; delayed payment of 251n2; of movie stars 32, 36–37, 246n7, 247n18, 247n19; raises in 248n25; in television and advertising 248n20. *See also* budgets

Saleh, Ahmad 104, 173, 175, 196–97

Sami, Salma: beginning point of film for 232; on classism 58; at *Décor's* premiere 205; expenditures by 119; logistics after screenplay adjustments 71; personal links 42–43; at planning meeting 1; scheduling 114; visualization by

150–51; visual mediators used by 102

Samir, Mohammed 49

Samuel, Sandy 77

satellite television channels: distribution loans by 31–32, 245n5; and film distribution 4, 186; labor market of 38; serial film production by 35

el-Sayeh, Adham 41, 80, 130–31, 136–37

scouting: in India 252n6; mediation of imponderable outcomes in 164; as operational sequence 233; in predigital times 164; reserves in 14, 159–60, 162; and traffic calculations 128; vignette 50–52; and visualizing film 149–50, 154, 156–64; visual mediators in 85, 150, 163–64. *See also* coordination; operational sequence; preparations

screenwriters and labor division 221

screenwriting 71–73, 97–99, 183–84, 232

script breakdowns 101, 113, 120–21, *122*, 197–98, 232

Seoud, Habi 36, 58–59, 96, 116–17, 140

Setohy, Mohammed: on coordination 143–44; at *Décor's* premiere 205; on delays in other film shootings 134–35; digital devices of 99; on digital technologies 106–107; as location manager, *The Cat and the Mouse* 130–32; personal links 41; at planning meeting 1; preparations for shooting 132; scheduling 113–14; scouting 2, 14, 50–52, 118, 149–50, 156; scouting, traffic problems 128; on success of *Décor* 188–89; technological devices used as reserves 80–81; transportation mode preferred 127

of imponderable outcomes;
mediators; reserves; technological
devices as reserves

Suniʿa fi Misr (Made in Egypt, 2014) 37

Supreme Council of Culture
conference 86–87

Taher, Bahaa 86

Tarek, Renad 77

taxes on film industry 31, 119–20

el-Tayeb, Atef 47

technological devices: and mediation
of unpredictable outcomes 13–14,
18–19; subject/object distinction
15–16, 83–84; and worktime
106–107. *See also* cinema equipment;
technological devices, digital;
technological devices as reserves;
technology, digital filmmaking;
tiknulujya

technological devices, digital: as class
markers and status symbols 84,
95–96; and creativity *(ibdaʿ)* 89;
enchantment with technology
87–88; generational divide in use
86–89; perceptions of 105–106,
250n11; *tiknulujya* 85–90. *See also*
cinema equipment; mobile
phones; technological devices;
technological devices as reserves;
technology, digital filmmaking;
tiknulujya

technological devices as reserves
14–16, 142–44, 210–11; analog
or digital 106; cameras 101–102;
computers 108, 124, 142, 164–66;
microphones 14–15, 104–105;
mobile phones/smartphones
14, 84–85, 99–102, 142; paper
and pencil 142–44; and parallels
with executive work 170; sound
equipment 174; video-assist

monitors 104; vignette 80–82;
word-processing software 96–97,
97–98. *See also* cinema equipment;
mediation of imponderable
outcomes; reserves; technological
devices; technological devices,
digital; technology, digital
filmmaking; *tiknulujya*

technology, digital filmmaking: as
"black-box" 94–95; design
software 164–65; improvements
expected in 246n12; skillfulness
(shatara) in 65–66, 94–95;
transition to 33–34, 90–93, 250n6;
and workflow 33–34. *See also*
cinema equipment; technological
devices; technological devices,
digital; technological devices as
reserves; *tiknulujya*

television sector: digital technology
use in 33; drama production 125,
247n14; film exhibition 35; labor
market network 39

El-Telmissany, Tarek 6, 188

Telmissany family 6, 39–40

theaters. *See* exhibition

Thompson, Edward P. 106

tiknulujya: as class markers 95–96;
as commodity-objects 84,
90; connotations of 85–87;
disembedding of technical from
social 83–84; perceived power of
87–89, 175, 252n5; as reserves
96–97; as undesirable progress
89–90. *See also* cinema equipment;
mobile phones; technological
devices; technological devices,
digital; technological devices
as reserves; technology, digital
filmmaking

TimeCode (postproduction studio) 33,
40, 91